DIVINE LOVE

DIVINE LOVE

A SERIES
OF
DOCTRINAL, PRACTICAL AND
EXPERIMENTAL DISCOURSES

JOHN EADIE

SOLID GROUND CHRISTIAN BOOKS
BIRMINGHAM, ALABAMA USA

Solid Ground Christian Books
2090 Columbiana Rd, Suite 2000
Birmingham, AL 35216
205-443-0311
sgcb@charter.net
http://solid-ground-books.com

Divine Love
A SERIES OF DOCTRINAL, PRACTICAL AND EXPERIMENTAL DISCOURSES

John Eadie (1810-1876)

Taken from 1856 edition by Lindsay & Blakiston, Philadelphia, PA

Solid Ground Classic Reprints

First printing of new edition August 2005

Cover work by Borgo Design, Tuscaloosa, AL
Contact them at nelbrown@comcast.net

ISBN: 1-59925-014-4

PREFACE.

The Discourses contained in this Volume are in no sense nor aspect critical, but are meant for ordinary readers — for the domestic circle, or the Lord's-day evening. The one effort of the Writer has been, to exhibit clearly and enforce earnestly the mind of the Spirit on this precious and delightful theme. No uniform style of composition has been followed, but the common form of Lectures has been adopted, as best fitted to bring out most naturally and fully the instruction contained in the verses or paragraphs selected for exposition. Some have not the accredited shape of public addresses, as they have never been delivered from the pulpit. But Love is the unvarying text, and who can ever weary of it? It is, in fine, the prayerful hope of the Author, that his readers may be stimulated to adore, with renewed ardour, the manifestations of the Divine Love towards them, and to feel more powerfully its influence within them, as they strive to obey 'the first and great command of the law.'

CONTENTS.

LECTURE I.
The Love of God: its Objects, Gift, and Design......... Page 13

LECTURE II.
The Love of Christ to His Church — its Fervour and Self-sacrifice—its Nearer Purpose and its Ultimate Result, 45

LECTURE III.
The Love of the Spirit — its Reality and Glory. (*An Argument*)... 73

LECTURE IV.
The Votive Tablet—or the Saint's Record of his Love. (*A Soliloquy*)... 93

LECTURE V.
The Adopting Love of the Father. (*A Lecture*)............. 116

LECTURE VI.
The Father's Love to the Son, the Model and Measurement of the Son's Love to His People............................. 142

LECTURE VII.
The Loving-kindness of the Lord, on the Wild, in the Dungeon, in the Sick-room, and on the Seas. (*A Meditation*), 161

CONTENTS.

LECTURE VIII.
                                                                Page
THE SIN AND DOOM OF THE LOVELESS.................................. 181

LECTURE IX.
THE LOVE OF INVITATION AND REVIVAL. (*An Exposition.*)
    Part I.—The Invitation and Welcome............................ 200
    Part II.—Revival 233

LECTURE X.
THE DIVINE LOVE IN ITS REFLEX POWER AND MANIFESTATIONS. (*Detached Annotations.*)
    I. The Momentous Question..................................... 250
    II. The New Commandment....................................... 255
    III. The Necessity and Growth of Love in the midst of Persecution.. 264
    IV. The Conscious Test of a Saving Change to Ourselves........ 266
    V. The Basis of the Christian Poor Law........................ 267
    VI. Love to the Bible... 270
    VII. The Walk of Love... 273
    VIII. The Apostle's Adjudication among the Graces.............. 278

LECTURE XI.
THE FRIENDSHIP AND SYMPATHY OF JESUS............................... 281

LECTURE XII.
THE LOVE OF CHRIST THE SUSTAINING MOTIVE IN THE MISSIONARY ENTERPRISE. (*An Appeal*).. 322

THE

DIVINE LOVE.

LECTURE I.

THE LOVE OF GOD: ITS OBJECTS, GIFT, AND DESIGN.

JOHN III. 16.

'For God so loved the world, that he gave his only-begotten Son, that whosoever believeth in him should not perish, but have everlasting life.'

AND is it so? Can this extraordinary announcement be received as actual truth? Dare we credit it, or lift up our guilty hearts to comprehend its terms? O it is so strange and thrilling, that it seems to stun us, and only on recovering from our amazement are we able at length to reflect on the blessed declaration. There is so much of God in it, that we recognise His awful presence, and fear as we are entering 'into the cloud.'

'God loved the world.' If I use the expression, God created the world, or God preserves the world, or God governs the world, the language which I employ is, to my mind, the symbol of infinite wisdom, power, and benignity; but when I repeat this statement, 'God loved the world,' the simple clause reveals at once a depth and an amount of meaning at which the mind is almost startled into incredulity; and it feels as if it were temerity to lay hold on this divine charter of human salvation. And yet these precious words afford the solution of many a living mystery. Why, for example, may the saint exclaim, have I been brought into the conscious possession of peace and joy, and the dark shadows that lay on my mind have all fled away; or why does the throne of the universe now stand out as a throne of grace, to which there is for me daily access, continual welcome, and rich response; or why are there in heaven the spirits of my human kindred, whose bodies are lying yet in the darksome pollution and thraldom of the grave — are not such changes, privileges, and blessings to be traced upward and backward to the grand and ultimate fact, that God has loved the world?

Now, the introductory 'for' shows that this verse presents itself as the reason of a previous statement. The reference in it is to a remarkable incident in the history of ancient Israel. They had, in one of their periodical fits of national insanity, so provoked their divine Guardian and Provider, that He sent among them 'fiery flying serpents,' and many of them were bitten, and died. But to modify and counteract the chastisement, and make its terror a means of salutary impresion, Moses was commanded to frame a brazen representation of one of the poisonous reptiles, and place it on the summit of a flag-staff, so that any wounded Hebrew might be able to see it from the extremity of the camp. And every one, no matter how sorely he felt the poison in his fevered veins, if he could only turn his languid vision to the sacred emblem, was instantly healed. It is then asserted that salvation is a process of equal simplicity, facility, and certainty—'so also must the Son of man be lifted up,' that every 'one believing in Him may not perish, but have everlasting life.' But why are belief and salvation so connected, and how comes it that any one, every one, confiding in the Son of man, is rescued and blessed—saved from the death which he has merited, and elevated to a life which he had forfeited? This pledge of safety and glory to the believer has its origin in nothing else but the truth under our consideration. Belief and life are in this wondrous and inseparable union: 'For God so loved the world, that he gave his only-begotten Son, that whosoever believeth in him should not perish, but have everlasting life.'

The scheme of salvation is here presented to us in its origin, its means, and its design. Or we may contemplate the love of God, first, in its object — the world; secondly, in the provision He has made for its deliverance—the gift of his Son; and, thirdly, in the instrumentality by which this provided salvation is brought into individual possession — the exercise of faith.

I. The Object of God's Love.

1. Again we recur to the starting thought, If God loved, and so loved this guilty world, what an unplumbed depth of grace must be in His heart. For the object of His love is not the world in its first condition, such as it was when His own eyes, resting on it with beaming complacency, pronounced it 'very good,' but that same world ruined by sin, and condemned for its apostasy. There would have been no wonder had the divine Lawgiver assumed the stern functions of Judge, and doomed our guilty earth to the death which it deserved. Might it not have been enveloped in flames which, gleaming far into other orbits, would have taught other races that 'our God is a consuming fire?' But though He had armed His law with a terrible penalty, and allowed the incipient elements of the menace to fall upon the sinner—though the holiness of His nature and the interests of His government seemed to demand that punishment shall instantly and immediately follow transgression — yet, without any change in our claims or character, He has loved us. And that love is not a mere relenting which might lead to a respite, or a simple regret which might end in a sigh, but, thrice blessed be His name, it is a positive affection. It is as true as His existence, as real as our sin. Now, there is no merit in loving what is lovely. By a necessity of our emotional nature, our affection throws itself out upon any object that presents an aspect of loveliness; and such

an instinct within us is only the reflection of a similar law in the character and actings of God. He cannot but love what bears His image; and therefore the bright and happy essences who surround His throne are for ever sunning themselves in His ineffable smile. But, ah! man has washed out and lost his moral loveliness. Originally like God, he is now as unlike him as he can be, and there is nothing about him but his misery to attract the divine attachment. Paradise loathed and expelled him, and the globe into which he was exiled out of Eden has been cursed for his sake. 'The whole creation groaneth and travaileth in pain together.' The bleak rock on which no seed can vegetate; the eternal snows where no animal can breathe; the blasted oak of the forest, stretching its leafless arms to the wintry sky; the beach spread over with the wreck and corpses of the hurricane; the desolations of the volcanic fires, and the rocking and chasms of the earthquake; the bed on which tosses the invalid to whom 'wearisome days and nights are appointed;' the hand which the labouring man uplifts to wipe the perspiration from his brow; and those monuments of victory that tell of thousands lying beneath them uncoffined and unknelled — these are the tongues by which Nature proclaims, in melancholy emphasis, that she has wandered from her God. And this sin of man is not his misfortune, but his fault. Sometimes those around us are overborne in providence; wave after wave breaks upon them, and as they stagger and fall, they are more to be pitied than to be blamed. Alas! on the contrary, man is not only a ruined, but a self-ruined creature. He has lowered himself to what he is — the victim of his own pride and disobedience. I presume not to solve the mystery of the origin of evil. I cannot tell why, with God's possession of infinite power, and purity, and love, sin was ever permitted to find its way into our world; but this I know, that amidst all subtle speculations on this dark theme — amidst all daring and devious attempts to climb these heights of eternal providence, this one truth is very apparent — 'God made man upright, but he has sought out many inventions.' There is therefore no palliation of our crime. Our Master is not an 'austere' one, 'reaping where he had not sown, and gathering where he had not strawed.' The law under which man was placed was 'holy, and just, and good,' and he was furnished with powers of perfect obedience. The test by which he was tried was an easy one, and he was, but 'for one restraint, lord of the world besides.' It was simply a respect for the Divine will which could lead him to obedience. There was no commingling motive, such as that which springs out of natural relationship and originates moral obligation. But man broke this simple covenant, and wantonly disobeyed the clear injunction not to eat of the tree. And yet that world, which has in this way made itself so guilty and helpless through its perversity and disloyalty, is not thrown off by God — is not flung into oblivion by Him, and covered with His frown — is not merely tolerated, or, like a condemned criminal, indulged with a few providential and minor kindnesses, but is really loved by Him. The marvel is this — there is nothing He hates so much as sin — and yet no one He has loved so much as a sinner. In spite of our alienation and our hostility, in spite of our low and loathsome repugnance, in the midst of so much that He hates, and condemns, and nauseates, God has loved, yes, has so loved the world. What infinite grace in this amazing love of God!

2. If God loved, and so loved this little world, surely His love was wholly disinterested in its nature. Should some large and important province of an empire rise in rebellion, the sovereign will use every means to induce it to return to its allegiance ere he proceed to arms against it; but should an insignificant region be involved in insurrection, summary vengeance will be taken at once on its folly. Now, our rebellious world was only a small portion of God's universe. What a melancholy thought, did we look up to the sky and see in every orb a wreck and in every star a prison of ruined spirits! The great unfallen universe is a vast territory on which its Creator can yet look with complacency. If, therefore, worlds unnumbered roll around His throne, brighter in their glories of light and mass, of structure and motion than ours; if the absence of our earth from creation would be as little felt as the removal of a single particle of sand from the mound which girds the ocean; and if another divine fiat could at once fill its room with a new orb and

with another population, whose obedience should be coeval with their existence and coextensive with their faculties — will it still be affirmed that it was from any selfish motive, or with any selfish purpose, that God has prolonged our existence, when life and all its enjoyments had been forfeited, or that we are of so much importance to Himself, His happiness, or the harmony of His empire, that, rather than allow us to perish, He gave up His only-begotten Son to the death? Far from us be such vain imaginations! 'When I consider thy heavens, the work of thy fingers, the moon and the stars, which thou hast ordained; what is man, that thou art mindful of him? and the son of man, that thou visitest him?' Higher beings are even the servants of believing humanity.

> 'O the exceeding grace
> Of highest God, that loves His creatures so,
> And all His works with mercy doth embrace —
> That blessed angels He sends to and fro,
> To serve to wicked man — to serve His wicked foe!'

The same truth has been pictured out to us by the great Teacher: The shepherd had a hundred sheep, and only one of them had gone astray. But his fond anxieties go out after it; and leaving the ninety and nine in comparative neglect, he flees into the wilderness and seeks everywhere, till he come upon the object of his solicitude—the one poor wanderer; and when he finds it, there is more joy in his bosom over the recovery of the solitary straggler than over the entire flock that had not deserted the fold. O there is more of the heart of God exhibited in our salvation than in all His benignity to the universe beyond us. This orb is truly a 'little one;' and yet it has called out emotions which other and mightier spheres had failed to elicit. Now, such is its moral magnitude, that in its connection with Christ it stands out in unrivalled glory from other worlds, and over its redeemed inhabitants is the chaunt raised, ' This my son was dead and is alive again, was lost and is found.' Surely this love to a world so insignificant, when compared with the gigantic and numerous planets that revolve in the heavens, must be purely disinterested. ' Our goodness reacheth not to Him.' 'Not unto us, O Lord, not unto us, but unto thy name give glory, even for thy mercy and for thy truth's sake.'

3. If God loved this world — this world of fallen men, and not the world of fallen angels — His love must be sovereign in its essence. For man was not the only sinner in His dominions. Beings of higher original nature, and having their position in heaven itself, were mysteriously involved in the guilt and doom of apostasy, and expelled from their bright domain. And yet, though they dwelt in heaven, they are not summoned back to it. No pardon is offered to them — no means of purity are provided for them — no mediator has taken on him the 'nature of angels,' in order to make atonement for them. They are left to the endurance of death, death for ever—ever sinning, ever suffering—while

pardon and restoration have been proclaimed to the human family — that weak and erring race, so nearly allied to the ground they tread, so proud in their debility, and so impious in their thraldom. Would it not have been a more natural operation, so to speak, to have saved these lofty exiles, and called them again to the heaven in which they once lived, and for which they were created, than to select this distant and miserable world, and, by an abnormal and mighty process, to purify and refine its wretched and earthy outcasts for a realm of existence to which they are strangers, and to which they would never have been able to penetrate? The reasons inducing the Infinite Wisdom to make this choice, we may neither search nor maintain. This preference of fallen man to fallen spirits as the recipient of divine love, can only be resolved into a mysterious exercise of uncontrolled sovereignty. He has loved earth and not hell. Both might have been punished with eternal penalty, and neither the one nor the other could have complained of the equity of its doom; and both might have been forgiven and redeemed, and the one and the other would have equally felt its salvation due to Jehovah's tender pity. Nay, though hell had been taken and earth had been left — though the earliest transgressors only had been saved, and brought again to the awful presence before which they once bowed, the bright myriads with which they once mixed, and the hallelujahs which they once choired, while this world was left to pine and groan hopeless and helpless — and this alternative one shudders to contemplate — who would have dared to impeach the God of grace, who has the right to give as He pleases where none have any claim on His bounty? But, let His name be extolled, earth has not been passed over — it has been selected in His sovereign regard. Ay, GOD SO LOVED THE WORLD. It was a vain conceit which supposed that redeemed spirits were taken up into heaven to supply the vacancy caused by the lapse and loss of the angels. 'Glory and life fulfil their own depletion;' and though God banished the apostates the one moment, their places might have been all filled the next, and the change might have been not merely compensative, but at the same time the source of augmented splendour. 'Be not highminded, but fear.' 'God spared not the angels that sinned; but cast them down to hell; and delivered them into chains of darkness, to be reserved unto judgment;' and if thou art spared in His patience, and kept on earth, drawn with 'cords of love,' plied with the offers of His grace, and set apart and sanctified unto glory, thou hast no reason to boast. O no; but every cause to 'rejoice with trembling.'

4. But the fervour and mightiness of this love arrest our attention — God so loved the world — loved it with such ardour and indescribable generosity—loved it so, that He gave His only-begotten Son. O the immensity of the gift! a divine gift from a divine Giver. The grandeur of His love may be seen in its results. If you can measure the gift, you may gauge the depth of the love which

bestowed it. But the gift is 'unspeakable.' That gift is God's own provision for the world's salvation; and while we contemplate the means, we shall also be able still to illustrate the greatness of the love.

II. The Gift of God's Love.

Now, we estimate the value of a gift by various criteria. First, the resources of the giver must be taken into the account. If a man be loaded with the blessings of fortune himself, and occasionally part with some of his superfluity, such a fraction, if estimated by its proportion to what remains behind it, is really far less in value than another gift that does not possess its semblance of magnitude. Our Lord reckoned by this scale when he declared that the poor widow, who cast her last mite into the treasury, gave truly more than the wealthy worshippers, with the ringing shekels and talents of their 'abundance;' for 'she gave her all.' Nor can the motives of the giver be left out of the calculation. One may heap favours on the head of a fallen foe to wound his pride and produce within him a rankling sense of his inferiority; but such a donation suffers a sad discount when compared with other, and, in themselves, smaller benefactions bestowed in cordial warmth and generosity of spirit. The manner, too, in which a gift is conferred must enter into the estimate. If it be withheld till it be wrung out of the donor by repeated and humiliating importunity; or if it be offered in a surly spirit, and its amount enlarged upon with undue exaggeration;

or if it be meted out slowly and with a prolonged comment upon the trouble and self-denial it has cost the benefactor, it sinks at once in importance, especially if placed in contrast with a lesser boon given in frank and spontaneous sympathy — the donor all the while looking and speaking as if he were the person obliged. Nor must the condition of the recipient be overlooked. Presents heaped on those who are themselves wallowing in opulence are not rated even at their intrinsic worth—a grain or two, more or less, passing unnoticed in the heap. But when the needy are benefited, they can appreciate the contribution, and if relief come to them in their deep necessity, in the very crisis of their necessity, and in the last moment of that crisis, and completely free them from danger and difficulty, then such discreet liberality, transcends alike description and gratitude. Especially does the blessing rise in utility and magnitude when it is adapted to him who receives it. To a man who had lost his way, and had wandered till faintness and hunger had seized him, a crust and a cup of water would be a largess far, far beyond a bag of gold, for his trembling arm could not lift it; or the charter of a lordly inheritance, for his eye, dimmed in death, could not decipher its contents.

Now, let the love of God be tried by any of these criteria, and you will at once conclude it to be beyond mensuration. Look, then, with enlightened veneration at the resources of the Giver. Are they not infinite and endless? The riches of the universe are at His disposal. But O, when He gave His Son, did He not give His all? What other gift remained superior to Him, equal to Him, or next to Him? There was no second Christ to confer. The divine treasury contained many gifts, which could easily have been conferred; but was it not exhausted when Christ was given? Beings of noble nature, yea, the 'sons of God,' might have formed the boon, and the vacancy would have been immediately supplied by the unwearied arm of Omnipotence. But in the donation of Christ, (we shrink from saying it, and yet we must,) you see at once the limits of possibility. For He is no creature, but the only-begotten Son. The epithet certainly implies His possession of a divine nature — one identical in essence and attributes with the Father, having in it the same majesty of uncreated existence, the same wisdom of universal range and grasp, the same power of unlimited operation, the same moral lineaments of character, and the same immutability that casts its bright mantle of perfection over them all. And as a Son did He enjoy the infinite attachment of the Father, and reciprocate it in eternal, boundless, and unchanging union.* If Christ be God, what gift superior to Him can be presented? or if He be the Son of God, what richer love could be exhibited? Donations might have chased each other from His hand, each greater and more godlike than the one which preceded it, and though the number and

---

* See Discourse on John xv. 9.

amount of such gifts might defy our arithmetic and outreach our imagination, such benefactions might continue through eternity; but when God loved the world, and gave His only-begotten Son, He gave a solitary gift, but one so immense and exhaustive that it could not be repeated. What unfathomed meaning in the monosyllable—so! God so loved us, that He gave His only-begotten Son — so like Him as to be His very image, and so loved by Him as to lie in His very bosom—Him he gave up to suffering and death to redeem a lost and rebellious world. Only in the infinite mind could such a love be cherished.

And the gift is enhanced by the motives of the Giver. There was in Him no selfish tinge. It was His profound pity for us in our low and lost estate that prompted Him to the unequalled gift. Undeservedly and unexpectedly were we saluted with the boon. There was no entreaty on the part of man. The sky was not rent with earnest and universal cries for help; the heart of God was not moved and melted because His ear was filled with the echoes of shrieking and clamorous humanity. No; His love was not so slow or reluctant; for salvation was provided for us, in purpose, ere yet we fell into the need of it. His love, in its eagerness, anticipated our fall, and made preparation for it.

Again, this gift of His own and only Son is the only donation that could have profited us. There is in Him every blessing we need, and every blessing is brought near us in the only form in which we can avail ourselves of it. For His complete salvation is also a free salvation, sealed and applied by the Holy Spirit. Guilt is pardoned and pollution is removed — our relations and our nature are equally changed — no element of perfection or felicity is withheld, and the germs engrafted now are destined for ever to mature and expand. No previous qualification is requisite, and no subsequent merit is anticipated. Works are wholly excluded as meritorious causes, and even the faith that brings a gratuitous justification is itself the gift of God. Christ includes a full and free forgiveness, an incipient and progressive sanctification — peace, hope, freedom, and joy — the deliverance of the soul, the final resurrection of the body, and the preparation of our entire nature to see, enjoy, and glorify God. What adaptation in this gift to a frail and guilty world, that could not win its way back to purity and paradise! Surely it comes in this its fitness from Him who 'knoweth our frame.' Is it not Infinite Love robed in Infinite Wisdom? O then, if the gift be of such a nature, in intrinsic value, in nobility of motive, in largeness of efficacy, and delicacy, of adaptation — if it be the Son of God, out of the heart of God, gifted to a thoughtless and hostile race, to bless it with Himself, and all the fulness that is in Him — will we not, under the impulse of such a reflection, be induced to exclaim, 'Herein is love, not that we loved God, but that he loved us, and sent his Son to be the propitiation for our sins!' God so loved the world that He gave, unsolicited and freely, the noblest gift in His means to confer—His second Self—His only-begotten Son. If you reason from the gift to the love which bestowed it, by what name shall you call it—where shall you find epithets to heap upon it? On this subject hyperbole is tameness, and seeming extravagance is actually sterility of language. Thus have we considered the amazing fact, that God has loved this guilty and insignificant world, and selected it to be the object of His tender attachment; and that He has so loved it, as to make provision for its deliverance, in the gift of His Son — that bright and matchless display of His boundless affection.

III. THE DESIGN OF GOD'S LOVE.

But the same fervour of the Divine love is seen, too, in the end contemplated, and in the peculiar instrumentality by which that end is achieved. He gave His only-begotten Son, for this purpose, 'that whosoever believeth in him, should not perish, but have everlasting life.' The language plainly implies that the race are in a lost condition. The Son of God is given to keep them from perishing — from sinking into irretrievable ruin. It was a perdition great and terrible which sin had produced. What a frightful spectacle! a soul in ruins — away from God, and hostile to Him — His image gone, His glory in the dust, a darkened mind, a distracted or sensualised heart, a spirit in thraldom, appetite predominant, the divine law forgotten, conscience bribed, hushed, or quelled; and the end of man's being not only unrealised, but, by a reversed polarity of inclination, fought against, and the end that was at the opposite extreme pursued and gained. And so the soul perishes — sinks, and sinks lower and lower still, till it fall into unending agony, and suffer the penalty of disloyal transgression. The most terrible imagery is employed in scripture to depict the fate of the wicked — the intensity of unquenchable fire — the blackness of unbroken gloom — ceaseless descent into a bottomless abyss — the gnawing of a undying worm — and the living spasms of the 'second death.' Not that any agony is needed in the form of material appliance; but the spirit of the language is, that the anguish of a soul, which, in another world, realises its severance from God, and feels itself to be the guilty cause of this alienation, which shuts out all hope or idea of return, and is ever reminded by all around it, in scenery and companionship, that it is lost, and lost for aye — must be an anguish so intolerable as to be above all description and beyond all relief.

Now, there may be many aspects of retribution. If memory recall the hosts of opportunities neglected, and wring the spirit with remorse, may not imagination create a torture by picturing out to itself the cross in fiery gleam, and be so haunted with the spectral symbol, as to be forced, ever and anon, to gaze upon it, while the vision must pierce the heart with unutterable pangs, because it looked not and was saved, when the day of grace was not gone, and a look of faith would have brought salvation?

Or may not fierce and turbulent passion, possessed in unchecked ascendency, and yearning for gratification and finding none, devour itself in increasing bitterness? If the teaching of the parable of the talents be listened to, there do we learn that gifts misimproved are taken away; that genius abused shall wither under the curse of sterility and impotence — for ever stung with the consciousness that itself has done it, and impelled to cry in agony to the Avenger, 'Thou art justified when thou speakest, and clear when thou judgest.' But no matter in what form this perdition is felt, the fact is, that a soul which comes short of the end of its being — the glorification and enjoyment of God — is a lost soul. If it cannot enjoy God, if it cannot look in His face, with confidence, if it cannot exult in His presence, if it do not feel Him to be its only portion and satisfaction, if it shrink and tremble before Him, and shun Him, conscious that it is hostile to Him and unlike Him — O then it is lost! for what can bless it or restore it? It must prey upon itself, and its essential immortality becomes its curse. It cannot die, or fall into the shades of non-existence. Could it cease to think or feel, there might be refuge; could it cast itself into stupor, there might be remedy. Without faith in God, or love to Him, it cannot but perish — there is no sphere where it can be happy, no state in which it can gladden or beguile itself.

Thus, the entire species having wrested itself from fellowship with God — having cast off His authority, and incurred His just displeasure — might have perished, and most certainly would have perished, if the mercy of God had not prevented. It had severed itself from the throne, and would have fallen, and fallen for ever, if the hand of Him that sits upon that throne had not arrested its descent, and a voice of ineffable love had cried, 'Deliver from going down to the pit: I have found a ransom.' But the object of the gift of Christ is not merely to free sinners from danger, keep them from doom, and bring them into a species of negative safety. He was given that positive blessings might be conferred; that rescue from danger might be followed by renewal of heart; that the fallen spirit might not only be stopped in its downward progress, but raised, and brought back, and re-united to the only source of life and joy. The disease is not simply checked, and the patient kept in weakness, but health and activity are fully restored. The prodigal son has not a portion sent him to keep him from starvation in the 'far country,' and among the unclean herds which he tends; nor is he detained at the spot where his father met him and embraced him, and there washed, and fed, and clothed; but he is at once brought into the household, to its inner chamber, clad in its best robe, feasted at its upper table, and upon its richest viands. The believer in Christ not only does not perish, but has 'everlasting life.'

What a mine of indescribable happiness in that term—life! It is the sum of all blessing—the elixir of all enjoyment. Life, how eagerly cherished by all! The young hope for it, the aged are loath to quit it, the sick man tugs for it, the bad man dreads its termination, and the good man prays for its continuance. The whole struggle of the world is for life — for means to enliven and prolong it. It is full of contrivances to shut out the idea of death. Now, if there be such anxiety for the life that now is, a life that is brief and chequered by clouds and trials; a life that is rarely stretched to threescore and ten years, and is ended amidst spasms and tears; O what intense aspirations, and prayers, and wrestlings should there not be after a life that is not measured by centuries or by millenniums; a life far above change and sorrow—a life serene as the bosom of its Giver, and endless as God's own eternity! For this life is not mere immortality, but a happy immortality. It is the perfection of our spiritual being, enjoyed in the presence of God; the intellect acting in an atmosphere of unclouded truth, and the heart throbbing in a region of universal love; life having found its highest aim and its noblest development in the praise and service of God. This is life — to be in Him, near Him, like Him — Himself the giver, and Himself the gift — Himself the portion, and Himself the song.

> 'And not to one created thing
> Shall our embrace be given;
> But all our joy shall be in God —
> For only God is heaven.'

'Sin has reigned unto death: but grace reigns through righteousness unto eternal life by Christ

Jesus our Lord.' How glorious, therefore, the purpose of the divine gift of the Son of God — to confer life; to give man the best of blessings — eternal life!

For this life never dies; it is 'everlasting life.' Ah! how chilly should our enjoyment of heavenly glory be, if we had any suspicions of its termination! The faintest doubt of its coming to an end would wither the laurel and unstring the harp. That all this glory should have the pall of gloom over it, and this life should come to its last moment, how saddening and vexatious must be the thought of such a possibility! No; the life is everlasting— as it springs from the 'fountain of life.' The grace that conferred it never wearies in giving, and never revokes its boon; the throne before which it throbs and sings is never eclipsed; the merit of its Redeemer's work can never be exhausted; the human spirit is possessed itself of an undying essence, and therefore this life of life lasts for ever. The lamp kindled at the divine radiance, and burning so near the source which feeds it, can never be extinguished. So long as God lives and dwells in love, so long shall the saved spirit live in Him, and dwell in His love. This is the high end of believing humanity — an end so godlike, that you cannot doubt that God has designed it, and prepared you for it. If there was love beyond measure in God's gift of His Son, is there not also affection beyond parallel in this high and happy purpose realised through faith in such a boon?

For salvation is not of works. Man is not summoned to some stupendous effort in order to win his way to glory. Nor are the terms of the divine law lowered in order that he may be able to comply. But salvation is provided, and you are summoned to accept it. The blessing is 'of faith, that it might be by grace;' and nothing stands between you and salvation, but your own unwillingness to take it; nothing between you and heaven, but your reluctance to enter it. How, then, is this blessing of everlasting life to be got? It is not flung lavishly and at random over the world, nor is it forced upon the acceptance of sinners. They are not compelled to live, nor do they unconsciously inhale the elements of this new life. No; only he that believeth 'shall not perish, but have everlasting life.' Faith is the instrument of life. Cordial belief in Christ Jesus, God's own gift, brings into the heart the first pulsations of the new existence. And tell me why should there not be faith? Why should not God get credit for His love? There might have been some tremulous sensation, if that love had been described as merely resident in the Divine bosom; but surely there can be no hesitation when you see it embodied in the gift of Christ, His Son — so loved by Him, and so like Him; and when you can trace it in its descent to earth, and see the babe in Bethlehem, scan the footprints of the man of sorrows and sympathy, and shudder at the expiring agony of the sufferer on Calvary. Faith in Christ is requisite for salvation by Him. Whosoever believeth in Him shall not perish. Belief in Him, as the manifestation of the divine love, brings you within the sphere of saving influence. It shows your acquiescence in God's plan of salvation, and your anxiety to avail yourselves of it. Of Christ's ability to save, there can be no doubt. It is said of Him in this gospel, that 'by Him all things were made;' and is not He that created the universe mighty enough to redeem a lost soul? The arm that upholds all worlds is surely able to lift a human spirit out of misery into glory. Can you doubt the resources of that Omnipotence which, amidst all its astounding operations, 'fainteth not, neither is weary?' And as is His power, so is His will; the persuasion of the one must be as strong as your conviction of the other. For He became His Father's gift, and took upon Him man's nature, and in it made satisfaction. If He was born as never man was born, spake as never man spake, acted as never man acted, loved as never man loved, suffered as never man suffered, and died as never man died — O who would refuse to confide in Him, or commit to Him the keeping of his immortal soul! Why then so reluctant to have faith in Him; what possible motive can there be for doubt? Surely He has said enough and done enough to quell every suspicion. And this faith, the result of divine influence, leads to the acceptance of Him as Saviour, to justification by His blood, and sanctification by His Spirit. He who believeth in Him shall not perish, but, pardoned and purified by His grace, shall ascend to the enjoyment of eternal life.

But who may possess this faith? Is any one debarred? No: 'Whosoever believeth in Him shall not perish.' Any one may believe, every one is summoned to believe, no matter what his character, country, rank, or age. The gospel is offered to the world without discrimination. It has no national restriction, no geographical peculiarity. It is presented, in all its fulness, to 'mankind sinners, as such.'

And thus, through the love of God and His infinite gift, whosoever, in any age, believeth on Christ shall not perish, but shall have everlasting life. The blessings of salvation were not all given away in the early centuries. The myriads saved in those epochs did neither diminish nor exhaust the treasury of redemption. The love of God and the gift of His Son have a fulness which is neither emptied by time nor absorbed by numbers; still any one responding to the invitation is welcomed. The blood shed on Calvary has not spent its virtue on the hosts which already have been pardoned and purified in it. Its power is still as fresh as when the thousands at Pentecost were washed in it, and myriads in Antioch and Rome were blessed with its atoning merit; as when the thief saw it shed on the cross, and the beloved disciple declared its efficacy to cleanse 'from all sin.' In every subsequent period the same truth will keep its blessed place, and down to the last moment of time shall each sinner that rests on Christ be ransomed and glorified.

Nay more, any one of any nation believing in Him shall not perish, but be saved. It was a son of Abraham, with Jewish blood in his veins, who died; but His atonement has an efficacy unlimited by race or country. It has no distinction of colour, clime, or language. Wherever fallen humanity is found, it receives the same glorious offer, be its hue what it may, and no matter under what sky it may live and breathe. The Shemite equally with the Hamite — the savage of Africa, no less than the educated European — he with the chain, and he with the crown, are all upon a level. Every man, even though he be a demon in ferocity or a brute in sensuality; every living man — a man on earth and not in hell, is warranted to seek and commanded to accept salvation. No one is excluded by position or distance. Yes, thou poor Aztec, stunted, and but the semblance of a man, thou too art welcome; and thou bleeding and fettered negro, thou art doubly welcome, for He came to 'proclaim liberty to the captive, and the opening of the prison to them that are bound.'

God so loved the world, that He gave His only-begotten Son, that any one, of any character, believing on Him might not perish. Jesus 'came not to call the righteous, but sinners to repentance.' Classical philosophy and religion chased away the vulgar and poor, and concerned themselves only with the refined and virtuous. But Christ does not spurn the sinner. His blessings are not only for those of fairer character and of better reputation; they are for sinners, even for the most abandoned. O yes! He pardons sins without number, and sinners without distinction. If any are specially invited, it is the very unworthy — the utterly depraved. 'He lifteth the poor out of the dunghill, and setteth him with princes, even the princes of the earth.' O how many such triumphs has the gospel witnessed! Let the veriest sinner that breathes turn to Christ, and he shall feel, ay and feel at once, that the 'blood of Jesus Christ cleanseth from all sin.' Who then can despair? Why not believe? Thou art not placed beyond the pale of His love. Sunk and low, proud and filthy as thou art — in rags and vice, the devil in thy heart, and blasphemy on thy tongue, thou art the object of the love of God most high. Christ was thy brother; and that loving brother's blood was shed that thou mightest believe and live. Thou art not cast off; the heart that bled for thee still yearns over thee. Feel this — how can you but feel it — and be saved. We proclaim a gospel of infinite merit and universal adaptation. The annals of the church are filled with examples of the conversion of the biggest sinners. 'Such were some of you,' says the apostle to the church at Corinth — sinners indeed above many — 'but ye are washed, but ye are sanctified, but ye are justified in the name of the Lord Jesus, and by the Spirit of our God.' Should there be a contest in heaven as to who is most indebted to the love of Jehovah, the claim will be awarded not to the 'babe thither caught from womb and breast,' whose early death prevented its pollution by the world; but to him who could say, 'I was a persecutor, a blasphemer, and injurious;' to him who had been a paragon of depravity; to him who had lived like Newton, and blasphemed like Bunyan: to him who had revelled in the darkness and impiety of the night, ere the blessed morning burst upon him. Yours was a noted example on earth, and yours is a thrilling song in glory; your crown is brightest among the bright, and your harp has a melody all its own. Among many wonderful trophies, surpassing wonder attaches to you; ye know more than most the tenderness of the divine heart, and the might of the divine arm. Christ has shown in you 'a pattern of all long-suffering;' and the Lord, of His infinite mercy, grant that we may rightly appreciate it and savingly profit by it.

Yea, in fine, God so loved the world that He gave His only-begotten Son, that any one, at any period of life, believing on Him might not perish. The young are welcomed: 'He took children in his arms and blessed them;' but the old are not placed under a ban. At any instant of any day, or month, or year, may the soul believe. The divine love never sleeps, and it is no intermittent emotion. At Bethesda, only one, and he the first one who stepped into the pool, was healed; but the whole band of invalids may all bathe in this fountain, and each in his turn will be saved. Its waters need no periodical stirring, for they possess a perennial efficacy. Seventy years may have passed over the impenitent sinner, and all that God has done for him may have been wantonly despised, and yet, should his spirit look to Jesus, a full forgiveness will be at once conferred. Yes, even at the last and solemn hour, and ere the heart cease its pulsations, it may find the preciousness of Christ. Its last look may be to the cross, and its last syllables, lost yet saved, may be, I believe . . . in Christ. But yet this last hour is not to be trusted to; for you cannot tell when it may come. The ninth hour approaches, the tenth hour is numbered, the eleventh hour strikes, and, ere you are aware, the twelfth hour tolls, and you are hurried into a lost and undone eternity.

How now shall we tell the immensity of this love, and the indescribable value of this gift, when their glorious end is contemplated—the salvation of sinners, of every age and country, of every character and period of life! What bosom but that of God's could contain such an emotion; what gift but that of Christ could have realised such blessed consequences! Whatever be the special relation of the love of Christ to His church,* this is the general aspect of the love of God to the world—His 'man-love,' as it has been termed by the apostle. (Titus iii. 4.) It has made provision for an indiscriminate and universal offer of the gospel, and it secures the salvation of all who will accept it. What more shall we say, or can we say, to induce you to 'believe on the Lord Jesus Christ?' Trifle not with time and invitation. Perplex not your spirits with

---

* See Discourse II.

theories about the nature and origin of faith. The question is not, how you believe, but what you believe; the value of your belief depends upon its object and foundation. 'I believe; help thou mine unbelief.' You may believe much of no immediate practical value — the devil believes the theoretic truth; but you are summoned to credit the statement of our text — this divine record, which forms the very pith and marrow of the gospel.

With what rapturous feelings the idea of this love should fill us, and with what fervent gratitude should we respond to it! With what prolonged hosannas should we hail the advent of Christ, and what unwavering confidence should we repose in Him! And if it be that we have ruined ourselves beyond self-recovery, how shall we admire the divine plan of restoration; for He that made the world, saves it; He against whom it had sinned, gave His Son to redeem it. But yet if you do not avail yourselves of these blessed provisions; if this love do not move you, and this gift do not satisfy you, and this faith do not fill you — then the hazard is terrible; for your original ruin will have a new aggravation, in your rejection of God's helping hand. If you do not accept God's salvation, having such an origin and instrumentality, and if the universe cannot present you with any other, then you must perish in your wantonness and crime. And that will be not because there is no pity for you, and no one cares for you; for God loves you, and the tenderness of a mother's love is not equal to His. Nor will it be because there is no deliverance provided; for the bosom of God is emptied of His only Son, and He loved you, wept over you, and died for you. Neither will it be because you are placed in circumstances which bar out the power of the gospel; for no one is frowned upon, and every one may turn, believe, and live. Will you madly wrestle against your happiness, and resolve to perish in spite of all this love felt for you, and all this provision made for you? What other help could you covet? Could you imagine a more ardent love, or a more glorious deliverance? Could heaven be brought nearer to earth than it has been, or could the heart of God be more truly laid bare before you? Shall you then doubt— doubt of His love—as He points to the cross and to His bleeding Son? O it is provoking to a fellow-creature to have his word doubted and his veracity suspected; how much more so to the most true God! There is nothing that brings such vexation and disappointment to a benefactor as to see his good intentions misunderstood, and the very benignity of his purpose called in question; and what must God feel when His love makes no impression on you, and you refuse to give Him any credit for His declaration of it? Can you commit a sin more wounding to Him after what He has said and done, one that so pointedly insults Him, and that so awfully ruins yourselves? Such unbelief hardening itself against such love must meet with very signal punishment, for it at once wooes and warrants its frightful and aggravated doom. Do homage, we therefore conjure you, to this love; extol it, and accept its mighty gift, and, according to the pledge of the text, you shall be saved. And the end shall at length be reached, and your perfected natures will pour out their grateful melodies in honour of this unceasing love, and in perpetual view of Him whose mission was its unexampled fruit. Then, indeed, of the truth and blessedness of this verse your own experience in heaven will be a living, glorious, and eternal illustration.

LECTURE II.

THE LOVE OF CHRIST TO HIS CHURCH — ITS FERVOUR AND SELF-SACRIFICE—ITS NEARER PURPOSE AND ITS ULTIMATE RESULT.

EPHESIANS v. 25–27.

'Christ also loved the church, and gave himself for it; that he might sanctify and cleanse it with the washing of water by the word; that he might present it to himself a glorious church, not having spot, or wrinkle, or any such thing.'

OUR last discourse was an attempt to illustrate God's love to the world — this is intended to describe Christ's love to His church. The emotion now to be reviewed is, therefore, the inner love of the Redeemer towards His own. In the former case, the love of God was seen to be broad, full, and indiscriminate, shining on the world like its sun, or enveloping the world like its atmosphere; in the present case, the Saviour's love will be found to be deep, ardent, and saving, but regarded as exercised toward those who have been or are to be justified by the blood and sanctified by the Spirit of its glorious possessor. For, as the solar beam often falls upon a hard and barren rock, and often nurses weeds and noxious herbage; and as the atmosphere sucks from the morass into its bosom the elements of pestilence and death: so the love of God frequently hardens where it is meant to bless; the reckless spirit presumes upon it, and becomes still more defiant in its tone and more resolute in its unbelief. But the Saviour's love to His own, works out its destined purpose; it has chosen and formed the church, and will glorify itself in it. For is not that church the great company of the redeemed — confined to no age or country, no class or character — the whole host of all who are, or are to be ransomed and glorified? No wonder that Jesus loved this bright assemblage, the entire circle of which was present from eternity to His all-sweeping eye. When He regards this church, and thinks of its origin and safety, He calls it, as He alone is entitled to do, 'those whom thou hast given me;' but when we survey it, and think of its distinctive character, we name it, the band of believers, disciples or brethren in Christ.

But this company, no matter how bright and joyous its destiny, had no more claim on the attachment of Christ than the world had on the love of God. The church was originally in the world and of it, though in God's grace it is taken out of it. Helpless and exposed it lay, till His fond and pitying eye looked and loved. It was no better than the world, and it was no superior worth that attracted Christ to it, no singular or exceptional loveliness that originated his affection. Scan the roll of its members, and you will find among them men who had been specimens of daring impiety and ferocious guilt, even the chief of sinners. For what says the apostle to the early churches: 'All have sinned, and come short of the glory of God.' 'Sin has reigned to death.' 'When we were enemies, we were reconciled.' 'Ye were the servants of sin.' The Ephesian church had been 'dead in trespasses and sins;' 'aliens from the commonwealth of Israel, strangers from the covenants, having no hope, and without God in the world.' 'They fulfilled the desires of the flesh and of the mind, and were children of wrath.' 'Ye were sometimes darkness.' These are but a sample of the clauses of that indictment which hangs over every member of the human family, and from which those who compose the church are in no sense or form by nature exempted.

In this passage we have the great theme, the love of Christ — the proof and result of that love in His death — the nearer intention of that love and death in the sanctification of His Church, and their ulterior purpose in the final glorification of His Church.

I. THE LOVE OF CHRIST TO HIS CHURCH.

'Christ loved the church.' What else than love could have selected, pardoned, purified, and redeemed the church? What other feeling could have stooped to such guilt, and raised it to such glory? To what other attribute in the nature of God could the apostle have appealed? What other divine property could have formed such a conception, and carried it out at so awful a sacrifice; would have come into the lowest depths, touched what is so leprous and impure, beautified it, and carried it up in its bosom to unending felicity? An idea like that of our salvation, so rich, glorious, and free, beginning on earth, and ending in heaven, could only spring out of infinite love. And this love was no incidental emotion, excited for the first time by the view of human helplessness and guilt. Even when He lay in His Father's bosom, His thoughts were thoughts of love — even then 'He rejoiced in the habitable parts of the earth.' As every one feels, we naturally associate ideas of height and splendour with heaven, the place of His past abode. The glory of God fills it. His throne is in it, and sheds all around it its royal radiance. It is the residence of the great Architect, fitted up for Himself with dazzling splendour. No taint of sin is there. The image of Jehovah enshrines itself in every heart. Wherever He looks, He sees the happy reflection of Himself; and His heart is regaled, and His ear is ever filled with melody from the highest creatures. For angels dwell there, and they are the noblest specimens of divine workmanship — of vast mind, prodigious power, and incredible swiftness; so like 'gods,' as to be called so in scripture. And yet the Son of God, looking beyond all this magnificence strewn through heaven, and all this homage presented to Himself, and gazing down through the blazing train of worlds that swept around His throne, could thus tell what were His emotions even in the depths of a bygone eternity, when He utters the wondrous avowal, 'My delights were with the sons of men.' Ay, and though the certainty of His own death was present to his mind, death involving such spiritual anguish and corporeal torture; and though those for whom He died were to nail Him to the tree, spurn His claims, and requite His kindness with unbelief and hostility, He flinched not, but loved and bled for guilty, and ungrateful humanity. Was it not, therefore, an eternal affection? and if it had no beginning, it can have no boundary, and it shall have no termination. Who shall gauge its fervour? What plummet shall sound the infinitude of the Divine bosom? As a divine love to a creature so far beneath Him, what matchless condescension there is in it! as the love of a holy God toward offending creatures, does not the contrast proclaim its gracious tenderness and strength?

'Christ loved the church.' But, in fact, to know the power and depth of the love of Christ, surpasses the limits of created intellect. It has a height, and we cannot climb it; a depth, and we cannot explore it; a breadth, and we cannot grasp it; a length, and we cannot compute it. Is it not infinite as its Author, and changeless and everlasting as the heart in which it has its home? Men may fancy what they cannot express, and feel what they are unable to describe; but on this momentous topic inability attaches to heart as well as tongue, to thought no less than language. O! do we not see in the incarnate Lord a pure and fervent love assuming a nature of clay, feeding the hungry, taming the demoniac, sympathising with the wretched, bleeding on the cross, and prostrate in the tomb! And we must not contemplate its mere warmth, but also its illustrious harmony with the sterner attributes of the Godhead. It is a love of the sinner, but it attempts no compromise with his sin. In its outflow toward us, it neither prostrates holiness nor bribes justice, but throws such a moral lustre over these attributes, as to reveal more truly their unchanged and original purity and brilliance.

'Christ loved the church.' But that love was no inert emotion. It did not lie in a waveless calm within Him. Nor was it a divine luxury on which He feasted, without leaving heaven and laying aside the robes of His majesty. No. He felt its keen impulses, descended from the throne, left the hallelujahs of angels, and threw the mantle of our manhood over His higher nature — became one of ourselves; and all from love to us. We have no means of enabling us to calculate the depths of His condescension, when in love to us He became man, and in order to suffer for us. Were a creature, even the highest and loveliest of heaven, to leave its station and descend to our world, the degrees of this humiliation might be counted and measured. For though he exchanged heaven for earth, and the free and buoyant energies of a spiritual nature for the tardy motions and limited capabilities of an animal frame, and unlimited range of travel from orb to orb for a stationary residence on this the meanest of planets; even then, with all this extraordinary contrast, the various steps of such a descent might be meted in depth and computed in number. But between the loftiest intelligence and Him who sits upon the throne as the Son of God, there is the immeasurable interval of infinitude, and none 'can by searching find' it out. The distance from the highest point in creation to the lowest, may be investigated and reduced to a scale, but, at an unapproachable height above all creation, sat He who loved the church, and came down to save it.

'Christ loved the church,' and He walked in that church in the radiance of love. Thoughts of love nestled in His heart; words of love lingered on His lips; deeds of love flew from His arm; and His steps left behind them the impress of love. It threw its soft halo over His cradle at Bethlehem, and it fringed with its mellow splendours the gloom of the cloud under which He expired on Calvary. It gave edge to His reproofs, and pathos to His invitations. It was the magnet that guided Him in all his wanderings. It bound Him to the cross and held Him there, and not the iron nails that pierced His hands and His feet. It thrilled in His bosom, and glistened in His eye. Yes; 'Christ . . . Love,' said the dying philosopher,* 'Jesus Christ—love—the same thing.' It prompted Him to impart miraculous aid on every opportunity. His meekness was but one of its features. It clothed itself in forgiveness towards His enemies, and its last pulsation was in a prayer for His murderers. It was the spi-

---

* Sir James Mackintosh.

ritual atmosphere in which He lived, moved, and had His being. There was love to His mother, love to His kinsfolk, love to His country, love to His disciples, love to His enemies, love to the church, and love to the wide, wide world. And all this love had His own for its central object, round whom it ever hovered with sleepless tenderness and assiduity.

'Christ loved the church;' but those exhibitions of love during His life are eclipsed by the displays of it in His death. It shines out with novel charms amidst the shades of dissolution, for it shrunk not from the shame and woe of the cross. There is a form of friendship in the world which scarcely deserves the name. It fawns upon and fondles the prosperous, but flees and spurns the victims of adversity. At its highest warmth it but evaporates in words, the fulsome incense of flattery being its only product. But the Saviour's love to His church was no mere profession, no verbal attachment. From heaven it came down to earth, and from divine immortality to human pains and dissolution. Abasement did not repress its impulses, hostility did not freeze its ardour, and the most terrible prospect which an omniscient fancy could depict neither abated its zeal nor subdued its courage. For the Saviour loved the church; and to give her the best of all proofs of the depth and sincerity of that love, He gave Himself for the church.

The strength and the sacrifices of love are indeed proverbial. Dangers incredible are treated with disdain, and enterprises which the sobriety of reason would be apt to pronounce impracticable are achieved with easy celerity. But man shrinks from death. He may suffer many things, subject himself to many privations, and conquer appalling difficulties; but he starts at the idea of death. 'Scarcely for a righteous man will one die; yet peradventure for a good man some would even dare to die. But God commendeth his love towards us, in that, while we were yet sinners, Christ died for us.' The 'righteous man' is one who is of sterling integrity, whose word is his bond, whose sovereign rule in all things is equity, who pays to the last farthing what he owes, and exacts to the last farthing what is due to himself. He is more revered than loved — men stand in awe of him; and scarcely will one die for him. The 'good man' is righteous, but he is more — he is not only just, but kind; not only equitable, but obliging; full of generosity and good deeds; and he is so admired and loved that, in the bond of friendship, 'peradventure some one would even dare to die' for him. But we had neither the one character nor the other. Righteousness and goodness were alike wanting in us; we were 'sinners,' 'enemies,' 'without strength,' deformed by impurity, when the Divine love not only displayed, but 'commended' itself in the death of Christ for us. In His love, Christ gave Himself for, or in room of the church. The language is sacrificial, and denotes that the death of Christ was a voluntary and a proper propitiation.

II. The Sacrifice, as the Expression and Result of Love.

In the stead of the church He died, to deliver her from death, the sentence which so righteously lay upon her. The death of the Son of God is a true and mighty sacrifice. That death might be viewed in a variety of aspects; for while it was an instance of exalted bravery, and a confirmation of His sincere attachment to men, it was also an example to all His followers, inspiring them with that patience which they must evince during their lives, and with that calmness and fortitude which must not forsake them even in the hour of trial and dissolution. But it was more than a tragedy or a martyrdom. To suppose the Saviour to be the victim of human persecution is true, but to suppose Him nothing more, is but to give an ordinary termination to His extraordinary existence. In what, if he only sealed his testimony with His blood, does He differ from apostles and prophets, who loved not their lives even unto the death? In what respects, on this hypothesis, is the death of the Son of Mary, who was crucified, of more honour and value than that of the son of Elizabeth, who was beheaded? How many since Christ's time have bled and been burned for the church — how many of the prophets of Israel were put to death by their apostate nation; yet which of all these is ever said to have given himself to God, or to have died in our stead, or to have been the propitiation for our sin? But the death of Jesus was an oblation: 'He loved us, and gave himself for us, an offering and a sacrifice to God for a sweet-smelling savour.'

The central idea of a sacrifice is vicarious suffering. Piacular victims have been frequent in all ages, as guilt is a load upon the conscience which no efforts can shake off, and the heathen, under this impulse, stained the altar with human blood. In no other way could sacrifices ease the conscience of the worshippers, than by being supposed to bear the penalty due to their guilt. The victim was accounted guilty, and punished as such. It was offered in the room, and made expiation for the sin, of the offender. 'So Christ was once offered to bear the sin of many.' And it is this quality which gives its solitary eminence to His death, and not the wicked means by which it was effected, nor yet the patient magnanimity with which it was endured. A violated law had uttered its curse, the sentence had gone forth and must be executed, and the moral administration of the universe was deeply involved in the result; and therefore the Saviour died that sin might be punished, and that the government issuing forgiveness might be confirmed in the very act of it, and that a more brilliant and impressive demonstration of the holiness of God should be afforded in the pardon of sin than if man had never fallen, or having fallen, should himself be visited with the full infliction of the penalty. In consequence of this self-exposure for us, his severest anguish was that of his soul. O! it was not shame, persecution, or crucifixion, for these terrible elements could have been easily borne; it was not the rage and malice of Satan — these also could have been trampled on; but it was the endurance in Himself of the punishment due to that sin which He had taken upon Him, that drank up His spirit, prompted the moan in Gethsemane, and the mysterious complaint on Calvary. The 'silver cord' was loosed, and the 'golden bowl' was broken by the ruthless violence of His persecutors; but 'the travail of His soul' was induced by vicarious pangs. It is the uniform testimony of Scripture that He ' suffered once for sins'—that 'He who knew no sin became sin for us' — that 'we are justified by his blood' — that 'the chastisement of our peace was upon Him'—that 'He offered himself without spot to God' — and that 'His blood cleanseth from all sin.' And in that world where theology is perfect, redemption is ascribed not to the birth of Christ with its mysteries, nor to the miracles of Christ with their splendour, nor to the life of Christ with its holy beauty, but only to His death: 'Thou art worthy to take the book, and to loose the seals thereof; for thou wast slain, and hast redeemed us to God by thy blood.' Thus did the Incarnation of love enter alone into that ominous cloud which, charged with terrible thunder, hung over our guilty race, and He gathered in upon Himself its dark and destructive elements; and the cloud, now bereft of them, assumes a hue of glory, and weeps itself away in soft and fertilising showers. Who can estimate the depth and fervour of a love which gave itself to such agonies, laid itself on the altar a perfect oblation, suffered that we should not suffer, and died that we might live?

For in His love He gave HIMSELF. It was no inferior gift He selected, for no inferior gift could be the adequate expression of His love. It found no donation worthy of itself but Himself. It would be content with nothing else, and nothing less. The Divine Lover gave Himself. The fires of Lebanon to consume the 'cattle upon a thousand hills;' the lightnings of Jehovah to reduce the universe to ashes,—these could not suffice to redeem a world. A Being originally above the law, and placed voluntarily by Himself beneath it, only He can so obey it as to satisfy it, and so suffer its penalty as to liberate from it the original transgressor. His obedience and suffering are not for Himself, since the law has no claim upon Him, and the merit of his voluntary sacrifice is made over to those who could neither obey nor suffer for themselves. Not that God does or can suffer; but the humanity of Jesus was one in person with divinity, and the union was not dissolved by the agony upon the cross. What an amazing gift! Himself—the Son of God —in earnest and loving self-sacrifice. Surely the voice of the Redeemer's love speaks in thrilling accents from the cross. That patient and holy victim suffered as never being suffered—that pure and susceptible heart was wrung as never heart was wrung;

and all to convince you of His love, and confer upon you its choice and saving blessings.

> 'Ah never, never canst thou know,
> What, then, for thee the Saviour bore,
> The pangs of that mysterious woe,
> That wrung His frame at every pore—
> The weight that press'd upon His brow,
> The fever of His bosom's core.

> 'Yes, man for man perchance may brave
> The horrors of the yawning grave;
> And friend for friend, or child for sire,
> Undaunted and unmoved expire,
> From love, or piety, or pride,
> But who can die as Jesus died?'

Himself, too, was both priest and victim — HE gave HIMSELF. Unlike the Jewish pontiff, He did not stretch some other victim on the altar, nor was He laid there Himself by the hand of any officiating minister. In sovereign generosity and heroism He offered Himself. And it was a solitary act. It needs no repetition. Its atoning merit can never be exhausted. 'It is appointed unto men once to die,' says the apostle; that is, our nature can only die once — and therefore Christ's real humanity is proof of the oneness of His death. That one death has infinite merit. Repeated oblations, under the law, were confessions of inefficacy. The atonement of the day had only an expiatory value of twelve months, and the scene was re-enacted every year — there was an annual propitiation and sprinkling of blood. But Jesus 'suffered once for sin.' The high priest remained but a few mysterious moments in front of the mercy-seat and the Divine presence ere he re-passed the vail, and on that same day of the next year he re-entered with the blood of another victim; but Jesus has passed into heaven itself, and still is there pleading the value of His blood, only once shed, and the merit of His sacrifice, only once presented.

How voluntary was the gift — He GAVE Himself! It was not extorted. The sufferer was no victim of circumstances. After he began to teach, there did not slowly dawn upon Him the painful necessity of suffering; but He came into the world for this very purpose — to bleed and die. 'Sacrifice and offering thou didst not desire; mine ears hast thou opened: burnt-offering and sin-offering hast thou not required. Then said I, Lo, I come: in the volume of the book it is written of me, I delight to do thy will, O my God: yea, thy law is within my heart.' The animal was tied by cords to the horns of the altar ere its life was taken; Abraham bound Isaac his son, ere he laid him on the wood, and stretched out his arm with the knife to slay him; but all our Lord's intellectual and moral energies were free and unfettered, for when He gave Himself for us He felt no curb, but that of self-imposed obligation, and was urged by no stimulus, but that of unquenchable zeal and fondness. Compulsory suffering would have been highest injustice, and would have damaged the entire worth of the oblation.

HIMSELF the offering — how pure! O, then, if you view Him as the priest, are not purity and perfection His characteristics; as He appears before the altar, His heart confesses no sin ere He makes atonement for the people — no prayer for personal absolution escapes His lips; His supplications arising from the depth of His sympathies, assume the form of intercessions; and though He plead with the yearning interest of a brother, yet has He no sinful likeness to that family of which He made Himself a member, and no participation in that guilt whose removal He implores. Standing as the 'daysman' between heaven and earth, His higher nature has received no contagion from its humbler partner. He was on earth, like His own 'word of prophecy,' a 'light shining in a dark place;' the Man of men — a spotless representative and advocate. And if you look upon Him as the sacrifice, what imperfection can be attached to the Lamb of God, bearing, ay, bearing away the sin of the world. That oblation, no matter what idea you form of the altar on which it was presented, was pure as the fire from God by which it was consumed; nor even were its ashes suffered 'to see corruption.' Surely the love which prompted such a noble gift is a love 'that passeth knowledge.' What imagination can grasp it — what penetration can fathom it! There was nothing in the church to excite it, but everything to repel it: 'While we were yet without strength, Christ died for us.' Yet He loved, and that love embodied itself in the noblest of gifts — the gift of

Himself — generous and self-bestowed; and not only so, but it was crowned in a death which was calmly encountered and triumphantly endured. Ye members of His church, as you look to His cross, will you not be always re-assured of His love: when you see Him groaning, bleeding and dying in agony and shame, under the deepest of shadows, and beneath the most mysterious and terrible of visitations, will you not feel that His love is without parallel in its unextinguishable fervour, and majestic results? It writes its name on every blessing, and its voice is the music of every invitation. Will it not glow in your bosoms, and thrill in your praises?

> 'Now to Him that loved us, gave us
> Every pledge that love could give—
> Freely shed His blood to save us,
> Gave His life, that we might live,
> Be the kingdom
> And dominion,
> And the glory, evermore!'

III. THE NEARER PURPOSE OF HIS LOVE AND DEATH.

Let us now consider the proximate purpose of the Saviour's love and death — the sanctification of His Church: 'That he might sanctify and cleanse it with the washing of water by the word.' This is a design worthy of such a love, and fitting such a death: to purify and ennoble its objects — to wash them from the stain of guilt, and clothe them in the 'beauties of holiness.'

The pardon of sin is not referred to, as it is but

as a means to an end. The imputation of righteousness precedes, and prepares for the infusion of holiness. The remission of guilt does not bestow purity, nor reconfer original innocence. Therefore in this salvation man is not only justified, but he is also sanctified; not only does he receive a full and irrevocable pardon of all his sins, but he becomes a new creature. Not alone to free him from hell, but to prepare him also for heaven, to elevate him to those holy joys he had lost and forfeited by the fall, was the great end and purpose of the Saviour's mission and death.

That death not only affects our state, but also tells upon our character. He died to sanctify the church. This sanctification, though it be the design of the atonement, has indeed its immediate source in the influences of the Divine Spirit. He regenerates the heart; and the radical change is one from death to life. Not only does He originate the change, but He sustains it; for He 'abides' within us. What He commences, He still fosters and perfects. The life which He imparts He nurses and cherishes till it come to maturity. The forgiveness of guilt is an act without us, or a sentence of release, which, on being pronounced, takes immediate and complete effect. But sanctification is a work within us, which is progressive in its nature, and which, owing to our waywardness, is often retarded. O! there is many a sigh and many a struggle when the heart is carried away by inferior motives — the law in the members warring against the law of the mind, and threatening to bring it into captivity. From the mysterious moment of regeneration, when the spirit is born again, or the more palpable moment when this hidden gift reveals its power in conversion, on till the instant of death, the work of sanctification advances, often very unequally, and amidst tears and prayers, conflicts and triumphs. The pardon of iniquity is a blessing that comes directly and without intervention from the cross; but the purification of our nature, though it have the Spirit for its agent, is yet carried out by various instrumentalities. Thus it is said in our text, 'He loved the church, and gave himself for it,' in order that, having cleansed it, He might sanctify it 'with the washing of water by the word.' The terms are expressive. The allusion is to a bridal ceremony, and perhaps to the usual ante-nuptial lustrations. As the church is the bride, there may be a reference to the water of baptism, but to that only as the symbol and pledge of spiritual influence. And the phrase, 'by the word,' we take to be a reference to the scriptures — 'the word,' 'the word of God.' The meaning, then, seems to be, that in consequence of the love and of the atoning death of Christ, men are now sanctified by the Spirit, acting generally by means of the word.

And that word does possess a sanctifying power. 'Wherewithal shall a young man cleanse his way? By taking heed thereto according to thy word.' 'Sanctify them through thy truth, thy word is truth.' How often does the word stir up the conscience, and appal it with solemn and deep conviction, pressing it to seek safety in the cross. 'It pierces even to the dividing asunder of joints and marrow;' throws the soul into such an agitation, as if the 'pains of hell' had taken hold on it, that it may be led to the refuge of the gospel. With what prominence and charms it holds up Christ as the one Saviour, amidst the terror of its thunders, and the earnest agony of its invitations. But to the believer it is also the standard of duty, the rule of manners. It shows him his defects, and urges him to progress. It warns him and encourages him. It preserves him from self-delusion, for it holds up the spirituality of the law, and the immaculate purity of Christ's example. So that, amidst his lamentations of weakness, he looks to the word of God for courage; and the more he drinks into the spirit of the Bible, and the more he feels its laws engraven on his heart, the more does he grow in sanctity, and realise his lofty destiny — 'to glorify God, and enjoy him for ever.' If the attainment of holiness be likened to a life, the word is the food; if to a race, it is a 'light to the feet;' if to a battle, it is the 'sword of the Spirit,' by which our antagonists are cloven down and dispersed.

Still the Bible is but a dead letter without the Spirit. It is His special function to give it edge and penetration. Not that He imparts any new truths, as such an idea would be a libel on the perfection of the previous revelation. But He enlightens the mind, and He so softens the heart, as to render it susceptible of impression from the word. Ah! how many read the scriptures, and, closing the sacred volume, retain not one idea in their intellect, not one fact on their memory, not one impression on their heart. The Spirit who gave the Bible has not been implored, and the study of His Book has not been imbued with His healthful influence. But when He impresses its truths on mind and conscience, and lodges its statements in the deep recesses of the soul, then does it evince its power, impelling the sluggish, warning the wayward, controlling the vehement, directing the unwary, deterring the presumptuous, cheering the downcast, and animating the feeble. In short, when the Spirit comes with the word, then the experience of the Psalmist is realised: 'The law of the Lord is perfect, converting the soul: the testimony of the Lord is sure, making wise the simple: the statutes of the Lord are right, rejoicing the heart: the commandment of the Lord is pure, enlightening the eyes: the fear of the Lord is clean, enduring for ever: the judgments of the Lord are true and righteous altogether. More to be desired are they than gold, yea, than much fine gold; sweeter also than honey, and the honey-comb. Moreover, by them is thy servant warned: and in keeping of them there is great reward.' And now, does not the love of Christ commend itself, in forming such a motive, and securing such a result? It was no idle attachment, no sentimental outburst, but a mighty and all-conquering affection, which did not expire in mere lamentation over man's fallen condition, for it has stooped and raised him to the likeness and enjoyment of itself.

Thus, though the Spirit be the agent, and the word the means of sanctification, the process is here ascribed to Christ. It is in consequence of what He has done that the Spirit has been given. The Holy Ghost descended only when Jesus was glorified. Moreover, the entire work of the Spirit has a close and a perpetual connection with Christ. 'He shall take of mine,' says the Redeemer, ' and show it unto you.' The entire *material* of the Spirit's operation is Christ's. When He enlightens, it is with the truth of Christ; when He sanctifies, it is with the blood of Christ; when He comforts, it is with the promises of Christ; and when He seals, it is with the image of Christ. Nay more, the atonement has another and vital connection with our sanctification. For not only has this spiritual influence been secured, but the most powerful of motives is also supplied by it. That love which so mightily works upon us, springs from faith in the atonement; for he who receives the atonement, cannot but love the Atoner — he who so profits by the death, gives himself to Him who died. That law which man had broken terrified him by its penalty, and as he hated it, and would not obey it, it served to reveal and exacerbate the corruption within him; but its penalty being borne, and itself being satisfied in the death of Christ, it no longer creates alarm; for, viewed now as the mind and will of Christ, it commands the affection and loyalty of the believing heart. The example of Jesus also derives its peculiar power of assimilation, not simply from its own purity and loveliness, but especially from the fact, that it is the example of Him who loved the church, and gave Himself for it, and therefore every member of that church is instinctively led to observe, admire, and imitate. Thus Christ has loved the church, and given Himself for it; and thus He sanctifies it 'with the washing of water by the word.'

IV. The Ultimate End and Result.

With what delight and satisfaction will we not now contemplate the ulterior purpose of these preliminary arrangements — 'That he might present it to himself a glorious church, not having spot, or wrinkle, or any such thing.' How noble such a destiny — perfect restoration and felicity. The nuptial figure is still continued, and the allusion is to the presentation of the bride to her husband. That presentation does not take place till he can look upon her with complacency. But spiritual perfection is pledged; the love of Christ would not be contented without it, and His death, in union with the eternal purpose, has effectually compassed it. For as that love was no meteor that flashed athwart the sky, and gave sunken humanity a momentary hope by its sudden gleam, but was as the vernal sun, whose splendour not only fills the heavens, but gives life and growth to what had been torpid amidst the frosts and snows of winter, so that death was not a peradventure or an experiment — its results were foreseen and secured in the counsels of eternity. Wherever there is this incipient sanctification, there is also the guarantee of this final completion: 'He who hath begun the good work, will perform it until the day of Christ.' Moreover all that is holy in nature is heavenly in tendency — and the elements of this progressive sanctification have an instinctive longing to climb upwards to that Divine bosom which is their origin and home. Grace is glory begun, and glory is grace consummated — the one is the bud, the other the fruit — the one is childhood, the other the maturity of age. But there is a necessary development; and the sanctified church becomes in due time 'a glorious church, not having spot, or wrinkle, or any such thing.' What is partial now, is then complete; the shades that hover around us are dispelled, besetting infirmities have vanished, indwelling sin is extirpated, chilling influences are removed, and, 'the perfect day' comes at length, whose light is liable to no revolution, and which shall never suffer any eclipse.

If it have no spot or wrinkle, O will it not be a glorious church? Now it has dark freckles, but yet it is 'all-glorious,' in spite of its many imperfections. The Spirit and word are still sanctifying it; and when its bright countenance is without stain, then has the appointed epoch revolved. It is of the church, as an organic whole, that the apostle speaks; and the presentation is deferred till the last and happy period, when the church shall be as perfect in numbers as it is in character. Though many have been gathered into the heavens, yet, not till all who are to compose the church are finally redeemed and translated, has the 'set time' come. And then when myriads of myriads are collected, and the blessed company is complete, no matter when they lived, or how they were converted—what was their previous condition, or the stage of spiritual progress they had reached ere they left the world — the Saviour, standing on His elevated throne, and surveying at one glance every secret thought and emotion, shall behold nothing to offend Him; the church will then appear in His vision, whose 'eyes are as a flame of fire,' 'without spot, or wrinkle, or any such thing.' And thus, having loved her in her impurity, so as to give Himself for her, how deep and ardent must now be His attachment, when he sees, in her perfection, the full success of His redeeming efforts and sacrifice. The union is at length consummated amidst the pealing hallelujahs of grateful triumph — a union never to be interrupted by one passing suspicion, but ever to become more joyous, and more fertile in the fruits of unbroken and mutual satisfaction and glory. Who but a God could have devised such a destiny; who but a God could have wrought it out? To think of uniting Himself to creatures, and such creatures — O, the very idea bewrays its origin. The love which, to prepare them for such a union, sustained the agonies of Calvary, could have no origin but in Him who is

Love. Let the church, as it contemplates this high and happy destiny, enter into its spirit, and seek in the meantime to realise it.

Members of the church of Christ, reflect on your past position, on its helplessness and guilt. How low and loathsome was your state—Paradise expelled you, and heaven could not admit you. And yet, when you were so unlike Him, He loved you —and O how He loved you! At what an expense have you been delivered: 'not with corruptible things.' God says concerning His ancient church, 'I gave Egypt for thee; Ethiopia and Seba for thy ransom;' but to His present church His moving appeal is, 'Ye are redeemed with the precious blood of Christ, as of a Lamb without blemish and without spot.' If He has loved you, and died for you, to sanctify and perfect you, and for ever unite you to Himself, will you not feel that you are His? Will not the cords of His love bind you to Him as His own? Are you not His; for He has bought you—paid a price beyond all calculation for you? Are not you His, for his authority governs you, and His law directs you? Nay, more, are you not His; for has not His Spirit, as His representative and in His name, taken possession of you? Are you not therefore really His? Will you not live and act under this hallowed consciousness, and rise above every form of temptation and sin? Let not present evil discourage you; for each of you can say, I have His love. So long as you enjoy that love, why should anything distress you? Will it not soothe and compensate you? If you have His love, you have everything. O, then, ever cherish this secret treasure, and feel within you, I possess His love.

And now tell me, can you imagine a nobler purpose for His love than this — to sanctify you, to bring you back to lost holiness and forfeited felicity? Will you not enter at once and thoroughly into the spirit of it, or will you dare to frustrate the design of His death by continuance in sin? With His glory as your aim, and His law as your guide—His love as your motive, and His Spirit as your power, O will it not be your intense desire to 'hate every false way,' and 'so to walk even as He walked!'

What an inducement, too, to commemorate His death as the result of His love, and to pray for more of its purifying and elevating power! Let the love of Christ thus 'constrain' you. Nourish the thought of it, cherish the nearer purpose of it, and long for its ultimate result. That love which has suffered so much for you, will not be content till it have you near itself, and its summons will soon say to you, 'Come up hither,'—

> 'Where keep the saints, with harp and song,
>   An endless Sabbath morning;
> And in that sea, commixed with fire,
> Oft drop their eyelids, raised too long,
>   To the full Godhead burning.'

Then, with all saints, so close to Him, and never more to be away from Him, His glory will fill and ravish your vision, for His love will have realised its end in your perfected and happy natures. 'Worthy is the Lamb that died;' yea, worthy of eternal tribute and praise. Such is the ceaseless minstrelsy of the exalted church, and such is the response of all its members now on their way to glory. Hallelujah! Amen.

LECTURE III.

THE LOVE OF THE SPIRIT—ITS REALITY AND GLORY.

AN ARGUMENT.

Rom. xv. 30.

. . . '*The love of the Spirit.*' . . .

IF we have dwelt on the love of the Father, and have illustrated that of the Son, it cannot be that we shall neglect the love of the Spirit. His attachment has not indeed had thrown around it the same visible and majestic mantle as that of Father and Son. But it is none the less real, nor is it essentially different. It exhibits the same divine features — the same characteristic phenomena of tenderness, fulness, and self-denial. For He is one with Father and Son. His functions, it is true, in the scheme of redemption are subjective, and are wholly occupied with human experience. It is not without us, but within us that He operates; for His work is not a spectacle to be contemplated, but a process to be felt. And His love has not one spot, like Calvary, for its surpassing manifestation, but it is everywhere exhibited in the church; and its genial glow, which burst into a flame at Pentecost, has been continuously diffused. Yet who shall say that though His love have clothed itself in no glorious externality, it is the less genuine, as it thrills in the renewed heart? His love, in short, is divine, for it is that of the Third Person of the Godhead. The one emotion of attachment dwells in the one God, and that distinction which we name personality, does not violate this unity of affection. The same elements of eternity, infinitude, and unchangeableness which distinguish the love of Father and Son, distinguish also the love of the Holy Ghost. Though He is named third in the inspired formulary of baptism and benediction, His lustre is not dimmer than that of God the Father, or that of God the Son. His name is last in reference, not to His essential nature, but to His place and sphere of operation in the scheme of redemption.

And that love, moreover, is saving love. That He has any part at all in the scheme of mercy, proves the depth and fervour of His love. For sin is as hateful to Him as to the Father; and must be so to Him who is specially named the *Holy* Ghost. Nay, human guilt must have touched Him with a peculiar sorrow. The 'Spirit brooded on the face of the deep,' and fitted up the world as the residence of the novel creature; and He took possession, too, of Adam, when the breath of the Lord God kindled life within him. What provocation must He have felt when He was forced to quit the soul which He had so recently entered, and when He beheld sin bring death and desolation over that earth, which He had so shortly before evoked from chaos! Yet He has loved man, and He has a position, and that a momentous one—a function, and that a vital one, in the economy of mercy. Gracious, disinterested, and sovereign must be the love of this Divine Spirit. Thus, though its modes of manifestation may vary, its essence is identical with that of Father and Son. The Father loved in sending His Son, and that Son loved in coming and dying; but the Spirit equally exhibits His love in His various modes of operation and residence.

1. And first, is not the love of the Spirit seen in preparing and publishing for us the Holy Scriptures? This blessed book is His precious gift. It was by His influence that prophets and apostles wrote and circulated it. The Holy Ghost is the source of inspiration; and He was the great promise of Jesus to the apostles to qualify them for their mission. They spoke in the words of the Holy Spirit. 'God hath revealed them to us by his Spirit.' 'Which things also we speak, not in the words which man's wisdom teacheth, but which the Holy Ghost teacheth.' What a boon was this — the revelation of God's eternal plan — the communication to men of that saving knowledge which they could never have discovered for themselves. Cast your eye over any part of the world where the divine word has not been distributed, and what crude and erroneous opinions of God and man, of duty and destiny, are universally and fatally prevalent. Worship is either

inanity, lust, or brutal fanaticism. Life is but a distracted fever, and death its dark conclusion. What benefits, then, have you not got from scripture — what knowledge as the basis of faith, what comfort and hope in your trials, what counsel as to the way of duty, and what bright glimpses of eternity.

And if you regard the Bible in its fulness — all necessary instruction is communicated; or in its clearness — 'he may run that readeth it;' or in its majesty — it is the voice and word of the great Jehovah; or in its impressiveness — it solemnises and awakens, it cheers and strengthens, it directs and purifies. In whatever aspect you take it, you cannot but feel it to be a product of love — love to the best interests of the best part of your nature. Think of it as the Book of books, the roll of promise which you clasp to your bosom. Remember its Moses and Paul, its Elijah and Peter, its Isaiah and John. Think of its pure truth, its tender invitations, its thrilling promises, and awful warnings; of its tears and its thunder, of its pathos and its sterness. Survey the altar of Aaron, and the throne of David; the birth at Bethlehem, and the death on Calvary; the sepulchre of Joseph, and the descent at Pentecost. Call to mind the united testimony of all saints to the sacred volume, as first in rank, and mightiest in effect on conscience and life, and surely you will be disposed to glorify the love of that Spirit who is really its author, who knows our frame, and has accommodated His book to our weakness and wants. Next to His own gift of Himself, is His gift of the volume of life; and the love that brightens every page, is proof of the love of Him who gave it. If I am benighted and wandering, with death before me if I proceed, is it not love to warn me and set me right? and if I am disposed to treat this counsel lightly, is it not kindest love to terrify me into compliance? O say not, therefore, that the threatenings of scripture are awful and agonising, and might be dispensed with. No; it was the tenderness of the Spirit's love that dictated them. You must be aroused ere you can be saved. It would be mistaken affection to fear to disturb the sleeper in the hour of peril. The alarms of scripture are the loud voice of Divine love in agony over you. The hundred and nineteenth Psalm, a prolonged eulogy on the Bible, is a sustained proof and demonstration of this love of the Spirit.

2. The love of the Spirit may be learned from His preparation of the human nature of Jesus, and His dwelling in it. Our argument now is, He who loves the means, loves the end. If the Spirit had such a connexion with the mediatorial nature of the Son of God, what love must He have had to those sinners whom Christ became incarnate to save! His union with Jesus was early predicted: 'Behold my Servant whom I have chosen. . . . I have put my Spirit upon him.' 'The Spirit of the Lord God is upon me: for the Lord hath anointed me.' Messiah, or Christ the anointed one, enjoyed the unction of the Spirit: 'The Holy Ghost shall come

upon thee,' said the angel to His mother, ' and the power of the Highest shall overshadow thee.' The Spirit came down upon Him at His baptism, and 'remained' upon Him. 'God gave not the Spirit by measure unto him.' 'By the Spirit of God' He wrought miracles. 'Through the eternal Spirit he offered himself without spot to God.' 'Put to death in the flesh, he was quickened by the Spirit.' He was 'declared to be the Son of God, according to the Spirit of holiness, by his resurrection from the dead.' His constitution and career are also described in those two parallel clauses — 'God manifest in the flesh, justified in the Spirit.' Thus, by means of the Spirit, was the humanity of Jesus created, endowed, and sustained for its arduous enterprise. And does not this agency of the Spirit argue His love to the great cause of our salvation? That body which was at length to be offered, and that blood so soon to be 'poured out for remission of sins unto many;' in short, that humanity which, in its glorified state, was to plead for us with God, and govern and defend us, was brought into existence, fitted, and furnished, by the operation of the Holy Ghost. Will you not appreciate His love to the saved in this union with their Saviour? And when you feel your relation to the Brother-man, and think how He wears your flesh, and has a fellow-feeling with you in it, and in it has been crowned with glory; when you partake of the sacramental symbols of His holy suffering humanity, and hear those awful words, 'This is my body broken for you'—'this cup is the new testament in my blood;' when you anticipate the falling of your own frame into the sepulchre, amidst the solemn cry of dust to dust, and ashes to ashes, and cherish the hope of seeing Him and being satisfied with His likeness, then, O then! will you not see in Him and His humanity a singular and touching proof of the love of the Spirit?

3. His love is evinced by the special position which He occupies in our salvation. And according to the New Testament He is Christ's representative and substitute. 'I will,' says our Lord, 'send you another Comforter'—another, implying that Himself was the first, and that the Holy Ghost was to be the second in His room. Other passages announce the same truth. 'I will pray the Father, and he shall give you another Comforter, that he may abide with you, even the Spirit of truth.' 'The Comforter, who is the Holy Ghost, whom the Father will send in my name, he shall teach you all things.' 'When the Comforter is come, whom I will send unto you from the Father, even the Spirit of truth, which proceedeth from the Father, he shall testify of me.' 'It is expedient for you that I go away: for if I go not away, the Comforter will not come unto you; but if I depart, I will send him unto you.' Such being the case, our plain argument is, that if the Spirit occupy such a position, love must have prompted Him to it. There lay no necessity upon Him — He was under no moral constraint. There was nothing in His essence or His character

that demanded this condescension of Him. That love which brought Jesus down to earth, that and none other brought down the Spirit to fill His room. He cannot be a substitute if He has not the attachment of Him whom He represents. Nor would Jesus have intrusted the completion of His work to one of less love than His own, for such a task needed all the love which led to the cross, and sustained under its agonies. Love of a lower temperature would have sunk beneath the enterprise. That enterprise was to be as Christ was — 'another Comforter;' to stand to the church as did the tender and sympathising Jesus, to speak as He spoke, to cherish as He cherished, and to lead as He led to communion with Himself. The ardour of such a love is equal to that of Christ, but its radiance is of a mellower and less dazzling nature. Like the light of the sun, which is of intolerable brilliance, and cannot be hidden, — the Son of God appeared in this commanding splendour of love. But the light which follows the setting of the luminary is softer, sweeter, and less majestic; so, though the love of the Spirit, appearing after the withdrawal of Jesus, may assume a milder form, yet it has not the less penetration or divinity. Feeling, then, the relation which the Spirit bears to the church — how He compensates for the absence of Christ's person and visible sympathies, and how all that you would anticipate from the Incarnate Brother is realised in and from Him, will you not discern in this tender and delicate position another proof and result of the love of the Spirit? If, therefore, believer, thou hast ever pictured to thyself what noble enjoyment thou mightest have had in following Christ incarnate were He upon earth, in ministering to Him, in listening to Him, in beholding the miracles of His grace, in telling Him thy sorrows, and soliciting His sympathy under thy bereavements; if this vision ever rise up before thee, then feel that it is all verified now in and through the love and presence of the 'good Spirit.' As Jesus was to Mary and to John, so is the Spirit now to thee. As He was to the widow of Nain — as He was at the tomb of Lazarus — as He was to her who bathed His feet in tears; so is the Spirit in His love to thee. Will not thy heart beat in responsive pulsation, and will not thy petition be, 'Take not thy Holy Spirit from me.'

4. The same truth may be inferred from the peculiar function which the Spirit discharges. The province which the 'Free Spirit' occupies is that of application. Christ provides, He applies. This work of His is distinctly told to us by Jesus: 'He shall glorify me, for he shall receive of mine, and shall show it unto you.' He applies the truth of Christ for our enlightenment, and not some new and unheard-of revelation. It is the blood of Christ which He sprinkles for our purification, and the image of Christ with which He seals us. What Christ has done for us was done in Judea, and what He now does for us is done in the court of heaven; but all that the Spirit does for us is within us, is in

our hearts. His work is subjective, and deep laid in our vital experience. The first impulse to believe, and the last polish and preparation of the departing spirit for eternity, are alike His gracious and sovereign gift. What special and tenacious love is there not in all these operations?

He awakens. It is His work to alarm the conscience, to throw the sinner into agony, and to leave him no rest until he lay hold on Christ. Now, it is His love which originates all this distraction. As we have already said, the truest love to the man in danger is to terrify him out of it. But it is not one simple impulse which creates this agitation, this wretchedness in the heart of a panic-stricken sinner. O what effort, continuous and prolonged, is put forth! The Spirit employs every means. He warns and He invites, He threatens and He persuades; He strikes a terror into the heart, or keeps up in the memory the echo of an arousing sermon; He sends some sharp visitation of providence, and brings the man so near the gates of death, that he sees the grim portals, and starts and shudders; or He brings some bereavement so close upon him that his heart bleeds in anguish,—and all this discipline, or a large portion of it, may be repeated, and varied, and multiplied year after year, till the end be achieved. For the heart appears often to close itself against the Spirit, and defy all His endeavours, and therefore He waits and wrestles, argues and implores. Did any man wish to impress some favourite idea on the mind of his familiar companion, and did he find him so reluctant to apprehend it as is the sinner to know and recognise his real position, the preceptor would soon abandon the task in despair, and declare his friend either stupid beyond hope, or perverse beyond recovery. But the Spirit of God perseveres, and stands and knocks. O nothing but divine and unfathomable love could sustain Him amidst such provocations! Ye who have felt His early workings, and are conscious that you did for a season resist them, O how thankful are you now that He did not leave you. Are not your present faith and grace and hope, a living and a lasting monument to the love of the Spirit? For did you answer when first He said, Come? Did you move when He essayed to lead you? Did you embrace salvation when first He proved its necessity and freeness? Ah no! Yet He persisted, and successfully persisted, in His efforts with you, for He loves you.

The Spirit also enlightens. The sinful heart is covered with gloom. Self-knowledge is absent, and there is no perception of the only path to felicity. Yea, though a revelation has been given to man, he does not practically understand it; 'for the natural man receiveth not the things of the Spirit of God, neither can he know them, for they are spiritually discerned.' It is necessary, therefore, that the Spirit which gave the word should apply it, and so illumine the understanding that it can experimentally comprehend it. When the famous statesman Pitt, on one occasion and in company with Wilberforce, heard Cecil, an eminent minister in London, discoursing on this subject, he confessed, at the close of the discourse, that he did not in the least understand it. The Premier of England, whose acute and mighty mind was equal to any emergency, could not comprehend what was realised by many a poor peasant and humble cottager. The Spirit begets within us a relish for spiritual truth, and He shows us very clearly its divinity and adaptation. 'Ye were sometime darkness, but now are ye light in the Lord.' They who have been so enlightened by the Spirit of wisdom wonder why truth so plain was never felt in its reality and power before. The spiritual vision was diseased, and refused to admit the light into its chambers. But the scales at length fall, and light is seen in God's light.

Now, this enlightenment by the Spirit is surely the fruit of His love. For such light is sweet, and a pleasant thing it is, by means of such a medium, to behold the Sun of Righteousness. But ah! how long men refuse the light, and coil their spirits up against it; how they even love the darkness rather than the light; and how numerous are the strivings of the Divine Spirit, ere

> 'On the eyeballs of the blind
> He pours celestial light.'

Many continue to 'see men as trees, walking,' and live under the dim and troubled shadow of an eclipse. To recur to an illustration analogous to our former one. Had any teacher a pupil so dull as is a sinner to learn the very alphabet of divine truth, he would, after a fair trial, dismiss him as either incorrigible or incompetent, and would not wait so many months and years as does the Spirit of God. He far outdoes, not in skill only, but in patience too, every human tutor. Nay, which of us has all the illumination he might possess? or which of us possessed it at the moment when it was offered to us? Is there no prejudice yet to be overcome, no twisted opinion yet to be undone? Is there not some lurking misconception, some obliquity of vision? And should none of these faults exist, who among us, even the most aged and intelligent, has arrived at the 'riches of the full assurance of understanding?' O! is there one who enjoys, to its utmost splendour, this spiritual light, or who can set his conscious seal to the statement, in its widest warrant of signification, 'Ye have an unction from the Holy One, and know ALL THINGS?' If, then, the Holy Ghost assist the memory, and bring precious truth to our remembrance, nay, leads us 'into all the truth;' and if such industrious patience with His awkward pupils be demanded, will we not rejoice in the assurance of His love? If we feel it to be 'eternal life to know the only true God, and Jesus Christ whom he has sent;' if we feel that the eyes of the understanding have been opened that we may know 'the hope of His calling;' if we have just conceptions of divine truth in its fairness and beauty; if, in short, 'the darkness is past, and the true light now shines,'—then, surely, our instruction and attainments are an irresistible and harmonious witness to the love of the Spirit.

And He also sanctifies. He changes the heart—restamps upon it the divine image—restores it to its pristine purity and perfection, and fits it for the glory of Heaven. Oh blessed work is this! a work which none but a divine agent could accomplish. He alone who created the heart, can re-create it. Human influence may achieve a great deal, but in us the springs of action and emotion must be laid hold of and changed. In this transformation the Spirit is the agent, and His own word is the instrument which he employs. In constructing that word, He has adapted it to his gracious purpose, and He gives it the requisite efficacy by His own accompanying influence. The Bible, in its various parts and style, so fits in to our nature, that it developes a full and healthy spiritual life. If, then, His special work be to make man what he once was; to fit him not for re-entering Eden, but for ascending to a heavenly inheritance; to make him the companion of the princes of the universe, and the very counterpart of its Lord,—does He not love the creatures whom He thus condescends to elevate and purify? If He had formed a being for this high destiny, we should have argued that love prompted His creative energy; and if He has taken a fallen creature, whose sin had so provoked Him, and led to His withdrawal—taken him in all his guilt and defilement, and washed him in the blood of the Lamb, sanctified and brought him back to a higher than his first estate, — is not this blessed, holy, and prolonged operation the result of love, and nothing but love?

And, then, remember how the Spirit labours in accomplishing this end — that He leaves no means unturned, and no motives unapplied; that He is often thwarted, rebelled against, and vexed, — and will not you ascribe every spiritual attainment, your growth in grace, and your advancing meetness for glory, to the love of the Spirit? And surely this love, tender as that of a nurse that guides a feeble and wayward child, and inweaving itself with all your experience, will be the theme of earnest and rapturous comment and gratitude. Every breath of your spiritual life is perfumed with the love of the Spirit.

> ' 'Tis He that works to will;
> 'Tis He that works to do;
> His is the power by which we act,
> His be the glory too.'

Can this love be less worthy of mention than that of either Father or Son? The patience of the Father is indeed marvellous. Long has He borne with men — with their unbelief and ingratitude. Six thousand years attest that He is 'long-suffering and abundant in goodness;' but during the same period the Spirit, too, has been striving with man, for he is even flesh. The Son of God, during His abode on earth, endured the 'contradiction of sinners against himself:' and has not the Holy Spirit, ever since the ascension, been experiencing similar treatment from rebellious and obstinate man. With all these truths before us, let us never forget the patient and conquering love of the Spirit.

5. The Spirit's love may be learned, in fine, from the abode which He has chosen. And that abode is no pure or princely mansion; for it is the human heart. He who knows it best, says of it, 'The heart is deceitful above all things, and desperately wicked.' He who 'needed not that any should testify of man; for He knew what was in man,' bears this testimony — 'Out of the heart proceed evil thoughts, murders, adulteries, fornication, theft, false witness, blasphemies.' And this heart is not fitted up or prepared for His reception; but He comes to it in its foulness and dilapidation, and cleanses and decorates it for Himself. Neither is He there as 'a wayfaring man, that turneth aside to tarry for a night;' nor yet as an accidental or transient guest — He is a resident, who dwells in it as His chosen habitation. 'But will God in very deed dwell with men upon the earth? Behold, the heaven, and the heaven of heavens cannot contain thee, how much less this house that I have built!' That was a noble national fane of which the royal dedicator spoke — a temple built in splendour to enshrine the resident glory of its divine Architect. But, oh, the human heart, so abject and vile, how will it contain divinity? Yet the Spirit of purity sets His affections upon it. He enters there to cast out all that is inimical to our happiness, and to fill it with every holy grace.

There He is as counsellor, friend, and comforter. When you commune with your hearts, you commune with Him, your bosom friend. What but love, we ask, could prompt Him to choose such a residence, and prolong His stay in it? It has no native attractions for one who is 'of purer eyes than to behold iniquity, and who cannot look upon sin.' And what provocations does He not meet with in it? No guest would endure them, but would leave the place of his sojourn under such wanton and undisguised insults. The apostle warns Christians, and says, 'Grieve not the Spirit of God.' When Israel 'rebelled, and vexed his Holy Spirit,' God 'turned to be their enemy.' Ah, how often do you refuse His counsels, and throw from you His authority, though you avow that He is your Instructor and Governor. Might He not in anger or in sorrow depart? Alas! how often have you resisted, or at least shown reluctance, when He would lead into deeper and holier experience, and give you a nearer view of God and eternity; when He would enable you to penetrate into the spirituality of His law, and give His love a firmer hold on your nature; when He would bring you nearer heaven in spirit, and fill your hearts with its cheering elements? Have you not too often in such a crisis remained passive and unexcited, and contented as you were? And if He be still within you, patiently bearing all those repulses, and working out the blessed end of His mission, can you doubt His love, or reckon it less than that of Christ? 'The Word was made flesh.' God dwelt in humanity. Jesus appeared in the world as an incarnate God. But does not the Spirit in His love experience a similar incarnation? Is not He also infleshed when He fills the bosoms of believers, and dwells in the heart of His church?

Nor will He desert His favorite abode. The body dies, but still He claims it. It is His. His love to it is not cooled by death. The fondest friend and tenderest relative is obliged to say, 'Bury my dead out of my sight;' but the beloved ashes are precious to the Holy Ghost as the dust of His own temple. And so in His love He watches over it, and at the appointed time He will re-animate and re-organise the scattered particles. 'If the Spirit of him who raised up Jesus from the dead dwell in you, he that raised up Christ from the dead shall also quicken your mortal bodies by his Spirit that dwelleth in you.' Thus a more glorious structure is reared up, in unison with the character of the pure Being who is to rest in it for ever. So that, if you know that God 'abideth in you by the Spirit which he has given you'—if you feel that you carry Him in your hearts, a friend of friends, innermost and attached, and realise His presence, and know the abiding, the joy, comfort, power, and hope of the Holy Ghost, surely you will need no further proof of 'the love of the Spirit.'

And, in fine, the effect of all this varied working and prolonged abode is the impartation of comfort. He is the 'Comforter;' and believers, as they walk in the fear of the Lord, walk at the same time in 'the comfort of the Holy Ghost.' He is ever present to assist you, and the effect of His assistance is comfort. There is comfort in his light and in His strength, in the intercession which He makes, and the progressive purity which He secures. There is no part of your nature left unhelped — intellect and will, memory and heart, share in His assistance. The result is peace, and joy, and assurance — the serenity which victory insures, and the felt approach to perfection which experience is able to testify. The saint is as one 'whom his mother comforteth,' calm, happy, and confident. O that this consciousness were the privilege of us all! Then should we have days of revival and apostolical triumph.

Will we not be ever on our guard against grieving this Holy Spirit of God? Whatever is dark and sensual, cruel and malignant, is specially opposed to Him, and hateful to Him. Flee such sins as war against Him.

Shall we now doubt His love, or undervalue His work? There may be mystery in that work, and it may be beyond the reach of our analysis; but our experience declares its reality and power. O let us adore Him with fervour, and pray for His presence with unceasing importunity. Thou promised Spirit of the living God, wilt not Thou come down upon us, and fill us more entirely? We long for Thee, we look for Thee, and we are ever in need of Thee. We are ignorant, but Thou art the Spirit of truth. We are impure, but Thou art the Spirit of holiness.

We are often in doubt of our spiritual state, but Thou bearest witness with our spirits. We are often straitened in prayer, but Thou makest intercession for us. We are in want of preparation for heaven, but thou makest ready the heart, and sealest it, and art Thyself the 'first-fruits' of the inheritance. Descend, we implore Thee, descend in the fulness of Thy blessing, and make us what we sigh to be, and so restrain and guide us that we may never be so far left to ourselves as at any time to grieve Thee. Amen and Amen.

LECTURE IV.

THE VOTIVE TABLET — OR THE SAINT'S RECORD OF HIS LOVE.

A SOLILOQUY.*

PSALM CXVI.

'*I love the Lord, because he hath heard my voice and my supplications. Because he hath inclined his ear unto me, therefore will I call upon him as long as I live. The sorrows of death compassed me, and the pains of hell gat hold upon me: I found trouble and sorrow. Then called I upon the name of the Lord: O Lord, I beseech thee, deliver my soul. Gracious is the Lord, and righteous; yea, our God is merciful. The Lord preserveth the simple: I was brought low, and he helped me. Return unto thy rest, O my soul; for the Lord hath dealt bountifully with thee. For thou hast delivered my soul from death, mine eyes from tears, and my feet from falling. I will walk before the Lord in the land of the living. I believed, therefore have I spoken: I was greatly afflicted. I said in my haste, All men are liars. What shall I render unto the Lord for all his benefits toward me? I will take the cup of salvation, and call upon the name of the Lord. I will pay my vows unto the Lord*

---

* So vivid is the rehearsal of experience in this Psalm, that, in our exposition of it, we have deviated so far from usual custom as to preserve the construction of the first person which characterises it, and gives it the form of a soliloquy.

now in the presence of all his people. Precious in the sight of the Lord is the death of his saints. O Lord, truly I am thy servant : I am thy servant, and the son of thine handmaid : thou hast loosed my bonds. I will offer to thee the sacrifice of thanksgiving, and will call upon the name of the Lord. I will pay my vows unto the Lord now in the presence of all his people, in the courts of the Lord's house, in the midst of thee, O Jerusalem, Praise ye the Lord.'

'I LOVE THE LORD.' I bless the Lord that I love Him, and that my carnal heart, which was once enmity against Him, has been enabled and induced by His grace to love Him. I complain often, very often, alas! that my love to Him is so cold and languid, as to be scarcely worthy of the hallowed name. I feel, at the same time, that what I should not love does hold my affection, and that, while I am convinced of its worthlessness, my wayward heart is drawn toward it. Still it is my study to love Him; and my prayer is, to love Him more. If I know myself—if I can form a right judgment of my ruling passion, it is to love the Lord. O for the baptism of fire to consume every earthy emotion, and give fervour and flame to all that is gracious and divine within me! O how I long for this blessed result! Thou Spirit of love, shed abroad this love in my heart; fan it, and feed it with the fuel it needs and craves. So reveal the Father in His loveliness, and the Son in His spiritual beauty, that I shall be ravished and overpowered; and so touch my heart with the 'live coal,' that I shall be brought to cry in an ardour yet unfelt—I love the Lord.

Nor am I ashamed of avowing this love; and while my lips pronounce the avowal, may my heart respond, and may my life be for ever a witness to seal it. Thou God hast bidden me love Thee — love Thee with all my soul. Alas! my love to Thee is not what Thou askest in amount, but it is sincere in nature; and wilt Thou not accept it for the sake of Him who does not 'break the bruised reed, nor quench the smoking flax?'

I was once hostile and indifferent to Him—and I shudder at the past and its sin; but then I did not know Him. I was a wilful stranger to His character and grace. I gazed on His universe, and bowed to His power. I looked on His sun, and was awed by its glory. The stars of the sky penetrated me with the idea of His immensity. I heard His thunders, and trembled. I surveyed hill and valley, wood and river, and drank in their beauty and gladness. I saw Thy hand in the seasons, amidst buds and flowers, fruits and harvests — amidst songs of birds, and the life and joy of nature around me; — and yet, how often in my delicious reverie, did I practically forget that 'God is love.' And even while glimpses of the truth stole upon me, how evanescent was the sensation. I sometimes called to mind the divine goodness to me personally, from early youth and upwards; how it had soothed me in grief, led me in difficulty, recovered me from sickness, and crowned me 'with loving-kindness and tender mercies;' yet the reminiscence awoke but a feeble gratitude; the frequency of His bounties strangely tending to diminish their value, and my daily familiarity with them leading me the less to esteem them. But when at length my heart, under deep conviction, could find no refuge but in God; when it poured its plaint into His ear, and He heard and blessed; when He pointed to the cross, and to His own Son stretched upon it; and when I looked as He pointed, and beheld the Lamb of God bleeding there and dying—O then I got a new discovery—I saw Him as I had never seen Him before, and saw Him as nature, providence, and my own history had never represented Him. I saw Him as my God in Christ, yearning for my salvation, and I could not but gaze and wonder—I could not but trust and love the Lord. My love is not love without a cause. It springs not from report, but from my own experience. He has loved me, and given me ample and repeated proofs of it. 'He hath heard my voice and my supplications.'

O it was a sad and melancholy time when my love to the Lord was formed and rivetted within me. I was in awful dismay when I obtained, for the first time, a view of myself and my position; and so agonising was my terror, that I felt as if life were about to leave me, and eternal ruin were to be my speedy and hopeless destiny. 'The sorrows of death compassed me; the pains of hell gat hold upon me: I found trouble and sorrow.' Mind and body were alike in pain. I grieved to think that I must die so soon, and I was distracted with the anticipation of what should befall me after death.

The shroud and the coffin were the least terrible part of the picture; there rang in my ear the knell of the awful doom, 'Depart from me, ye cursed.' 'My bones were filled with pain, and the multitude of my bones with strong pain.' 'I was weary with my groaning—I watered my couch with my tears.' 'Day and night thy hand was heavy upon me.' 'Thou scaredst me with dreams, and didst terrify me through visions.' I felt that 'I was deprived of the residue of my years,' and I said, 'I shall behold man no more with the inhabitants of the world.' For it was on a sick-bed that those awful visitations reached me—in a period of suffering and retirement. And where could I find relief? Every false refuge was laid low, when I was brought face to face with God. Where could I find relief? I durst not venture on my own righteousness, for I felt that I had none. I could not harden my spirit, the crisis was so sharp and frightful. I could not sleep on in indifference, for the ghastly portals of death, and beyond them the 'great white throne,' rose up before me. What could I do?—whither could I betake myself? I yielded at length to the necessity, and I prayed—'Then called I upon the name of the Lord.' 'This poor man cried, and the Lord heard him.' And O what relief in such prayer! I laid open my bosom to the God of love. I confessed my trespasses, bemoaned my utter unworthiness, and cast myself on His mercy. The burden of my prayer still was, 'O Lord, I beseech thee, deliver my soul.' Again and again, when my spirit was overwhelmed within me, did I betake myself to the 'Rock that is higher than I.'

The change was wonderful beyond expression. He whom I had so often offended, and of whose character I had heretofore possessed so dim and imperfect a conception, He in His infinite tenderness and pity 'inclined his ear unto me.' He stooped to hear, and He was not slow to answer. As He listened, He forgave and blessed. He delivered my soul. Yes, of all thy terror He freed thee — gave thee a lasting proof of His affection — hushed all thy distractions — soothed thee, and bade thee live. Love the Lord, O my soul. These were the throes of thy birth, when His power and grace took possession of thee, purged thy guilt, gave thee the sense of His favour, quickened thee, and began to impress on thee His own glorious image. Never forget the memorable epoch — it was a day of days; and aye as thou revertest to it, ratify the vow — 'therefore will I call upon him as long as I live.' He heard me then, and He will hear me again. I will wait for Him, and He will always answer. In whatever strait I am, whatever is my perplexity or my want, I will always make it an errand to Thy throne. Thou hast been so kind that I will make Thy kindness my unceasing plea. If my faith should falter, I will recall Thy generosity, and it shall 'fill my mouth with arguments.' Nor do I fear that Thou wilt be wearied with me for my continuous importunity, or that Thy gifts will soon be exhausted. Though others get, I can get too; and by my getting, they are not deprived. Thou canst 'do exceeding abundantly, above all we ask or think.' What Thou hast given is only a pledge of what Thou art willing to give. O fill me with desires, and deepen them, for Thou wilt abundantly satisfy them. I now rely on Thy promise. I will call upon Thee, and yet more and more, 'while I have any being.' So long as one aspiration remains — so long as any blessing is not given in its full extent — up to the time that prayer shall be changed into praise, will I call upon Thee. Let my last words be an invocation, and my last sigh a prayer; let the accents of supplication here be gently blended into those of praise above!

O is there not every cause why I should love the Lord! He did not put me off, or refuse to listen. And if I have been so welcomed and so delivered; if in that period of dark days and troublous nights I cried and He heard me; if then, when earth was vain, and all 'refuge failed me,' I found immediate succour in God; if He has forgiven all mine iniquities, healed all my diseases, and redeemed my life from destruction, there is surely every reason why I should love Him, and proclaim my love to Him. Yes, let me repeat it, as the daily emotion of my heart, I love the Lord.

And why need I conceal my reason — it is not peculiar to me: 'Gracious is the Lord, and righteous; yea, our God is merciful.' The God who afflicted me, and in my affliction so drew me to Himself, is a God of equity. I did not complain of

Thee or to Thee. 'I know, O God, that thy judgments are right, and that thou in faithfulness hast afflicted me.' My sins merited far more than I endured. But 'grace reigned through righteousness.' I now can understand what Thy servant meant when he said, 'Our light afflictions.' Then I regarded the declaration as unearthly romantic, and far beyond the truth, and I was inclined in anger at it to cry the more fiercely, 'Behold, all ye that pass by, and see if there be any sorrow like unto my sorrow.' I thought myself a 'mark' specially set up for an extraordinary stroke, and I indignantly wondered why I should be so singled out. 'So foolish was I and ignorant.' But now I acknowledge His righteousness and grace, and I trust I can say, sincerely and intelligently, 'My light affliction.' Is it not 'light' compared with what I deserved, and light in comparison with what Jesus endured for me? Is it not 'light,' for it lasts 'but a moment,' in contrast with eternity? And I cannot but regard it as 'light,' when I think of its effectual connection with the 'far more exceeding and eternal weight of glory.' O what kindness I enjoyed — what promises to soothe me, and what influences of the Comforter. What before was theory to me, then became matter of experience. I understood because I felt. Grace and mercy waited on me, in tenderness and sympathy. There could be no higher love than to chastise me — to alarm in order to convince me, and to convince in order to bless and save me. And do not I love Him because He is so 'righteous' as to show me my sin in my suffering, and so 'gracious' as to lay His hand on me so lightly, remove it so speedily, sanctify the dispensation, and make it the means of permanent health to my soul! I LOVE THE LORD.

They who cannot save themselves are saved by God. They who have no means of self-defence are shielded by Him. 'The Lord preserveth the simple;' but the proud, the wary, and the self-satisfied look not to Him, but to themselves, and therefore are enveloped in ruin. 'I was brought low, and he helped me.' He helps the helpless. I was weak and poor, and He had compassion on me. Low indeed was I, feeble and depressed—my health gone, and my spirits sunk; but He restored me. There was a soft slumber, and a placid awakening — then came convalescence, growing health, renewed serenity, and final recovery; but along with all this there was given me assured possession of my Father's love — of Him who knew my frame, and remembered that I was dust. Can I ever forget Thy kindness in my distress? Thy one hand did strike, but Thy other hand did heal me. Surely I must love the Lord, my Physician.

No wonder is there that, 'O my soul, thou hast said unto the Lord, Thou art my Lord.' Thou hast had many wanderings. Far and near hast thou flown in thy vexing search. From flower to flower hast thou flitted, delighted for an instant with each, and never finding in any what thou didst crave. Disappointed in one region, thou hast travelled to another; dissatisfied in one pursuit, thou hast resorted to another. Philosophy only tantalised, and pleasure only cloyed thee. The deity of Science was vailed, and the beauty of Art was without spiritual fascination. Fatigued and chafed, whither wilt thou go? Return to thy rest, O my soul.' Thou hast now got what thou wast so vainly in quest of. In the bosom of Him who created me, I have found repose. There is no rest for any spirit Thou hast made, save in the bosom of Him who made it. And now abide in thy rest; what should tempt thee to leave it? All thou wishest and hopest is there, — a spring of joy to drink of, and an atmosphere of love to revel in. O never, never cast thyself loose again. That rest which thou enjoyest shall be thy eternal haven. It was long open for thee ere thou wouldest enter it, and it might have been shut upon thee, but 'the Lord dealt bountifully with thee.' I must surely extol the grace which has brought me into it; and while I am in it,

> 'I must love on; O God,
> This bosom must love on; but let Thy breath
> Touch and make pure the flame that knows not death,
> Bearing it up to heaven, Love's own abode.'

I have seen the infant worn out, nestle on its mother's bosom, and sink into slumber. I have seen the ship, driven by the gale, glide into the land-locked harbour, and at length drop her anchor, gather up her canvas, and repose peacefully on her own shadow. I have seen the bird beat up against the storm, till she found a spot of shelter, and folded her weary wing under the cover of a rock. I have seen the streamlet tossing and leaping from the brow of the mountain, till it descended into the plain, and found rest in the great and undisturbed waters. But all I have seen cannot image out the sweetness and joy of that tranquillity which my spirit has in God. 'Return unto thy rest, O my soul, for the Lord hath dealt bountifully with thee.' Thou hast lavished every kindness upon me. From the most awful of evils hast Thou freed me. Thy love alone could prompt to it, and Thy power alone could effect it. For 'Thou hast delivered my soul from death.' O chiefest mercy! 'from death'—a death of deaths — in the loss of Thy favour, and under the withering of Thy frown. And Thou didst also deliver 'mine eyes from tears, and my feet from falling.' Thou hast wiped away the sad and bitter tear. Thy hand alone has the requisite softness and power. Thou didst preserve me in life, when Thou didst save my soul; 'the life that now is and that which is to come,' was Thy double and simultaneous gift. The tear started at the thought of death; but Thy love threw its radiance on it, and it glistened as it fell. Thou hast 'set my feet on a rock, and established my goings'—'Thou that liftest me up from the gates of death.' That blessed period must ever live in my memory—nothing can obliterate it; years may pass away, but that epoch will still stand out in its brightness and grace. All that happens to me but reminds me of it. Every blessing I enjoy, every prayer I present, every psalm I chaunt, every hope I cherish, all the evil I escape, and all the good I possess, carries me back to the primal benefaction— when 'all old things passed away' with my agony, and all things put on an aspect of gladness with my renewal. And what shall keep me from again declaring, with a fuller heart and in a bolder tone—I LOVE THE LORD.

Nor shall this love be inactive within me. As it throbs in my heart, it shall give fervour and freshness of consecration to my life: 'I will walk before the Lord in the land of the living.' If I have life, shall I sit and mope; shall I fold my arms, and enjoy the luxury in supineness and indolence; shall I still have the attitude of an invalid, — when such life beats in every pulse? No; 'I will walk before the Lord in the land of the living.' I shall occupy myself in serving my God; my whole life shall be devoted to Him. 'Lord, what wilt Thou have me to do.' As I walk, my tongue shall carry Thy praises upon it; whatever my hands find to do, shall be done in Thy presence, and as a sacrifice to Thee. Before Thee let my every thought be opened, and my every purpose be formed. Before Thee let my every wish originate, and my every word be uttered. Before Thee, and Thy smile beaming on me—before Thee, and Thy Spirit guiding me, let me ever walk. There are those who seek not to walk before Thee, and I was once among them; who try to lounge behind Thee, as if they could evade Thy vision, and find a genial gloom in the shadow of Thy throne.

They wish not Thy presence, but would flee from it. 'God hath forgotten,' say they; and thus they repeat their dream, 'He hideth His face, He will never see it.' The first man sought away from Thee; but the thunder of Thy voice brought him trembling to Thy feet. Thy prophet of old attempted to flee from Thee; but thy storm caught him and yoked him again to Thy message. But let me ever rejoice in Thy presence; let me feel it, as Thy flowers feel Thy sun-light—to be life and joy. Before Thee let me ever walk, and Thou wilt anticipate every wish, ward off every danger, and select for me every step. Nearer and nearer let me come to gaze on Thy radiance and love, till at last I approach that presence more closely than angels dare, and chaunt a melody which the seraphs cannot learn to sing. There love shall still be the music of the anthem, and the spirit of every occupation and enjoyment shall be in harmony with my dear and delightful avowal, I LOVE THE LORD.

The troubles that passed over me would have flung me into desperation, but 'I believed' in God. Ah, how dark and wretched should I have been without such faith — like a withered leaf of autumn, tossed by the winds into the swollen current. I did not let go my confidence. Though I have told my afflictions without abatement, it is only to enhance the glory of my deliverance. In no sullen fit 'have I spoken' of my sufferings. 'I was greatly afflicted,' and my mention of my agony has been to glorify my Saviour-God. After He revealed Himself to me

I never doubted. No, never; and 'though He slay me, yet will I trust in Him.'

As I looked around me, I felt the vanity of all human things. There was no refuge in man. They could not do for me either as they desired or as they professed. Trust in them brought only chagrin and vexation. Indeed, what can any human aid do for a wounded spirit? The balm of Gilead cannot minister to it — words of earthly solace fall on the ear without effect: 'miserable comforters are they all.' What is the world to one under suffering; to one labouring under disease, and under conviction of sin? To me it was all hollowness and vanity.

> 'Earth's cup
> Is poisoned; her renown most infamous;
> Her gold, seem as it may, is really dust;
> Her titles, slanderous names; her praise, reproach;
> Her strength, an idot's boast; her wisdom, blind;
> Her gain, eternal loss; her hope, a dream;
> Her love, her friendship, enmity with God;
> Her promises, a lie; her smile, a harlot's;
> Her beauty, paint and rotten within; her pleasures,
> Deadly assassins masked; her laughter, grief;
> Her breasts, the stings of death; her total sum —
> Her all — most total vanity!'

So that 'I said in my haste, all men are liars.' But the contrast cheers me. From men I turn away, and lift my gaze upwards to the source of refuge and blessing. O it is He, and He alone who gave me comfort, who heard my prayer, and bade me live. Such is my sense of His mercy; such my overwhelming consciousness of His love, that I know not what return to make: 'What shall I render unto the Lord for all His benefits toward me?' I cannot answer my own question. I find no gift worthy of the occasion; none can I commend as an adequate expression of my gratitude. For everything I have is His already; and I can only offer Him His own. The gem and the victim, the gold and the incense, come not up to my estimate of obligation; and they are but a mean offering after all.

> 'The best return for one like me,
>   So wretched and so poor,
> Is from His gifts to draw a plea
>   And ask Him still for more.
>
> 'I cannot serve Him as I ought —
>   No work have I to boast;
> Yet would I glory in the thought
>   That I shall owe Him most.'

'What shall I render?' I have no substantial gift; but I will give my ardent praise, and seal it in the sacramental goblet: 'I will take the cup of salvation, and call upon the name of the Lord.' Such a thank-offering — loving and ardent — the devout and genuine consecration of the heart He will prefer. With the cup of 'the communion of the blood of Christ' in my hand, Lord, I give myself to Thee. For Christ's sake accept me; wield me for Thy service, and fashion me for Thy glory. If thou sendest suffering, I will bear it in Thy patience; if Thou layest on me any commission, I will execute it in Thy strength. Bid me go, and I will go; beckon me to come, and I will come; say to Thy servant do this, and I will do it. Lord, I am Thine, pledged in this cup of salvation; and again will I record it — I LOVE THE LORD.

Nor shall my gift be rendered in secret. Mine was a public deliverance, and mine shall be a public thanksgiving. 'I will pay my vows unto the Lord now in the presence of all His people.' What I vowed I will pay cheerfully: 'what my lips uttered, and my mouth spake when I was in trouble.' Ye who were around me; who saw me laid low, so abject and agonised; who beheld the turmoil of my soul, and the fevered sufferings of my frame; who witnessed my moaning cry for help, and were spectators of my relief; — in your presence will I ratify my vows; and the Lord I love will accept them: 'The humble shall see it and be glad, and your hearts shall live that seek the Lord.' 'My praise shall be of thee in the great congregation.' 'I cried unto him with my voice, and he shall be extolled with my tongue.' 'He did not turn away my prayer,' and He will not turn away my praise. 'I will praise the name of the Lord with a song, and will magnify him with thanksgiving. This also shall please the Lord better than an ox or bullock that hath horns and hoof.' 'I am as a wonder unto many,' and many shall listen to my grateful acknowledgments. 'Let my mouth be filled with thy praise and thy honour all the day long.' 'Open unto me the gates of righteousness, I will go into them and I will praise the Lord.'

> 'Here in Thy courts, I leave my vow,
> And Thy rich grace record;
> Witness ye saints, who hear me now,
> If I forsake the Lord.'

My soul drew nigh unto death, but Thou hast brought me up. 'The dead praise not thee, neither any that go down into silence.' 'The Lord hath chastened me sore, but he hath not given me over unto death.' Now I know that 'precious in the sight of the Lord is the death of his saints.' Precious is that death, for He helps them in life, and does not abruptly dismiss them from the world; precious to Him, for He vouchsafes to them His gracious presence, and His Son for their sakes has conquered death; precious in His sight, for it happens only when He permits. Their soul was precious, for He redeemed it, and He has sanctified it; and unspeakably precious does He feel it to be at the moment when it leaves its tabernacle, and ascends upward to His bosom. And I have seen upon the death-bed of a saint how precious was his death! When Thy hand was first laid upon him, he submitted indeed, but with sore struggle, and there was intense desire for recovery. He had pictured to himself a long, happy, and useful life. But as days passed, Thy grace gained the victory, and gradually was he enabled to say, 'Not my will, but thine be done.' One who saw him daily might have marked step after step of the visible progress, not in resignation only, but in faith as it brightened, and in hope as it reached its 'full assurance.' O how unspeakably precious such a training — when Thy grace lays hold of the soul, and fetches it 'out of the depths;' reveals Thy glory yet more fully, brings forth one promise after another yet more forcibly, unvails the tender and indissoluble relations of the covenant, imparts triumph over every temptation, and so prepares for death, and ripens for future glory! And thus the dying believer comes to have no will but Thine — is ready to leave the world without a pang — can speak of his departure with an animating smile, and extol the love of His Father who is soon to bring home His child. He feels that he is Thine, and that Thou vouchest for the safety of Thine own. There may be pains, but he murmurs not; spasms of expiring nature, but he complains not; a dark step, but he shrinks not. At length he pillows his dying head on the bosom of Immanuel, and falls asleep in Jesus. Farewell, but for a season. Thou art before us, but we dare not envy thee. What wonders thou hast now seen, what praises thou hast now sung, what a full tide of joy is now in thy bosom! What are now thy thoughts of Him who died? Couldst thou express them in human words? As we gaze on thy coffin lid, and lower the precious and beloved dust, our eye fills, and the tear falls. But we dry it. For soon, very soon, shall we be with thee, to be locked again in friendship, and to walk with one another while we both walk with God.

'I saw when the time of his release was come,
And I longed for a congregated world to behold that dying saint.
As the aloe is green and well-looking till the last, best summer of its age,
And then hangeth out its golden bells to mingle glory with corruption —
Such was the end of this righteous one.
His filmy eye was bright with love from heaven;
His every look it beamed praise, as worshipping with seraphs.
What honey-comb was hived upon his lips, eloquent of gratitude and prayer;
What triumph shined serene upon that clammy brow;
What glory, flickering, transparent, upon those thin cheeks;
What beauty on his face!'

Yes, surely and beyond all doubt, 'precious in the sight of the Lord is the death of his saints.' That death is of high price, for it is to the saint great 'gain.' When I think of leaving earth, with its imperfect society and occupations — its brief and scanty enjoyment, I think, at the same time, of entering heaven, where those around me are robed in purity and 'walk in white,' and where I shall see His face, and praise Him in rapturous hallelujahs; where no sin shall cloud, and no infirmity shall distract; where the Sabbath never comes to an end, and the congregation never breaks up; where the heart shall never be out of humour, and the harp never out of tune; where the Lord I love shall be loved with an intensity of which I cannot now dream, and where the cup of which I have now partaken shall be replenished, fresh and full, out of the fountain that rises up from beneath the throne. Love the Lord, O my soul, for these precious hopes.

> 'Thou shalt walk in robes of glory;
>   Thou shalt wear a golden crown;
> Thou shalt sing redemption's story
>   With the saints around the throne.

> 'Thou shalt see that better country
>   Where a tear-drop never fell,
> Where a foe made never entry,
>   And a friend ne'er said farewell.
> Where upon the radiant faces
>   That will shine on thee alway,
> Thou wilt never see the traces
>   Of estrangement and decay.'

And now, as the Lord I love has done so much for me — has thrown around me the arms of His power, I feel that I am bound by peculiar ties to Him. I am under obligation (and I gladly own and record it) to prove the reality of my affection and homage by activity and labour. 'O Lord, truly I am thy servant.' Give me the spirit of a servant. Show me my work as a servant, and fit me for it. Then shall I find that all service is easy and pleasant. O that this love I profess had a deeper fervour, that it filled my entire nature, that it nursed every motive, and threw its radiance over every labour — then should I exult in declaring again, 'I am thy servant.' Thy service is no drudgery, for Thy will is always 'holy, and just, and good.' The work Thou assignest elevates and ennobles him who does it. Ye servants of Satan, how I pity you. Your task is ignoble; you are degraded into serfs, and your 'austere master' plunges you deeper and deeper in the mire, gives you no respite, and holds out no hope of reward; for 'the wages of sin is death.'

That I was early given to Thee, is my joy and gratitude. The seed sown in maternal love, and watered by maternal tears, has at length borne its fruit. 'I am the son of thy handmaid'—the child of many prayers. She travailed 'again as in birth' for me, that I might be born again. She was one of Thy servants, dear and devoted to Thee; let her son be ever a welcome servant. Thus race unto race shall fear Thee, and the promise of Thy covenant,—'to you and your children,' is fulfilled. Surely I cannot but value early parental instruction—'the son of thy handmaid,' who now says of himself, 'truly I am thy servant.' Have I not seen many trained from infancy, some to carelessness and some to sin; ay, and some, too, have I seen setting all parental nurture at defiance, burning their mother's Bible, and cursing their mother's God. That 'I am what I am,' 'bless the Lord, O my soul.' Nay more, I was once enslaved — the fetter was tight, and it galled me; the iron was heavy, and I could not break it. My soul was enthralled to the past, and I could not flee from painful recollections; it was chained to the future, and I could not shake off gloomy forebodings; it was tied down to the present, and I could not unfasten the sinful indifference that held me in captivity. and there I lay like —

> 'An infant crying in the night,
> An infant crying for the light,
> And with no language but a cry.'

But 'thou hast loosed my bonds.' My mind was in bondage to error, and my heart was in bondage to sin; but Thy truth has freed me — Thy Son has made me 'free indeed.' Relieved from such servitude, I am Thy servant, and grateful for my emancipation, 'I will offer to thee the sacrifice of thanksgiving, and will call upon the name of the Lord.' 'My praise shall be of thee in the great congregation, I will pay my vows before them that fear him.'

And thus, the longer I meditate, the more is my heart crowded with reasons for serving the Lord. And shall I not declare my love with a public acknowledgment? 'I will pay my vows unto the Lord now, in the presence of all his people; in the courts of the Lord's house, in the midst of thee, O Jerusalem.' Thy servant Hezekiah got it from Thyself as a pledge of his recovery from sickness, that 'on the third day he should go up to the house of the Lord.' The God who healed him, knew that the royal heart would like to give public thanks for the divine goodness. 'If,' said Thy servant David, 'I find favour in the eyes of the Lord, he will show me his habitation.' The exiled sovereign felt that his return to his capital would be one not only to his palace, but to Thy sanctuary. And shall not I love Thy house—the scene where Thou hast so often manifested 'Thy power and glory?' Am I not drawn to Thy people? 'Come and hear, all ye that fear God, and I will declare what he hath done for my soul.' While I began by saying of myself that I love the Lord, may I not conclude by saying to you — 'Praise ye the Lord' — 'O magnify the Lord with me, and let us exalt his name together?' Bear me witness, ye who share a kindred affection, when in the midst of you, I inscribe on my votive tablet —

'I LOVE THE LORD.'

'I love Thee, Lord, but with no love of mine,
  For I have none to give;
I love Thee, Lord, but all the love is Thine,
  For by Thy love I live.
I am as nothing, and rejoice to be
Emptied, and lost, and swallowed up in Thee.

Thou, Lord, alone art all Thy children need,
  And there is none beside;
From Thee the streams of blessedness proceed,
  In Thee the blest abide.
Fountain of life and all-abounding grace,
Our source, our centre, and our dwelling-place.'

LECTURE V.

THE ADOPTING LOVE OF THE FATHER.

A LECTURE.

1 John III. 1–3.

'Behold what manner of love the Father hath bestowed upon us, that we should be called the sons of God! therefore the world knoweth us not, because it knew him not. Beloved, now are we the sons of God; and it doth not yet appear what we shall be: but we know that, when he shall appear, we shall be like him; for we shall see him as he is. And every man that hath this hope in him purifieth himself, even as he is pure.'

ONE object of the beloved disciple in the composition of this inspired essay, is to show and prove that a holy life ought to be the invariable result and accompaniment of a pure and orthodox creed. For the surest proof of being in God, is to be like God. They who hope for salvation from Christ's death, ought to be conformed to His life; and they who trust in His righteousness, are bound to obey His law. But such spiritual assimilation implies a previous, radical, and permanent change — a change which is not self-produced, but is the result of divine influence. There lurks in the bosom of fallen and wrecked humanity no latent elasticity, by the operation of which man may recover himself to God and to goodness. Power not his own, power from on high, must therefore descend upon him, and transform him. This is the truth announced in the last verse of the preceding chapter, and in these words: 'If ye know that he is righteous, ye know that every one that doeth righteousness is born of him.' Genuine righteousness is the fruit of the second birth. Those who are thus born of God, own God for their Father — the twice-born alone are his spiritual children, and among themselves 'all they are brethren.' But while the power which translates and renews them is so great, that power has been excited into action by infinite love. And now, as the apostle looked on the spiritual brotherhood, and saw them all to be begotten of one Father; as he remembered what they once were, and by what grace they had been rescued; and as he reflected on the character enjoyed by them, the blessings heaped upon them, the privileges possessed by them, and the destiny awaiting them; as these thoughts lay in his deep and susceptible heart, they prompted him to exclaim, in the first verse, 'Behold what manner of love the Father hath bestowed upon us, that we should be called the sons of God.'

Such language is the expression of wonder and gratitude. And the point of the exclamation lies not in its reference to the mere fact of the Father's love, but to the 'manner' or kind of it. It is love of a peculiar species; unique in its nature, and unparalleled in its results. 'His ways are not our ways, nor his thoughts our thoughts.' Behold what *manner* of love; yes, it is worthy of all admiration, and deserves to be ever contemplated and adored. What then is its 'manner?'

Let us look, first, at the result or purpose of this love, and we shall be the better prepared to understand its 'manner.' If we know what it contemplates and what it has secured for us, then we shall rise to the recognition at once of its fervour and its strangeness. Now, the apostle says this affection has been lavished upon us, 'that we should be called the sons of God.' O the indescribable honour of such an appellation — to be called by the great Parent, His sons! This God-given name is an index to the reality, and is no ornamental epithet or appendage. Men of the Hebrew nation had often the name of God incorporated into their own, and a claim of divine descent was often boasted of by the heroes of classical antiquity. Thus, Isaiah is the 'salvation of Jehovah,' Jeremiah is 'exalted of Jehovah,' Daniel is 'judge appointed by God,' and Ezekiel is 'supported by God.' Thus, too, the idol Nebo is found in the royal name, Nebuchadnezzar; and Baal forms a part of such surnames as Jezebel, Hannibal, and Belshazzar. The common Moorish title, Abdallah, signifies 'servant of God.' This earnest desire to be named after the object of worship, springs out of universal religious instinct, and men have clung to the symbol after they had become strangers to the reality. But God's children are His in verity. The unnatural sin of their unfilial rebellion is blotted out, and they become sons by adoption. They had made themselves exiles from His family, but He brings them back, and the Spirit of their Father is bestowed upon them. So that, first of all, they bear His image, as the test and token of their sonship. The lineaments of His moral character are reflected in them. As the father lives again in the countenance of the child, so the likeness of God is communicated to His spiritual offspring; and as by gazing on the son, you can tell the paternity, so the lustrous features of the inner man proclaim at once his heavenly origin. The sons are conformed to the image of Christ, and Christ is the 'brightness of the Father's glory,' and the 'express image of his person.' What a change, so profound and joyous—out of the family of Satan into the household of God. O, then, prove your descent, by exhibiting your likeness! Disguise not your lineage. Live, we entreat you, in the thought of being the sons of God, and act always under a sense of this high relationship. Never tarnish your dignity by ungodly pursuits. Let the sons of God be like Him. Let not the heir of the crown be found among the slaves of the mine. Be ye 'the sons of God without rebuke, in the midst of a crooked and perverse nation.' What 'manner' of love is this, in transforming those who were once so unlike Him, and who had so terribly provoked Him; and in clothing them, not with a dim and distant similitude, but with the ethereal dignity of His very image.

The sons of God also possess His special love: 'Ye shall be my sons and daughters.' Love prompted Him to adopt them; and after they are adopted, He has peculiar delight in them. Being His children, they are His friends. His paternal arms are thrown around them. Angels are loved by Him with a single and a common love, but saints are loved by Him with a special and a double affection. The blood of His Son has been shed for them; they have cost Him much, and His heart has therefore a tender complacency in them. What 'manner' of love is this, that the fallen should at length have a place in His bosom which the unfallen can never occupy!

Still more, a glorious destiny awaits them—a rich and noble legacy is secured for them: 'If children, then heirs; heirs of God, and joint-heirs with Christ.' Fathers on earth sometimes leave their children a heritage of shame, and the shadow of the gallows looms over their cradle. But God has set apart an inheritance for us—rich, substantial, and permanent. All that He is, and all that He has is ours; yes, all that God is, and all that God possesses is the heritage of His children: 'All things are yours; whether Paul, or Apollos, or Cephas, or the world, or life, or death, or things present, or things to come; all are yours; and ye are Christ's.' When the years of minority are expired, the children are taken home to the household on high, where their filial likeness is perfectly developed, and their Father's love is fully enjoyed; where the whole family form one unbroken and vast assemblage—heart knit to heart in the secure possession of their celestial patrimony.

Can you now doubt that you 'should be called the sons of God?' You are not forgiven and kept at a distance — are not constituted servants inferior and apart; but you are made sons. The confession of the prodigal was, "I am no more worthy to be called thy son,' and his prayer was, 'make me as one of thy hired servants.' But the father at once reinstated him; calls him in the fulness of his joy — 'my son;' puts on him a robe, which no slave durst assume, and covered his feet with sandals, which no menial could wear. There was love in pitying you, special love in redeeming you from the curse; but there is an unearthly 'manner' of love, in not only plucking you from danger, but in placing you in the near and dear relation of sons. It would have been unspeakable grace to have made you servants, and kept you in the outer court to obey Him as your Master; but O it is past all thought and record, that you are children, and that you love Him as your Father—bear His image, share in His tender affection, and are preparing for His glorious home. 'What manner of love' in this triple privilege; yea, God represents it as a problem, and as a matter of surprise to Himself: 'How shall I put thee among the children, and give thee the goodly heritage?'

The extraordinary love of the Father is also seen

in the entire circuit of discipline which has been arranged for His children. As they occasionally transgress, so are they chastened, but not in anger or 'hot displeasure.' When a parent punishes a beloved child, it is the highest effort of a self-denying love. God's genuine affection lifts up the rod, and he does not spare the rod, for He does not hate the child. Such a visitation is a proof of sonship. Will you not take it joyously, as the evidence of a Father's love, and as the means of preparing you for a Father's home? 'If ye be without chastisement, whereof all are partakers, then are ye bastards, and not sons.' And you possess, in fine, a blessed privilege in prayer. Your Father's ear is ever open, and His hand is ever full. You have but to unbosom yourselves before Him, and without reserve. 'Ye have not received the spirit of bondage again to fear, but ye have received the spirit of adoption, whereby we cry, Abba, Father.' Your confidence in Him can never be misplaced. Children in the dawn of youth have perfect trust in their parents — in their ability to supply every want, to grant every request, and to impart all needed information and assistance. Such tender faith only leaves them after repeated disappointments have taught them an opposite conclusion. But all wisdom is God's to direct you, all power His to defend you, and all goodness His to secure your felicity.

And will not such a child be content in any circumstances? What is good for him His Father will give him. As much of temporal blessing will he get as he can improve. Nor does he need to possess the world in order to enjoy it. He can look around him on earth and say, 'My Father made it all.' He spends his life in a habitation provided by parental skill and love. And were he always conscious of his sonship, what peace and confidence would he not feel in all conditions and at every moment. As if he said or sung —

> 'Why should I stranger be
>   In my Father's dwelling,
> While hill and river, rock and tree
>   Of His love are telling?
> Always heard their simple voice,
> Bidding childlike hearts rejoice,
> Whispers me, this love is near;
> What I hope in yonder sphere,
> Love can find it now and here.
> See how every tree and flower,
> For a century or an hour,
> Rests in one upholding power.
> All their food to them is brought,
> Nothing wanted, nothing sought;
> Why should I, with anxious thought,
> Mar the good my Father wrought?'

Having now learned what God had in prospect, and how He has wrought it out; having seen that in making us His sons, the end and the process are alike marvellous and uncommon,—we are now prepared the better to comprehend the singularity of the divine affection. And first, the love that leads a man to call a child his own, which is not by his natural descent, has not such a 'manner' about it.

For when among men a child is adopted, it is usually because the adopter thinks it worthy of his regard; because there is something in its features or character that pleases him. He likes it and thinks it a likeable child, and so he takes it to his heart and home, gives it his own name, feeds it, clothes it, educates it, and prepares it for the duties of life. But no such motive could prompt the divine affection; for we were utterly lost and loathsome before Him. There was nothing about us, in our character or position, to attract the divine affection. All was unruly, defiant, and ungrateful. The pride of our apostasy bade us cry, 'Who is Lord over us?' 'Depart from us,' shouted we to the Almighty. The wonder is, that we were not consumed in wrath. For we were once in His family; but we scornfully left it, and in the pride of rebellious independence sought for ourselves another household. The door might have been righteously closed upon us for ever. But He welcomes us; ay, He takes us, disgraced and filthy as we are, to His bosom. He has loved us; and His love is like Himself. He has loved us, and in defiance of every repelling element, He has laid His gracious hand upon us, translated us into His family, and made us His sons. 'This is not the *manner* of men, O Lord God.'

Again, if one adopts a child, it is commonly because himself is childless, or his hearth may have been desolated by war or disease. He longs to have some object near him on which to set his heart, and expend his instinctive attachment. But Jehovah had myriads of a flourishing progeny — uncounted hosts of bright intelligences, who have never disobeyed Him. His heart rejoices over them; so numerous and so closely arranged are they around his throne, that in its reflected splendour they appear like moving and living clouds of radiance. It was not because His glory was unseen, or His praises were unsung, that He has loved us. There was no unsupplied craving in Him, which led Him to adopt us; for the 'many mansions' were crowded with a happy household. But yet He has loved us; and though He had so many children, He wishes to have more; nay, His heart is set on bringing 'many sons to glory.' What 'manner' of love is this; how noble and disinterested in its nature! How intense, too, in its warmth; for ere this adoption could be effected, the 'first-born among many brethren' must suffer and die. The Father gives up His only-begotten Son to agony and the cross, that the human slaves of Satan might receive the 'adoption of children.' Such love is in the manner of it above all conception and parallel, and has no shadow of itself among created attachments. Feeling, then, how He hath adopted you, and what blessings are implied in your adoption — how, as His children, you are so like Him, and are so loved by Him; how you have the prospect of a blessed heritage, and are enjoying necessary and wholesome tuition and discipline during your present minority — O will you not be induced to cry out with the apostle of love, who revels in the idea of such love, 'Behold what manner of love the Father hath bestowed upon us, that we should be called the sons of God!'

But the present condition of the sons of God is vailed and incomplete. 'Therefore,' the apostle adds, 'the world knoweth us not, because it knew Him not.' That is, the world did not recognise Christ; and on the very same principle, the world does not recognise those who are Christ's. The mission of the Son of God was spiritual. It was not in harmony with the vulgar expectation, and therefore the world did not and could not appreciate it. Had the Son of David come to confer earthly franchise and national independence; had He unfurled the banner of the Lion of Judah, and drawn a sword to expel the hated and crushing usurper — thousands would have flocked around Him with acclamations and hosannahs, and proclaimed Him the hero and head of Israel. But His character and errand were very different, for He came to free men not by the sword, but by suffering, and to deliver them not from political vassalage, but from the kingdom of darkness. His enterprise was too ethereal for the coarse vision of the world to detect, or its sordid heart to admire. The world recognises and loves only what belongs to itself — distinction in birth or rank, in arts or arms, in legislation or science, in poetry or architecture, in oratory or philosophy. Its great ones, and not its good ones, divide among themselves the world's homage. 'They are of the world, therefore the world loveth them.' Not that the world is able to ignore christianity.

But it admires it not for itself, but for its splendid results — for the beneficial effects, in the form of patriotism and philanthropy, which it has produced. It is not Wilberforce the saint, but Wilberforce the queller of the slave trade, that men admire. Spiritual christianity is as distasteful to the world as ever it was — 'the natural man receiveth not the things of the Spirit of God.'

The dignity and prospects of the sons of God are not of a secular and visible nature. 'The world knoweth them not.' Were they the scions of a royal house, or were their inheritance on earth, the world would very soon come to know them; but their Father is in heaven, and their dominion is with Him. They wear no mantle, with symbolic decorations, to attract attention; their pure robe is the righteousness of Christ, invisible to such as are strangers to the cross. But should this ignorance on the part of the world dispirit you? By no means. Your case is not solitary. It 'knew Him not' — even Him it did not recognise as the Son of God. 'It is enough for the disciple that he be as his master, and the servant that he be as his lord.' If the world did not know Him, though the glory of His Sonship so often flashed around Him, how can it be expected to know you, with your fewer and feebler tokens of relationship to God. Cicero says that if virtue were to descend to the world in a human shape, so enamoured would men be of the spectacle, that they would fall down and worship it. And yet virtue did descend in a true humanity — the incarnation of loveliness itself; and so far from doing homage to it, they nailed it, in the person of Jesus, to the accursed tree. 'Therefore the world knoweth us not, because it knew him not.' But it matters not. Were you to be tried by a jury of the world, and were your eternal destiny to depend upon their verdict, based on their knowledge of your filial dignity, then you might feel anxiety, and might use every means and embrace every opportunity to bring men into acquaintanceship with you. But your future welfare is in your Father's hands, and no member of His vast family is too mean to be overlooked, or too distant to be forgotten. He who ' counts the number of the stars, and names them every one,' has a perfect knowledge of all His children — of the least and the lowest of them — of the babes as well as of those of full age. The beggar that lay at the rich man's gate, feeding on the crumbs and waited on by the dogs, might die in solitude and neglect — no friend might receive his parting sigh, or close his drooping eyes — no stone would mark the spot of his unrecorded sepulture; and yet the angels carried his spirit into Abraham's bosom, on which he lay a cherished guest at the heavenly banquet. Out of a world that did not know them the children shall all be assembled; for the eye of a Father is on them, the heart of a Father is with them, and the arm' of a Father shall guide them home to His loved abode.

Verse 2, 'Beloved, now are we the sons of God; and it doth not yet apper what we shall be: but we know that, when he shall appear, we shall be like him; for we shall see him as he is.' Our sonship, we rejoice to be thus informed, is not a blessing awaiting us in some distant sphere of being. It is a present privilege: 'Now are we the sons of God.' Despite of this non-recognition on the part of the world, we are the sons of God. The reality of our adoption is not modified by the world's oblivion of it. It may be undiscovered by others, but our own experience gives ourselves the full assurance of it. So soon as faith springs up in the heart, are we reinstated in the family of God, cherished, protected, and sanctified — enjoying the children's privileges, eating the children's bread, possessing the children's prerogatives, and being made meet for the children's home.

But noble as is our present condition, our ultimate dignity surpasses conception. 'It doth not yet appear what we shall be.' It has not been revealed. It is matter of faith, and it is still wrapt in mystery. It may be questioned if human language has nerve and sinew enough to bear upon it a description of the 'far more exceeding and eternal weight of glory.' It might be doubted, too, if we were qualified to comprehend it though it had been revealed — if the words of such an oracle would not have been to us like the algebraic symbols of an unknown quantity. For our own present experience, blissful though it be, scarce lays a foundation for augury as to our future state. Even though we now revel in the divine favour, and are blessed with the divine image, though the joy of such a state does often make us mute from its very rapture, yet such transcendent felicity is scarcely a premiss to reason from as to the glory of our ultimate heritage. We know, indeed, that in harmony with usual divine procedure, there is a necessary development. The acorn springs into a sapling ere it spreads out into an oak, and the infant passes through childhood and youth to the maturity of manhood. It may be a slow and invisible growth, but there is sure result. Look on the blade—it doth not yet appear what it shall be, 'for it shoots into the ear,' and bends at length with the weight of the 'full corn in the ear.' When Pharaoh's daughter opened the basket of bulrushes on the bank of the Nile, it did not then appear what that weeping babe should be—the hero, legislator, and saint. We are not therefore to expect too much in the meantime. The apostle Paul, as he speaks of the children, and affirms that they are heirs, adds in the same spirit, 'If so be that we suffer with him, that we may be also glorified together.' Suffering and depression are not incompatible with sonship, for the children are spiritually related to Him who was the 'Man of sorrows.' There is so much about us that clogs and confines us—so much that is sinful and oppressive—so deep is the shadow that earth throws over the children of God, that any inference as to coming freedom and glory is all but an impossiblity. Such being the present eclipse of our sonship, there is the less wonder that 'the world knoweth us not.' The Son of Mary—a carpenter—a man of sorrows—

poor and persecuted — was not Himself, in such a disguise, seen to be the Son of God.

Yet there is a leading thought which the apostle presents as a guide, and by following it we may obtain some glimpse of future blessedness. It is as a central picture which stands out with peculiar prominence, and though we be not able to fill up its entire outline, or throw over it the living lustre of eternity, yet may we argue and imagine from the portion unvailed as to the nobleness and splendour of what is concealed: 'We know that, when He shall appear, we shall be like Him; for we shall see Him as he is.' In this declaration Christ is not formally mentioned. It needed not. The apostle's readers could not mistake the reference. Only one Being could possess that peculiar excellence and position. 'When Christ shall appear, we shall be like Him; for we shall see Him as he is.' This truth is an unshaken first principle on which all our conclusions are to be based.

Christ shall appear. This is the blessed hope of the church — 'The appearing of our great God and Saviour Jesus Christ.' He left the world with the promise of revisiting it. He has peculiar interest in it; the scenes of His nativity and suffering must have a special charm for Him. When He ascended, and the eleven were straining their aching eye-balls to obtain a glimpse of His lessening form, so fast disappearing among the clouds, the angels said to them, 'Ye men of Galilee, why stand ye gazing up into heaven? this same Jesus, which is taken up from you into heaven, shall so come in like manner as ye have seen him go into heaven.' He shall appear in majesty: 'In his own glory, the glory of his Father, and in that of his holy angels.' That bright humanity shall outshine the sun, and supply its place to a startled world. For 'He shall appear'— in the glory of His original Godhead, blended with the majesty of crowned Redeemer; arrayed in the regal apparel of Universal Governor; surrounded by a dense and innumerable retinue, and about to exercise His last and loftiest prerogative of judgment,— then — then — 'shall we see Him as He is.'

The inference is, that we have never yet seen Him as He is — never beheld His unshaded splendour. We have been privileged only to gaze upon His portraiture, sketched indeed by the pencil of inspiration; yet a likeness, no matter how exactly limned and naturally coloured it may be, can never be compared with the living original. But we shall see Him face to face, without any intervention. Yes; that same Jesus who lived and died, who wept and conquered — the Man-God, in His actual person — 'as He is'—the brightest and loveliest Being of the universe. Yes, 'as He is;' no semblance of Him, no cloudy phantom; but the Lord of glory before us, near us, as really as when He walked, and spoke, and lived among the houses and hamlets of Judea. For it is no dim glimpse we are to obtain — no sudden coruscation to dazzle us, no partial view which shall only create a longing for a fuller inspection; but leisurely and at large 'we shall see Him as He is.' Who can tell the bliss or glory of such a vision? There is no being like Christ. In His mysterious constitution He combines divinity and humanity, and the highest glories of the universe sit in gracefulness upon Him. That crucified Man is now 'Lord of all;' and 'as He is'—without veil shall we behold Him. He was seen of old in symbol, and at length was He beheld in flesh; but the symbol was dim in its transparency, and the flesh hid in its mantle the splendours of His Godhead; but He shall now be revealed in the radiance of divinity, mingling with the brightness of a glorified humanity, and heightened by the imperial lustre of the 'great white throne.'

On seeing Him, 'we shall be like Him.' The meaning is not that we shall be like Him, and therefore shall be qualified to see Him; but that when we see Him, completed likeness to Him shall be the result of the wonderful vision. If a partial and interrupted view of Him beget partial similitude on earth, the vision of 'Him as He is' will surely bring us into full and final conformity. In the same way as, by a discovery of modern science, the rays of the sun falling on your countenance transfer its features in an instant to a surface of metal or glass, so this vision of Jesus will at once communicate to His people His blessed and ineffaceable image. Only when He comes again do they wear their entire nature, so as to be capable of being universally like Him; for their bodies shall then have been raised, and they shall stand before Him in the fulness of their human constitution.

And what pencil can sketch the features of this likeness! We can only speak vaguely about it. Blessed are they who shall wear it; and even they may be unable to describe it; ay, and the tongue of angels may not be stocked with a sufficiency of epithets.

There is no doubt, however, that we shall be like Christ in mind. Our knowledge is at present limited and confused. There are murky shadows which float over the intellect, and there are special forms of bias which delude and fascinate the heart. Our conceptions are unworthy of those noble objects about which they are formed; and if a blush may cover the cheek of the redeemed, it will be excited by the memory of those low and limited views of divine truth and glory which they occasionally cherished on earth. Even when we think of our Father; of His love, His power, and His glory; of His household, in its occupations; and of His home, in its immortal blessedness, — our ideas are tainted with the earthliness of those human relationships on which they are based. But we shall rise above the relative into the region of the absolute and pure. Light direct from the throne shall pervade the mind, and, like the mists at sun-rise, all shadows shall fade away and disappear: 'Now we know in part, and we prophesy in part. But when that which is perfect is come, then that which is in part shall be done away. For now we see through a glass, darkly; but then face to face.' 'The new man,' put on by the believer, 'is renewed in knowledge, after the image of him who created him.' What lessons of sublimity may then be imparted; what large and unanticipated conceptions of the divine nature and works, and of the vast and far-reaching relations of the economy of grace! God shall be seen in everything, and everything seen in Him. We shall 'have the mind of Christ,' and shall find that all that philosophy has expounded, and all that the Bible has discovered are 'childish things,' and as such, are completely superseded. 'Now I know in part; but then shall I know even as I am known.'

And we shall also be like Him in heart; for our spiritual nature shall be perfected. The last and loftiest attainments of holiness shall be reached. Love shall hold an undivided empire within us. What is foreign to our nature shall be taken out of it, and itself 'filled with all the fullness of God.' Whatever you venerate as holy or admire as good, shall be concentrated in the person of the glorified saint. Every grace in Christ's heart shall have a reflection of itself in the hearts of all His worshipping brethren. There shall be 'no more conscience of sin;' all its forms and all the evils it has brought shall be for ever done away. 'The glory of God' now seen in the face of his Son Jesus Christ,' shall then be seen also in the face of all the members of the household. The perfection of Christ shall distinguish every one of them; for they 'shall be satisfied, when they awake, with his likeness.' Who would not hope for this, and who would not willingly die in order to reach it? Such a perfected nature must also enjoy intimate fellowship with His Father and their Father, His God and their God. The children, as they see Him, and adore His glory, shall feel for ever as one with Him. Nothing shall be a barrier to their communion; for though the person of an angel should pass between them and the throne, it would cast no shadow upon them. Their happiness, too, will be unalloyed — no pang can be felt, and no tear can ever fall. No one shall ever say, 'I am sick,' and the symbol of mourning shall never be seen on their robe; for the elder Brother 'has abolished death.' 'They shall hunger no more, neither thirst any more; neither shall the sun light on them, nor any heat. For the Lamb, which is in the midst of the throne, shall feed them, and shall lead them unto living fountains of water; and God shall wipe away all tears from their eyes.'

> 'Ye wheels of nature, speed your course,
>   Ye mortal powers decay—
> Fast as ye bring the night of death,
>   Ye bring eternal day.'

And, lastly, we shall be like Him in physical constitution. The brightness of heaven does not oppress Him, nor shall it dazzle us. Our humanity dies, indeed, and is decomposed; but when He appears, it shall be raised and beautified, and fitted to dwell in a region which 'flesh and blood cannot inherit.' Man has been made to dwell on earth, and on no other planet. If he is to spend a happy eternity in a distant sphere, his physical frame must be prepared for it. If he is to see God and yet live — to serve Him in a world where there is no night and no sleep — to worship Him in company with angels which have not the clog of an animal frame, and like them to adore with continuous anthem and without exhaustion—then, surely, his nature must be changed, for otherwise it would soon be overpowered by such splendours, and would die of ecstasy amidst such enjoyments. The glory of heaven would speedily become a delicious agony. But here is the blessed promise — 'The Lord Jesus shall change our vile bodies, and fashion them like unto his own glorious body.' Therefore these bodies shall cease to be animal without ceasing to be human bodies, and they shall become 'spiritual' bodies—etherealised vehicles for the pure spirit which shall be lodged within them. 'This corruptible must put on incorruption, and this mortal must put on immortality.' And thus, in our entire nature, 'we shall be like Him' — so like our illustrious Prototype, that none can mistake the family relation.

Now it is only when He shall appear that this universal conformity shall be enjoyed—for then shall the bodies of His people be raised and fitted for heaven. Up to that period salvation is only partially enjoyed and by instalments, but then total redemption is possessed. No wonder, then, that this epoch is held out to the church as the 'blessed hope' it is 'looking for.' And yet, strange to say, this period fills many minds with alarm. The 'last day'—how terrible the time, how many sights and sounds to fill the spirit with consternation! Are we not to anticipate the dissolution of nature, the wreck of the elements, the ominous fires which no power can control, the sable blank of the departing heavens, the innumerable congregation summoned out of earth and ocean by the peal of the 'trump of God,' and the wicked calling on the mountains and hills to hide them from the wrath of the Lamb. But oh! we are too apt to forget the bright side of the picture —that then, and not till then, shall we be like Him —that then, and not till then, shall we see Him as He is, whatever view of Him our spirits in the meantime may have, and whatever likeness to Him in the interval they may possess. Even in heaven, and up to the second coming, happiness may consist as much in expectation as in positive enjoyment, so that His appearing is the hope of His church universal.

But that hope is on earth no dull and passive emotion, for the apostle adds, as a practical conclusion—

Verse 3, 'Every man that hath this hope in him, purifies himself, even as he is pure.' The words 'in him,' should be 'on Him'—that is Christ. The apostle alludes to the basis of the hope—Christ Himself. The hope of being like Christ rests on Christ Himself, and on His pledge to come again. And that hope incites to self-purification, and that self-purification, has for its perfect and lovely model, the example of Christ. 'He is pure'—the incarnation of purity. His friends who knew Him best, affirmed, 'in him was no sin.' He threw out this challenge to His enemies, 'Which of you convinceth me of sin?' Of him whose delight it would have been to find a flaw, and who would have found it if he could, He said, 'The prince of this world cometh, and findeth nothing in me.' The traitor, who would certainly have laid his conscience to rest if he had been able, cried out, as he cast from him the coveted wages of his treachery, 'I have sinned, I have betrayed the innocent blood.' And the voice from the 'excellent glory' crowned every attestation —'This is my beloved Son, in whom I am well pleased.'

To the life of Christ, every child of God will always turn his eye. The more earnestly he looks, the more beauty he will find. Painters speak of making some work of the old masters their 'study.' Their meaning is, that they devote day after day to the inspection of the picture, and as they gaze upon it, beauty after beauty bursts upon their enraptured vision. Thus the sons of God must make the life of Jesus their study, and hold it up before them as the one model, till they understand it more fully, love it more cordially, and copy it with a closer uniformity. And it is the hope of ultimate success in this imitation that leads them now to make a vigorous, prolonged, and prayerful effort. Their aim is to be as like Him as they can be here, in the hope that they shall be perfectly like Him hereafter.

'Every man that hath this hope in him, purifieth himself.' Who would engage in this work, and for it pluck out his right eye or cut off his right arm, if he had not the hope or assurance that such self-denial and 'labour shall not be in vain in the Lord?' Wherefore, the coming of the Lord is vitally connected with our whole spiritual life; all our graces and feelings, as well as prospects, have it ever in view; so that, when He says, 'Behold, I come quickly,' the response, ay, and the welcome of our souls is, 'Amen. Even so come, Lord Jesus.'

And now the main question is, Are we the sons of God? Does His Spirit so bear witness with our spirits? Are we able to say that we are in the divine family? Is it the language of your true experience, that you 'have received the adoption of children?' O do not deceive yourselves. I do not ask whether you have resolved to return, or have travelled back a portion of the journey, or have even come to the threshold; but, have you crossed that threshold, and are you really in the house? Be not contented with saying, We wish it were so, or we hope it is so. Ah! the wish may never be fulfilled, and the hope may never be realised. Many a one, with such a wish on his lips and such a hope in his heart, has lulled himself into eternal ruin. And O remember that if you are not in God's family, 'ye are of your father the devil.' Will you not disown such a frightful paternity, and will you not shudder at its terrible destiny — 'everlasting fire, prepared for the devil and his angels.' Delay not, we implore you, in coming back; live no longer in such society, and with such empty enjoyments. The Father waits you; the whole house will be moved to greet you at your return.

And if you be the sons of God, what love will you not cherish towards such a Father, and what obedience must you not render to all His commandments? Be 'obedient children, not fashioning yourselves according to your former lusts in your ignorance;' but 'prove what is that good, and acceptable, and perfect will of God.' He will not overtask you, and you will find highest happiness in filial devotion and service. Need we bid you love also the whole household of faith—every one that bears your Father's image.

And, in conclusion, as long as you are here, feel that you are 'strangers and pilgrims.' 'This is not your rest,' your home is on high. When another and yet another of your brethren dies, be not alarmed, it is only his Father calling him home. When you think of your own mortality, ever regard it in this light—as the child crossing the disturbed brook which separates him from home. And the elder Brother will guide you—'I will come again,' says He, 'and take you to myself.' Thus shall you reach your Father's house, and then shall you fully know 'what manner of love the Father hath bestowed upon you, that you should be called the sons of God;' and then also shall you feel what it is to be like Him, when you shall have seen Him as He is. To Him, with the Father, and the ever-blessed Spirit, be glory and power, now and ever. Amen.

LECTURE VI.

THE FATHER'S LOVE TO THE SON, THE MODEL AND MEASUREMENT OF THE SON'S LOVE TO HIS PEOPLE.

JOHN xv. 9.

'As my Father hath loved me, so have I loved you.'

'I HAVE LOVED YOU.' Blessed Jesus, we know it, and we cannot doubt it. There is not a moment of our lives in which we are not reminded of it. Every blessing we possess leads us to the cross, the scene of Thy love in its noblest victory, and impels us to look up to the throne on which Thou sittest in benign and generous supremacy. The church is filled and fragrant with it; 'it drops as sweet-smelling myrrh upon the handles of the lock.' The life and joy of every holy bosom, is this precious truth from the lips of Him whose heart was the home of love. May He not appeal to His birth, His baptism, His agony, His death and burial, as tokens of His vast and ineffable fondness, and say, 'I have loved you.' These facts are irresistible evidence; for they are the elements of a history imbued with love. The babe on his mother's lap; the boy in the temple; the man on the bank of the Jordan, receiving the

Spirit, and in the wilderness, wrestling with the tempter; the victim scourged and crucified; the corpse wrapt in linen and spices, — are features of a picture on which the eye is never tired of looking, while the tongue is exclaiming in rapture, 'Herein is love.'

But the Lord's assertion of this cheering fact, 'I have loved you,' is preceded by a bewildering statement — 'As the Father hath loved me.' Amazing thought, that the Father's love to the Son should be the model and the measurement of the Son's love to His people! We may not comprehend the statement. How indeed can we? 'Who can by searching find out God, who can find out the Almighty unto perfection?' We do not plead for identity in all respects, between the Father's love to the Son, and the Son's love to His people; but we plead for a similarity which really amounts to it. For men can never bear the same relation to Christ, that Christ bears to God. In the one case, the subject and object are the same, and the affection of a divine person is lavished upon a divine person; but in the other case, they are widely different — as we are at once guilty creatures, who have no claim on Christ's attachment, and are also finite creatures, who cannot therefore absorb the whole of it. Yet we may glean something to satisfy us; we can wander along the frontier, though we may not enter the unexplored territory. We may look at the clusters brought from Eschol, though we may not scan the luxuriant foliage and fruits of its vineyards.

If the Son's love to us be as the Father's love to Him, we are surely warranted to rest upon it as an eternal, infinite, and unchanging affection.

I. The Father's love to the Son is an eternal love, and, therefore, so is the Son's love to His people. For Father and Son have co-existed from eternity, and their mutual affection, like themselves, had no commencement. Both being perfectly holy, no other feeling than love could subsist between them. The Father must love His own image, and that 'express image' being ever before Him, love must have for ever glowed in His bosom towards Him who lay there. Had there been a period when the Son was not, or when His likeness to His Father was not complete, this affection might have begun to exist only when the Son sprang into being, or when He began to assume, in their fulness, the features of the paternal resemblance. But the Son claims a co-equal eternity, an underived divinity, and being so pure and so lovely, must have been from everlasting the object of the divine complacency. 'The Lord possessed me in the beginning of his way, before his works of old. . . . Then I was by him, as one brought up with him: and I was daily his delight.' Yes, the Son is eternal and self-existent, and is styled 'He who was, and is, and is to come.' He is 'before all things;' for he summoned them into being, and He preserves them in it. What an unhallowed perversion to ascribe the commencement of His existence to the date of His birth, or even to regard

Him as the earliest and highest of the creatures of God? Is He not the same in His moral and physical attributes with the Father? For they are both objects of worship, wielding the same prerogatives, and clothed in the same holiness and majesty. If, then, we are warranted to apply to eternity the phraseology suggested by the duration of time, we may surely say that the eternal Father has loved His own eternal Son in all the past periods of their co-existence.

And if so, if the Father's love to His Son never began to be, but always was; so, in a similar way, the Son's love to us never began to be, but always was. Being eternal Himself, all the emotions of His heart are unbeginning. Affections of love or hatred rise in the heart of man, as objects amiable or hostile present themselves. No one of us can tell how soon any emotion may be created within him, or what may be its sweep or character. It may be fear, if danger be apprehended; or hope, if good be anticipated; or sorrow, if ill be borne; or joy, if blessing be received; or anger, if injury be inflicted; or gratitude, if unmerited favour be conferred. But in the mind of the Son, there can be no such changes or vicissitudes: 'All things are naked and open to the eyes of him with whom we have to do.' The guilt and misery of man were present to Him from eternity; and, therefore, He can say, 'I have loved thee with an everlasting love; therefore with everlasting kindness have I drawn thee.' There was no epoch when His mind was charged with enmity towards us; neither did the sin of our world so take Him by surprise as to convert a previous affection into enmity. O, then, what origin can you assign to His love, if it be not coeval with His nature?

Supposing that His love did not exist from eternity, what posterior source could you possibly imagine for it? Could you ever dream that your existence would be necessary to His happiness, and that He must therefore love and save you; or that the repair of the ruin was a natural and indispensable work on the part of Him who had first erected the structure? Or, if you turn your vision upon yourselves, can you be so vain as to believe that you can discover within you anything having power to excite the affection of the Son of God? Did you even mourn over your lapse, and sigh and cry unto Him to save you? What more provoking to Him than your sin, or more revolting than your spiritual pride, hostility, and deformity! True; but His love had no temporal beginning; for it pre-existed you, and it pre-existed time. It was ever in Him, and prompted Him from eternity to make provision for your recovery. It is no momentary compassion produced by your unexampled wretchedness; no incidental commiseration stirred up within Him for the first time, when He saw you 'lying in your blood.' It is not an impulse, but an eternal emotion, sublime alike in the awful remoteness of its past, and in the unvarying nearness of its present existence. 'As my Father hath loved me, so have I loved you.'

II. The love of the Father to the Son is an infinite love, and therefore so is the Son's love to His people. Every emotion in God is co-extensive with His nature, and that nature is infinite — its centre being everywhere, but its circumference nowhere. 'Whither shall I go from thy Spirit? or whither shall I flee from thy presence? If I ascend up into heaven, thou art there: if I make my bed in hell, behold, thou art there. If I take the wings of the morning, and dwell in the uttermost parts of the sea; even there shall thy hand lead me, and thy right hand shall hold me.' We believe, too, that all that has been eternal in its existence is also and necessarily limitless in its extent—that He who inhabited eternity, must also fill immensity. That God loves Himself with infinite complacency, will not be questioned; and as His Son is His other Self, the affection cherished towards Him will also be without limitation. What has God which His Son has not —what attribute which his Son does not possess in a similar degree — what property does He love in Himself, that he does not equally love in the 'Only-begotten?' And if these properties be all of them infinite in the Son, the love excited by them will correspond in its measure.

Therefore, like His Father's love to Himself is the Son's love to His own. O who can mete out its bounds! You might number the sand on the sea-shore, or tell the stars of the firmament — the difficulty of calculation might be surmounted; but never could you compute the depth and extent of the Lord's affection for you. Alas that we have so low and unworthy conceptions of it! Could we expand our souls to its full idea, we should create heaven upon earth. Yet we may have some notion of it. 'Ye know the grace of our Lord Jesus Christ, that, though he was rich, yet for your sakes he became poor, that ye through his poverty might be rich.' Ineffable condescension! Rich He was in the possession of divine glory, and the enjoyment of unsurpassed felicity, receiving the ardent homage of the noblest intelligences, and the hymn of the great universe ever rising before Him in mighty and varied minstrelsy; and yet He became poor — born in penury — 'for low lies His bed with the beasts of the stall'—living a life of privation—earning His bread by the sweat of His brow as a village mechanic — ' a worm and no man' — His character aspersed, and Himself branded as a wine-bibber, a Sabbath-breaker, and an associate of publicans and sinners — threatened to be stoned for blasphemy— mocked, and set at nought — scourged, and put to death by a public and ignominious execution. What but infinite love could have stooped to such sufferings, or sustained Him under them? A love that might be measured would have shrunk or fainted when its energies were overstepped. It would have trembled as it counted the cost; thus far, and no farther, would have been its resolve. And within the sphere of such sufferings there must have been intense anguish too, when 'it pleased Jehovah to bruise him, and put him to grief.' 'Why hast Thou forsaken me?' was a deep and mysterious complaint, wrung from Him who never complained before. As if the only woe which He felt was this desertion, it was the only lamentation which He uttered. Can that love be fathomed which could voluntarily bear such an infliction from the hand of a loving Father? And is He not still before the throne, pleading and guarding — provoked, but yet loving — often grieved, but never withdrawing His attachment? Man's love would weary, but Christ's is unquenchable. It is not a stream whose waters might fail, but an ocean of immeasurable depth and volume—infinite like Himself, and like His Father's love to Him. If, then, Jesus has taken upon Him our frail and fleshly nature, compassed with infirmities, and doomed to die; if, under the judicial infliction of His Father, he groaned, and bled, and expired; if He lay in the grave a lifeless and mangled corpse; if now He intercede, and govern, and hold heaven in our name, and be unsatisfied till all His own are gathered around in the 'perfection of beauty' — is not the love that leads to this self-denial, labour, and sacrifice, boundless in its extent, as well as eternal in its origin?'

Nor can we fail to refer to the rich variety of blessings which are provided for us in the fulness of His love. Everything needed by us, and everything as we need it, is copiously supplied. His exhaustless attachment is not worn out by our perversity and unbelief. 'Behold, I stand at the door and knock: if any man hear my voice, and open the door, I will come in to him, and sup with him, and he with me.' Look on this picture. Look on Him, at the door, not upon the throne; at the door, not in the gorgeous livery of state, but as a guest expecting admission; not merely glancing at the door, as if its portals were to be thrown open in instinctive and loyal rapidity, but standing and waiting our time; standing, and not departing under the insult of refusal and procrastination; nay, so bent is He on admission, that He is knocking, as if craving a boon, when He might demand it as a right, and on being denied, might shatter to pieces the surly and ungrateful mansion. The very idea of His salvation springs from infinite love. He descended to earth, that we might rise to heaven. He became a servant, that we might be sons. He was made a curse for us, that we might experience blessing in Him. He wandered without a place to lay His head, that we might have a settled home in the skies. He hungered, that we might be filled. That we should be reckoned among the saints, 'he was numbered among transgressors.' 'He offered up supplication, with strong crying and tears,' in order that we might sing immortal melodies. He died, that we might live; and He lay in the grave, to secure for us a blessed resurrection. Ay, and how many have reaped the fruits of this love, and yet it is not spent—how many have been saved, and how many will yet be translated to heaven! The darkest and worst have been met by His love; and though they had 'lain among the pots,' yet in the reflection of His love they appear like 'doves whose wings are covered with silver, and their feathers with yellow gold.' O how it descends to the impure and wretched! Myriads of all ranks and classes, of all characters and occupations, shall be blessed by it, and shall bask in its unquenchable sunshine for ever and ever. Their happiness is of the purest and most exalted nature — they live in light, and they walk in love. They 'receive double' of the Lord their Saviour. 'They have no sorrow in their song' —they are comforted for all their past tribulations, the tears are wiped from off all faces, for death has died, and mortality has been swallowed up of life. Tell me, then, thou saved one, is not the Saviour's love beyond the reach of thy comprehension? It stretches away on every side as far as thou canst see. The more thou dost penetrate into its extent, it still shifts like the horizon before thee, still encircling thee, and still receding as thou wouldst attempt to near its limits, or define its circuit.

III. The love of the Father to the Son is an unchangeable love, and therefore so is the Son's love to His people. The immutability of God is derived from His necessary existence. He depends on no other will or power; there can, therefore, be no cause of change without Him. Nor within Himself can there be any source of mutation, for already being the best, He cannot change to the better, and any alteration to the worse would be an abdication of divinity. Our confidence is based on an unchanging God. The uniformity of the laws of physical nature declares Him to be 'of one mind,' and, at the same time, answers the question, 'Who can turn Him?' His proclamation to His universe is, 'I AM JEHOVAH: I CHANGE NOT.' The orbs in the sky rise and set, but He is the 'Father of lights: with whom is no variableness, neither shadow of turning.' Any suspicion of change on the part of God would throw an eclipse over all His works, and bring upon them a suspense—the very image and shadow of death. There may be a change of dispensation, but there can be none of character.

As the Father is thus immutable in His being, therefore is He immutable also in His affections and purposes. He loves His Son, and that love can admit neither of alteration nor diminution. He cannot love Him more, and He will not love Him less. And if there can be no change in Him who feels the love, neither can there be any in Him who is its divine recipient, for He is perfect as the Father. Of Him specially it is said, 'Thou, Lord, in the beginning has laid the foundation of the earth; and the heavens are the works of thine hands: they shall perish, but thou remainest; and they all shall wax old as doth a garment; and as a vesture shalt thou fold them up, and they shall be changed: but thou art the same, and thy years shall not fail.' Ere He came into the world He enjoyed an unvarying attachment, and 'the voice from the excellent glory' said of Him after He assumed humanity, 'This is my beloved Son, in whom I am well pleased.'

And thus as His Father's love to Him is changeless, so is His love to us. 'One day is with the Lord as a thousand years, and a thousand years as one day.' And He who loves us is 'the same yesterday, to-day, and for-ever.' The affections of men are apt to vary, and they do vary, for they are liable both to increase and diminution. A fault may be forgiven to-day, but if repeated to-morrow it may be visited with its appropriate penalty. One transgressor may be pardoned, but some other, guilty of the same offence, may be severely dealt with. One class of offences may be overlooked, and another species of crimes not worse, or more aggravated, may have meted out to it the whole rigour of law. Man is moody and capricious, and feels and acts from momentary impulse, sometimes from unaccountable whim. According to the frame of spirit in which you find him, or the peculiar associations which are passing through his mind, or have occupied his previous thoughts, are the anticipations you form of his kindness. But the love of Jesus, like the Father's love to Himself, has no caprices. It will not cool and it cannot rise higher, for it is infinite. Glowing with quenchless ardour, it needs no additional excitement. He 'endured the cross, despising the shame;' and if it carried its possessor through these agonies of Calvary, will it flag in His bosom now when every obstacle to its free egress has been so gloriously removed?

Could you suppose His love capable of change, how melancholy and dark would be your prospects!

There would be no certainty of your attaining life — nay, there would be a 'way to hell even from the gates of heaven.' Let a prince pick up a gipsy child as it wandered in despair and hunger; and let him clothe it, educate it, and refine it, till the style of its assumed station was felt to be essential to its happiness; and then let him, in a freak, dismiss the youth from his palace, and all its coveted and appreciated luxuries, and send him to the 'hedge and highways,' would not such a procedure be a refinement and excess of torture? And, oh, would it be different if Jesus were to love us for a season — throw his mantle over us — declare us to be his brethren — fill us with new desires and majestic hopes — and then suddenly, and in a dismal moment, frown upon us and exclude us from His heart! Would it not be exalting us to heaven, and then thrusting us down to hell; allowing us to taste the cup of life, and then, as we began to relish it, dashing it from our lips! The bare thought of it is enough to madden us; and we feel the supposition of it to be almost an impious reflection on the Son of God. Our hopes depend on the immutability of Thy love — Jesus, thou incarnation of love; for those Thou lovest Thou lovest unto the end — supporting their souls by Thy grace — supplying all their wants out of Thine own fulness — still deepening their faith, and lifting their spirits to Thyself — forgiving their waywardness — assimilating them to Thy image, and giving them indubitable proofs of Thy undeviating and endless attachment. Who can forget the fervent and lofty tone of the apostle's challenge: 'Who shall separate us from the love of Christ? shall tribulation, or distress, or persecution, or famine, or nakedness, or peril, or sword? Nay, in all these things we are more than conquerors, through him that loved us. For I am persuaded, that neither death, nor life, nor angels, nor principalities, nor powers, nor things present, nor things to come, nor height, nor depth, nor any other creature, shall be able to separate us from the love of God, which is in Christ Jesus our Lord.'

Beyond change, or possibility of change, is the love of Christ. When we look on the ancient ridges of the Alps or Andes, so firm on their base, and so huge in their aspect, which have so long reared their lofty summits to the sky, and borne upon them the snows of unnumbered winters, we naturally regard them in their sublimity and vastness, as types of stability. More glorious and secure is the divine love, for a sudden shock may upheave 'the everlasting mountains' and 'the perpetual hills may bow,' but Jehovah exclaims in blessed triumph, 'The mountains shall depart, and the hills be removed; but my kindness shall not depart from thee, neither shall the covenant of my peace be removed, saith the Lord that hath mercy on thee.' So that again and joyfully we revert to the conclusion, As the Father's love to the Son is immutable, so the Son's love to us partakes of a similar immutability. May not He, therefore say, 'As my Father hath loved me, so have I loved you?'

IV. But, fourthly and lastly, as the Father's love to the Son did not prevent Him from punishing sin in the person of that Son as our substitute, so the love of the Son to us will not keep Him from inflicting on His people any requisite chastisement. Though Jesus 'were a Son, yet learned he obedience by the things which he suffered.' The law is to be satisfied ere pardon be dispensed, but the Son of God became our surety. God's intense and unchanging hatred of sin must show itself in and by an atonement. Therefore, the incarnate Jesus died, became ' a curse,' ' suffered once for sins, the Just One in the room of unjust men.' 'He hath put him to grief.' 'He spared not his own Son.' Marvellous thought! did not spare Him, with every motive to do so, if we might employ the language of human analogy. Yes, it was upon His Son—inconceivably near to Him, inexpressibly dear to Him — the object of His eternal, infinite and unchanging complacency, that He laid ' the chastisement of our peace.' Had it been from some creature who stood in a distant relation to God that such exaction was made, the wonder might not have been so great; but our iniquity was laid, in its guilt and penalty, on the Son of His bosom, who had ever been with Him in mysterious and reciprocal attachment.

Nor did He cease to love Him, when 'he was wounded for our transgressions,' and when it 'pleased' Him, as Righteous Governor, 'to bruise him.' His affection abated not for an instant; for there was no vindictive enmity on His part, and the desertion upon the cross was judicial and not personal manifestation. Nay, we are told that God's love for His Son was one motive which urged Him to commit to Christ the salvation of men; and the Son's love to His Father was shown and glorified in His acceptance of the enterprise. 'The Father loveth the Son, and hath given all things into his hand.' 'But that the world may know that I love the Father; and as the Father gave me commandment, even so I do.' And if you could imagine any purer intensity of an infinite love, or any crisis when its thrill was deeper, might we not point to the scenes of the garden and of Golgotha; for then was displayed, in high and hallowed majesty, the love of that Son to His Father, when ' he bowed his head, and gave up the ghost;' then was reflected, in bright serenity, the purest virtue and the tenderest grace; then was developed, under suffering, what the man Jesus really was, how perfect and noble; and then was laid a foundation for 'glory to God in the highest,' and for 'peace on earth.' Therefore doth my father love me, because I lay down my life, that I might take it again.' The suffering laid upon Jesus by his Father was in no way inconsistent with His Father's perfect love, but rather showed its august and mysterious depth and power.

Now, in a similar way, Christ's love to His people is in complete harmony with His administration of discipline. Though they are brought within the bond of the covenant, they are liable to sin, and such liability exposes them to chastisement. But O do not imagine that His love changes. Parents on earth chastise 'after their pleasure; but he for your profit.' Afflicted brother, do not hang thy harp upon the willow; but tune it to a high melody: 'Though he slay me, yet will I trust in him.' He loves thee dearly, and never more dearly than when He chastises thee. His love at such a time has a special penetration—it searches thee and knows thee, finds a way to thy heart of hearts, and works out glory for thee. It is surely sinful and wayward on the part of Zion to moan and say, 'The Lord hath forsaken me, and my God hath forgotten me.' Let your afflictions be what they may, never doubt His love. It may be that these afflictions are complex, heavy, and prolonged, and that your sorrow is deeper than any to be seen around you — yet why should you despond; your agony is not penal evil, but benign castigation. There is some lesson which you must learn, and the fraternal preceptor is striving to impress it — something which is as yet but a mere element of theory, but which needs to be deepened into one of experience. He who knows your frame adopts this method of promoting a spiritual revolution within you. O, then, in the day of gloom, rejoice in the inspired soliloquy, 'Why art thou cast down, O my soul? and why art thou disquieted within me? Hope thou in God; for I shall yet praise him, who is the health of my countenance, and my God.' Christ's love is without bound and without end, and when it impels to your discipline, it 'worketh out the peaceable fruits of righteousness.'

Feel, then, that His love is quite compatible with your correction, nay, that it is love in its tenderest form, and under its most practical adaptation to your present and eternal welfare.

O, then, surely the statement we have been considering will deeply and permanently impress us. What ground have we not for confidence? Can any believer perish when such a love encircles him? What purity and fervour should characterise our love to Christ! How indelibly should the commands be engraven on our hearts, 'Continue ye in my love;' 'Keep yourselves in the love of God.' To forfeit such a love would be to forfeit all: 'If ye keep my commandments, ye shall abide in my love; even as I have kept my Father's commandments, and abide in his love.' 'Ye that love the Lord, hate evil: he preserveth the souls of his saints.'

Besides, Christ's love to us should picture out that kind of love which we ought to bear to the brethren. 'This is my commandment, that ye love one another, as I have loved you.' Our duty is to regard them with undeviating fondness, loving Christ in them, loving them without reserve and without interruption. Alas! how feeble is our imitation of Christ's love — as a drop in comparison with the ocean — as a cloud in front of the deep and impenetrable blue of the sky beyond it.

And, in fine, let the idea and consciousness of this love reign within you. Amidst all the sin and the discipline, the trials and crosses of life—even when conscience accuses, and deep confession of unworthiness is poured out before the throne, and prolonged and earnest prayer bursts from the heart surcharged with sorrow—let this be your consolation—your bow in the storm — that the Father's love to the Son is the model and measurement of the Son's love to His chosen ones. 'He that hath an ear, let him hear,' and lay up in his heart, the amazing declaration, 'As my Father hath loved me, so have I loved you.' Thus, by divine grace, shall be fulfilled in you the Lord's own prayer, 'I have declared unto them thy name, and will declare it, that the love wherewith thou hast loved me may be in them, and I in them.'

LECTURE VII.

THE LOVING-KINDNESS OF THE LORD, ON THE WILD, IN THE DUNGEON, IN THE SICK-ROOM, AND ON THE SEAS.

A MEDITATION.

Psalm CVII.

' *O give thanks unto the Lord, for he is good; for his mercy endureth for ever. Let the redeemed of the Lord say so, whom he hath redeemed from the hand of the enemy; and gathered them out of the lands, from the east, and from the west, from the north, and from the south. They wandered in the wilderness in a solitary way; they found no city to dwell in. Hungry and thirsty, their soul fainted in them. Then they cried unto the Lord in their trouble, and he delivered them out of their distress. And he led them forth by the right way, that they might go to a city of habitation. Oh that men would praise the Lord for his goodness, and for his wonderful works to the children of men! For he satisfieth the longing soul, and filleth the hungry soul with goodness. Such as sit in darkness, and in the shadow of death, being bound in affliction and iron; because they rebelled against the words of God, and contemned the counsel of the most High; therefore he brought down their heart with labour: they fell down and there was none to help. Then they cried unto the Lord in their trouble, and he saved them out of their distresses. He brought them out of darkness and the shadow of death, and brake their bands in sunder. Oh that men would praise the Lord for* his goodness, and for his wonderful works to the children of men! For he hath broken the gates of brass, and cut the bars of iron in sunder. Fools, because of their transgression, and because of their iniquities, are afflicted; their soul abhorreth all manner of meat; and they draw near unto the gates of death. Then they cry unto the Lord in their trouble, and he saveth them out of their distresses. He sent his word, and healed them, and delivered them from their destructions. Oh that men would praise the Lord for his goodness, and for his wonderful works to the children of men! And let them sacrifice the sacrifices of thanksgiving, and declare his works with rejoicing. They that go down to the sea in ships, that do business in great waters; these see the works of the Lord, and his wonders in the deep. For he commandeth, and raiseth the stormy wind, which lifteth up the waves thereof. They mount up to the heaven, they go down again to the depths; their soul is melted because of trouble. They reel to and fro, and stagger like a drunken man, and are at their wit's end. Then they cry unto the Lord in their trouble, and he bringeth them out of their distresses. He maketh the storm a calm, so that the waves thereof are still. Then are they glad because they be quiet; so he bringeth them unto their desired haven. Oh that men would praise the Lord for his goodness, and for his wonderful works to the children of men! . . . Whoso is wise, and will observe these things, even they shall understand the loving-kindness of the Lord.'

'WHOSO is wise, and will observe these things, even they shall understand the loving-kindness of the Lord.' May we be enabled to exercise the power of observation, may we be filled with the grace of understanding, and may we find the theme to be possessed of increasing attractions, so that 'gladness and joy shall be found therein, thanksgiving and the voice of melody.' The Psalmist selects some rich and remarkable instances of God's gracious interposition, bids his readers study them and form their own conclusions from them. If we wish to 'understand' the loving-kindness of the Lord, we need not speculate, we have only to 'observe;' and we have not anxiously to cast about for examples, as they are gathered and classified for us in the induction which distinguishes this inspired song. Let us then be 'wise' and 'observe' them — let us interrogate them, and find what they say, singly and collectively, of 'the loving-kindness of the Lord.' Besides the miscellaneous illustrations that occur towards the end of the Psalm, there are four special instances set before us: the wanderer in the desert; the prisoner reduced to slavery; the poor and helpless invalid; and the mariner overtaken by the storm; while the record of each instance ends with the hearty refrain—'Oh that men would praise the Lord for his goodness, and for his wonderful works to the children of men.' If, then, we 'will observe these things,' and if we analyze the form, the period, and the result of these divine manifestations, we shall, by the divine blessing, 'understand' something of the loving-kindness of the Lord. And,

I. If one 'is wise and will observe these things,' he 'shall understand the loving-kindness of the Lord' to be effectual loving-kindness. It gives complete relief. It is no mockery of favour, no semblance of love. It deals not in half measures, but secures complete deliverance. In order to prove this, let us obey the Psalmist and 'observe.'

The wanderer in the wilderness has lost his path, and knows not whither he is going; there are no marks to guide him, no footprints which he may select and follow; all about him is monotonous sameness, the sultry sky above him, and the dreary waste, as far as his eye can reach, on every side of him. And what is now done for him? The divine care does not pave a path for him through the quagmires, remove a few sand-hills, vail the heavens to cool him, open a spring for his thirst, or create an oasis on which he may refresh his weary limbs. No; it does a more thorough work for him, for it guides him out of the desert—keeps him in the 'right path,' and leaves him not till it brings him 'to a city of habitation.' It also effectually provides for him — gives him not a scanty repast, the tasting of which only whets his appetite for more, but 'He satisfieth the longing soul, and filleth the hungry soul with goodness.' The deliverance is complete, and safety is secured.

Again, the slave is shut up in the dungeon, into which 'the shadow of death' has collected itself, the 'iron' gnawing his limb, and 'affliction' preying upon his heart. Now the divine love does not simply lighten his chain, or abridge his hours of labour, procure him some compensation for his drudgery, or teach him a song to gladden his captivity. No; but the intervention is decisive, and the prisoner is fully and finally liberated. 'He hath broken the gates of brass, and cut the bars of iron in sunder.'

Father, in the case of the invalid, sick, restless, and to all appearance about to die, the sympathy of God does not merely grant him an hour of respite, or a slight amelioration, a calmer pulse, or a less feverish brow—prolonged life with broken health. No; but it restores him, and so restores him as to leave no lingering weakness, no remnant of his previous malady. 'He sent his word and healed them, and delivered them from their destructions.'

Lastly, there are the mariners, 'that go down to the sea in ships.' The hurricane sweeps over them, the winds rise in their anger, and the sea rolls in wild disturbance; so that 'they mount up to the heavens, they go again to the depths.' Now, the divine watchfulness does not content itself with abating the blast, lowering the crest of the billow, or effecting a lull in the tempest, leaving the 'shipmen' still at the mercy of the elements and far from the spot of their destination. No; but 'he maketh the storm a calm, so that the waves thereof are still.' Nay more, Himself pilots the vessel, and 'so He bringeth them unto their desired haven.' If thus we 'observe these things' as the Psalmist instructs us, we shall learn the lesson, that His kindness is effectual in every emergency. The same perfection of rescue is seen in our salvation. The sinner is not let alone at any point of his history, but is at length guided to glory. He gets, not an occasional, but a full forgiveness; and, on being pardoned, he is not then left to find the means of his sanctification, but he becomes, by divine grace, a new creature, undergoing, not a partial, but a total renovation. Nor is he sanctified, but left unprovided with sources of happiness, for he is taken up to complete and eternal enjoyment in heaven. Why should not we invoke His kindness, and trust in it; and why should not those who have felt it to be so effective themselves, or seen it to be so in the experience of others,—why should not they join in the chorus, 'Oh that men would praise the Lord for his goodness, and for his wonderful works to the children of men!'

II. If we obey the Psalmist, and 'observe these things,' we 'shall understand the loving-kindness of the Lord' to be seasonable loving-kindness. Let us again review the instances—

The wanderers could not find their way. It was a solitary path which they so feebly trod, and on which they so often stumbled. They were fast being bewildered. Their stores were exhausted, 'hungry and thirsty their soul fainted in them.' No wreath of smoke hanging in the air indicated a human habitation. They were about to lie down on the sand and die, when heaven descended to their aid, led them out of the danger, and brought them to those who had mourned them as lost, and who were filled with gladness on their return.

The bondmen could not achieve their emancipation, and the fetter only cut the deeper into their flesh with every effort to break it or wrest their limb out of it. They could not dispel the 'shadow' that lay upon them, nor win their way back to freedom.

'They fell down, and there was none to help.' Their heart sank under their suffering. They were preparing themselves for the prospect of a hopeless bondage, and looked for release only in that world 'where the wicked cease from troubling, and where the weary are at rest,' when the Divine Liberator came down and achieved their deliverance, said 'to the prisoners, go forth; and to them that sit in darkness, show yourselves.'

The sick and suffering patients had been using every remedy, yet were 'nothing bettered, but rather grew worse' — 'their soul abhorreth all manner of meat, and they draw near to the gates of death.' They are given over by their friends, and they make up their minds that they must soon die. But just as they turned their 'back to the wall, and wept sore' under this terrible sensation, the great Physician visits them, lays His hand on them, and bids them live. The malady is arrested at the moment when it seemed to triumph, and they are rescued from the grave as they were at the point of falling into it.

The sailors were on the tempestuous deep, and the gale still grew in wildness — 'the sea wrought, and was tempestuous.' The mast was strained, the cordage loosened, and the canvas torn to shivers. The ship had been 'lightened,' but was still 'covered with the waves.' No anchor could hold, the yawning seams could not be kept together by being 'undergirded;' all the resources of their nautical craft had failed, and their 'soul is melted because of trouble.' But when they could do no more, and 'were at their wit's end,' and the bark, struck by a few more seas, must have foundered, then,— He who 'gathers the winds in his fist,' and 'measures the waters in the hollow of his hand,' looked on them in pity, dispersed the storm-cloud, and took the vessel safely into the harbour.

Thus God interferes in the crisis, and waits till it come, ere He show His power and love. Man is allowed to feel his own weakness, and feel it so thoroughly as to be convinced, that if God do not save him he must perish. He is suffered to make an experiment upon human help, nay is allowed ample time to make a series of experiments upon it, so that he may himself come to the conclusion, that his only refuge is in God. And when this conclusion in the end is pressed upon him, then does God step in to his rescue. It is often at the moment of sharpest agony, that the peace of God enters the heart; it is at the point when sorrow comes to be past all endurance, that 'He healeth the broken in heart, and bindeth up their wounds.' The angel of the Lord did not retard Abraham's journey to Moriah, but he intercepted the patriarch's hand as it trembled in the act of descent with the fatal knife. Isaac lay bound on the altar, ere the rustling of the ram was heard in the thicket. Thus man learns to appreciate God's kindness, for it is so seasonable; and thus the interference of God is ever at the best time, for it is His time. And surely it becomes us to wait for it. If it be delayed, it may be to try our faith; or it may be that the moment of our preparation to receive it has not come round. Some lingering remnant of self-reliance about us may retard the arm of the Lord. 'It is good that a man should both hope and quietly wait for the salvation of the Lord.' The apparent delay is explained by His servant—' That he might humble thee, and that he might prove thee, to do thee good at thy latter end.' And if, when the hour of peril came, His loving-kindness has come too—if our extremity has always been His opportunity, then should we raise the anthem for ourselves—for all, 'Oh that men would praise the Lord for his goodness, and for his wonderful works to the children of men.'

III. If we will 'observe these things,' we 'shall understand the loving-kindness of the Lord' to be undeserved loving-kindness. For it is manifested to those who did not merit it—to those who had brought themselves, by their own temerity and sin, into danger and difficulty. Let us again, in evidence of this, follow the Psalmist's guidance, and 'observe,' so that we may 'understand.'

First, they who had lost their road in the desert should not have been-there at all. Why did they leave the common haunts of life and expose themselves to such jeopardy? Why should they prefer the 'solitary way' to the trodden and frequented one? Why did they leave the scenes of cultivation, or the green banks of the stream, and be found at length 'hungry and thirsty?' The motive was either restlessness and dissatisfaction, or a mere spirit of adventure, or the ambitious desire to explore new tracts, or farm a more fertile glebe, or found a new colony, and raise a new city. They do not seem to have been in the way of duty, when they ran the terrible risk. They might therefore have been suffered to faint and die; and their bones, bleached in the shower and breeze, would have been an ominous warning to future rovers and malcontents.

In the second instance which we are asked to 'observe'—the sin is expressly stated—those who 'were bound in affliction and iron,' had brought upon themselves such a penalty: 'Because they rebelled against the words of God, and contemned the counsel of the Most High, therefore he brought down their heart with sorrow.' They would not serve God, and therefore they are forced to serve man. They would not serve God willingly, and now they serve man by compulsion. They would not wear His 'yoke, which is easy,' and therefore they were shut up 'and sit in darkness and in the shadow of death.' And in God's righteous judgment they might have drooped in hopeless captivity, and have found no freedom but in death; and these 'gates of brass' might have opened only that their corpses might be carried to an ignoble sepulchre— the spot where 'the servant is free from his master.'

In the third case, those bowed down by disease are expressly called 'fools,' who, 'because of their transgressions, and because of their iniquities, are afflicted.' Their own folly chastises them, and they might, as they well deserved, have pined and died. They had no claim for health, and they might have been suffered to feel that 'the wages of sin is death.'

The mariners, however, are described as those 'that do business in great waters.' It was not sin that led them to follow out their useful and exciting profession. But perhaps their error is, that they forget their close dependence upon God. They tread with perfect security that thin and frail plank, which is the only partition between them and the devouring billow. They trust in the skill of their captain, and in the quick eye and steady hand of their helmsman, but omit to place a higher confidence in God. So often have they ploughed the deep—so often have they been placed with only sky above and sea around, that the sublime scene creates no impression, and his 'wonders in the deep,' seen so frequently, raise no feelings of amazement or devotion. They look on the glorious mirror, but they recognise not the Almighty's form glassing itself. In time past, when 'the Lord sent out a great wind, and there was a mighty tempest in the sea, so that the ship was like to be broken,' they had found that their pilot did weather the storm, and they looked not above to Him who sat 'king upon the flood;' who rode in the whirlwind, and so controlled the blast, that 'the sea ceased from her raging.' So often had they been preserved, so firm had been the 'tackling,' so accurate the 'soundings,' and so often in their distress had they 'discovered a creek into the which to thrust in the ship,' that, when again 'the sea arose by reason of a great wind that blew,' they still had reliance on themselves. And they are therefore punished for their temerity and self-confidence, and might have perished. 'When thou didst blow with thy wind,' they might have sunk 'as lead in the mighty waters,' and remained in the abyss till the time when 'the sea shall give up its dead.'

Thus, if we 'observe,' we shall find that the loving-kindness of the Lord is always undeserved. It is free and sovereign. We forget Him, but He does not forget us; and when our sins expose us to imminent peril—and that peril is a righteous and appropriate punishment, even then does He 'make no tarrying,' but He swiftly comes to save us. Thus, 'when we were without strength, Christ died for the ungodly.' Paul was racing on an errand of blood when the divine grace laid hold on him. If, then, we have no claim upon Him, and yet He so effectually and seasonably aids us, will we not respond, 'Oh that men would praise the Lord for his goodness, and for his wonderful works to the children of men!'

IV. If we are wise, and will 'observe these things,' we shall 'understand the loving-kindness of the Lord' to be habitual loving-kindness. The Psalmist does not mean that God has done those acts of beneficent intervention once, and only once; but

He means that God is in the habit of doing them. He has special pleasure in doing them. He often takes the wanderer by the hand and leads him, often brings liberty to the captive, often heals and raises up the sick, and often quiets the foaming surge. Had He shown this power and affection but once, had 'these things' been solitary operations, men would hesitate to place confidence in Him; might have supposed that His love had expired, or that His power was exhausted. Our question would have been, shall such loving-kindness be again exhibited, and to us? if we need it, shall we get it? But we learn that it is God's daily and customary work, and so each of us can say, 'My soul, wait thou only upon God; for my expectation is from him.' He has often vouchsafed relief to others, and will He not to thee: 'The Lord's hand is not shortened.' Similar is His loving-kindness in redemption; for He 'daily loadeth us with benefits.' He bestows not one pardon, but myriads of them; not a solitary spiritual impulse, but a long series of them; not a single deliverance, but a succession of them; not one answer to prayer without a second, but a host of them beyond memory or calculation: 'Many, O Lord my God, are thy wonderful works which thou hast done, and thy thoughts which are to us-ward; they cannot be reckoned up in order to thee; if I would declare and speak of them, they are more than can be numbered.' And thus, if the Divine Benefactor never wearies in blessing us; if we partake so often, and as often are warranted still to entertain the hope that we may and shall partake again, will we not express our own gratitude, and invoke humanity in all conditions and countries to enter into the same exercise—'Oh that men would praise the Lord for his goodness, and for his wonderful works to the children of men.'

V. If we take pains and still 'observe these things,' we shall find 'these things' all to be acts of simultaneous loving-kindness. God is not so occupied with one case of misery as to overlook the others. All these deeds of loving-kindness may happen, and very often do happen, at one and the same time. While He is engaged in the wilderness, He is not so wholly absorbed as to forget that He has work to do on the ocean. When He descends 'to hear the groaning of the prisoner,' He is not so wholly engrossed as to desert the bed of affliction. But when He is filling the hungry, at that very moment He is gladdening the heart of the sailor; when He is breaking the chain of the captive, He is at the same instant quickening and restoring the invalid. His loving-kindness does not travel in narrow tracks, but it is ever active and is universally diffused. It may be found on the steppes of Tartary at the same point of time as amidst the waves of the Atlantic— equally and at the one minute among the icebergs of the poles and the torrid plains of the equator. He is everywhere to bless and save. Never do His worshippers, like those of ancient Baal, need to cry to Him in frenzy, under the idea that 'He sleepeth, or is in a journey,' or is otherwise occupied. Others may be receiving assistance, but you may receive it too. Their getting does not prevent you from getting. The blessing does not pass you as it goes to them. When Sir Philip Sidney was about to moisten his fevered lips on the battle-field, and beheld a wounded soldier look up wistfully at the draught of water, he at once denied himself, and ordered the cup to be handed to his wounded comrade in arms. But no one of us needs so to deny himself, for his reception of the gift is no stealthy anticipation of others, nor does he snatch to himself what might be divided in common with them. There is ever 'enough and to spare.' Why, then, should there not be unbounded confidence in God, in whom each one of us, be he where he may or how he may, lives, moves, and has his being? O let us rejoice in such omnipresent goodness, and trust in it. Let us ever feel that God's kindness to others does not shade his benignity to us — for the desert far inland, and the sea in its remote latitudes, the dungeon and the couch of suffering may be all at the same moment the scene of seasonable and effective intervention. As we cannot exile ourselves from His presence, or pass beyond the pale of His energy, shall we not, as we survey His unbounded and sleepless munificence, cry out in the fulness of our joy, 'Oh that men would praise the Lord for his goodness, and for his wonderful works to the children of men!'

VI. If we 'observe these things,' yet further and finally, we 'shall understand' that the loving-kindness of the Lord is manifested in answer to prayer. When they who had lost their way in the sandy waste, 'wherein were fiery serpents, and scorpions, and drought, where there was no water,' found the vanity of every shift, and became conscious of their own utter helplessness, — 'then they cried unto the Lord in their trouble, and he delivered them out of their distresses.' They who had been loaded with fetters, and guarded by 'bars of iron,' were so convinced of their feebleness and of their desperate condition, that 'then they cried unto the Lord, and he saved them out of their distresses.' The sick and suffering, 'to whom wearisome days and nights were appointed,' as they lay and tossed on their couch, feel that He alone could befriend them, and then 'they cry unto the Lord in their trouble, and he saveth them out of their distresses.' And the mariners also, as the gloom of the hurricane closes on them, and they drift wildly before it, cast themselves on the divine pilotage, and 'cry' at length 'unto the Lord, and he bringeth them out of their distresses.' In all these instances of danger they cry, and that cry is heard. 'His ear is ever open to their cry.' The ear of man may be too distant to listen. The cry of the wanderer might be borne on the breeze, and its echo might startle the beast that roams in the desert, but it could bring no relief. The groan of the slave might sink to the earth where he lay and pined, but it penetrated not through doors and walls, and his tyrant heard it not. The moan of the sick man might fill his own chamber, and be too feeble to pass beyond it; and the shriek of the mariner might be lost in the howl of the storm — but each cry came up before God, and brought down instantaneous, appropriate, and effective succour.

'Is any among you afflicted? let him pray.' Such prayer, indeed all prayer, is the instinctive cry for help. It is not a daily penance, or a formal repetition, but the natural outburst of a spirit yearning for deliverance. And when it asks for Christ's sake, it is assuredly heard and answered: 'Out of the depths have I cried unto thee, O Lord. Lord, hear my voice.' The spirit, in the hour of its weakness, looks up to God, and He blesses and saves. O, then, ask and wait; wrestle and triumph. What has not God done in answer to prayer—' what terrible things in righteousness?' Human entreaty has shut up heaven, and has again opened it. At the voice of a man the sun stood still. Prayer has sweetened the bitter fountain, divided the sea, and stilled its waves. It has disbanded armies, and prevented conflict; it has shortened battle, and given victory to right. It has conferred temporal abundance, as in the case of Jabez; and given effect to medical appliances, as in the case of Hezekiah. It has quenched the mouth of lions, and opened the gates of the prison-house. As Jesus prayed by the river, the dove alighted on Him; and as He prayed on the hill, He was transfigured. The glory of God was manifested to Moses when he asked it, and the grace of Christ to Paul when he besought it. Not a moment elapsed between the petition of the crucified thief, and its glorious answer. Ere Daniel concluded his devotion, the celestial messenger stood at his side. The praying church brought down upon itself the Pentecostal effusion. Will we not be encouraged by such examples to 'look up;' and will not this be the experience of each of us: 'I sought the Lord, and he heard me, and delivered me from all my fears. This poor man cried, and the Lord heard him, and saved him out of all his troubles.' If we will not ask, how can we expect to enjoy? and if we do ask and get, then surely may we not sing, 'Oh that men would praise the Lord for his goodness, and for his wonderful works to the children of men!'

One word more: if we observe the miscellaneous 'things' which conclude the Psalm, we 'shall understand the loving-kindness of the Lord' to be often startling in its nature and results. The good it does is amazing, and the penalty it sends is confounding.

On the one hand 'He turneth the rivers into a wilderness, and water-springs into dry ground;' and, on the other hand, 'He turneth the wilderness into a standing water, and dry ground into water-springs.' At one time 'He turneth the fruitful land into barrenness, for the wickedness of them that dwell therein;' and at another time He converts the desert into a fertile landscape, 'and there He maketh the hungry to dwell, that they may prepare a city for habitation, and sow the fields, and plant vineyards which may yield fruits of increase.' At one epoch such colonists are loyal to Him, and 'He blesseth them also, so that they are multiplied greatly, and He suffereth their cattle to increase;' and at another epoch, 'again' when they forget Him, 'they are minished and brought low through oppression, affliction, and sorrow.' Sometimes He sends a terrible revolution which convulses society, and turns it upside down. Then, 'He poureth contempt upon princes, and causeth them to wander in the wilderness where there is no way;' and 'yet setteth he the poor on high from affliction, and maketh him families like a flock.' Such acts are of loving-kindness — not only those of prosperity, but also those of adversity. These sudden and terrible reverses are meant to teach and humble—for they show the justice of God, exhibit the evil of sin, and induce man to forsake it. Therefore adds the Psalmist, 'The righteous shall see it and rejoice, and all iniquity shall stop her mouth.' Such a history says, 'unto the fools, Deal not foolishly; and to the wicked, Lift not up the horn, lift not up your horn on high; speak not with a stiff neck. For promotion cometh neither from the east, nor from the west, nor from the south. But God is judge; he putteth down one, and setteth up another.'

In conclusion, 'Whoso is wise, and will observe these things, even they shall understand the loving-kindness of the Lord.' We have endeavoured to 'observe,' and we trust that now we 'understand the loving-kindness of the Lord' to be effectual, seasonable, undeserved, habitual, simultaneous, and exercised in answer to prayer. And as we see it so strikingly exemplified in the wanderer, the slave, the invalid, and the mariner, let us always adore it, and ask grace to enable us to 'walk as the children of so many mercies.'

LECTURE VIII.

THE SIN AND DOOM OF THE LOVELESS.

1 Cor. xvi. 22.

'If any man love not the Lord Jesus Christ, let him be Anathema Maran-atha.'

ONE that was not aware of the debasing and hardening nature of sin might think it very improbable that any man should not love the Lord Jesus Christ. Were the revelation made to a sinless world, that its Creator and Preserver was about to pay it a visit, would it not be so thrilled by the intelligence as to arouse itself and bestir its mightiest energies, and 'rejoice before the Lord; for he cometh; for he cometh?' Would it not be forward to exhibit its love to Him in prolonged and ardent outbursts of loyalty; and if its affection were susceptible of increase, would not His advent be the epoch and means of such revival? But what would His visit do to such a world compared with what His descent to our earth has secured for us? For surely if this world has sinned, and guilt lies upon it, and He in our nature has come, not to see it, but to save it; not to visit it, but to bear away its curse ; if He has walked in it and taught in it, wept for it and died for it, and if ascending to heaven He still pleads for it, governs it, and blesses it,— might it not be anticipated that men, privileged with such a manifestation of divine love, would be attracted at once to the Benefactor; willing to give their lives for Him who had given His for them, and loving him with a passion which, in its nobleness and ardour, should be the image and reflection of His own? God Himself is represented as under the influence of a similar expectation when He says, in resolving to send the Only-begotten, 'Surely they will reverence my son.' Ah! but the world has been indifferent to its Saviour-God—that world that bore His cross and contained His grave. Alas! how awfully sin has darkened the understanding and seared and perverted the heart. Fallen humanity is certainly beside itself; for passions, sordid and worldly, so fill it and so usurp the supremacy, that no room is left for love to Him who is 'altogether lovely.' What need, then, to repeat and enforce the startling declaration —' If any man love not the Lord Jesus Christ, let him be Anathema Maran-atha.'

In illustration of our awful theme, let us then ask —

I. Why the Lord Jesus Christ is to be loved? There is no doubt that love to Him characterises the church of the New Testament, and throws its fragrance over the pages of inspiration. It was the pervading emotion of early times. Every bosom felt it; every life was hallowed and moulded by it. The song of praise rose to a joyous melody under its influence, and its fervour quailed not at agony and martyrdom. The memory of the cross was young and fresh, and faith wrought by love. That love was a distinct and personal attachment. Christ was enshrined in the soul, and lighted it up with unquenchable ardour. He was indeed represented on earth by His people and by His cause; but especially to Himself did love surge upward in continuous and irrepressible tides.

And there is every reason that it should still be so. For this love is a rational affection. It is based on ample grounds. It is not an emotion which springs up, none can tell how or why. It is no mysterious instinct that acquires a sudden and wondrous predominance. Nor is it any caprice or feverish excitement. It rests on a sure foundation — on a 'tried corner-stone.' Such affection toward the Redeemer has been sometimes supposed to be a species of dreamy enthusiasm, and many have given countenance, by their language and actions, to the unjust supposition. Mystics have in their fond fanaticism applied freely to the Saviour such terms of endearment as would at once destroy all distance and reverential abasement, and impel the spirit into a presumptuous familiarity. But the temperament of this love will be always that of profound humility and awe. It must never forget, even in its highest ecstacies, what it was once, and what, by the grace of God, it has now become.

Our love to Jesus is the most rational of feelings, for it rests on a knowledge of His person and claims; of His character and enterprise. Is He not 'the chiefest among ten thousand?' As a man, and were He not more than man, you cannot but love Him. 'Thou art fairer than the sons of men. Grace has been poured into thy lips.' For Christ was truly perfect — the only perfect being that the world has seen. The sexes appear to divide between them the elements of perfection, and a perfect man or a perfect woman might not be a perfect human being. But all that is tender and graceful in woman, and all that is noble and robust in man, met together in Jesus. Nature is never prodigal of her gifts. Birds of gay plumage have no song; strength is denied to creatures endowed with swiftness. Thus it is often said, and with justice, that as one man is generally distinguished by the predominance of one virtue, or one class of virtues, and another man by the ascendency of a different kind of excellences, so the union of both might realise perfection. Had the peculiar gifts of John and Paul been blended, the result might have been a perfect apostle. Were the intrepidity of Luther, the tenderness of Melanchthon, and the calm intellect of Calvin combined in one person, you would have the model of a faultless reformer. Had Whitfield possessed Wesley's tact and power of management, or Wesley Whitfield's restless vigour and burning eloquence, would there not be the type of a complete evangelist? Out of the distinctive talents and acquirements of Coke, Bacon, and Hale, might be evolved the ideal of a finished judge. And would not he be a paragon of statesmanship who had the tongue of Chatham, the soul of Fox, and the shrewd and practical energy of Peel? But Jesus was distinguished by the rarest union of integrity and goodness. Every grace that adorns humanity was in Him, and in Him in fulness and symmetry. No virtue jostled another out of its place. None rose into extravagance — none pined in feeble restriction. There was room for love to a mother in a heart filled with love to the world. He felt that He was dying as a Son, while He was making atonement as a Saviour. His patriotism was not absorbed in the wide sweep of His philanthropy. What amiability in His character — what meekness and patience in the midst of unparalleled persecution! No frown was ever upon His face, and no scorn was ever upon His tongue; but His eye was often filled with tears, and His bosom overflowed with sympathy, and His lips with consolation. His one pursuit was the good of men. For that, by night He prayed, and by day He laboured. Opposition did not deter Him, and ingratitude did not sour Him. With what pains and patience He taught — with what dignity and heroism He suffered. To attain the noblest of ends, He died the most awful of deaths. He lived in the luxury of doing good, and expired in the triumph of a perfected enterprise. There was no step for self. No unworthy taint soiled His purity, or alloyed His merit. He realised the end of humanity — the glory and the enjoyment of God. The multitude hungered, and He fed them; they erred, and He rebuked them. The disciple trembled at the storm, He arose and rebuked it. He summoned out of his bier the young man of Nain, and when He might have claimed him as a follower and an apostle, He gave her only son back to his mother. Wine was exhausted at the marriage feast, and not to expose the poverty of the newly-wedded pair, He created a farther supply. He took the little children in His arms, and blessed them. He could not keep the weeping mourner in suspense, but said unto her — 'Mary.' The sisters of Lazarus sobbed in sorrow, and He raised their brother. Peter denied Him thrice, and thrice He comforted and commissioned the penitent. Judas saluted Him with a kiss, and in the blandness of His sorrow for the traitor He called him 'Friend.' So perfect in every relation of life — so wise in speech, and so pure in conduct — so large in compassion, and intense in beneficence — so replete with everything that charms into attachment and rapture, He was the incarnation of universal loveliness. We repeat it, were He but a man, who would not love Him, and caress His memory, as an honour to His species — a man standing out from all other men in spiritual fascination and beauty? 'As the apple tree among the trees of the wood, so is my beloved among the sons' — of deeper verdure than the greenest of them, and of richer and more fragrant blossom than any of its blooming companions.

But we must bear in mind that Christ's humanity was assumed into a personal union with a higher nature. It was neither by a fate which He could not control, nor a change which He could not explain, that the Son of God found Himself on our world. He voluntarily took to Himself humanity, and it was love that induced Him — love of unspeakable fervour. To take a nature so low, and come to a world so distant; to save a race so guilty and polluted, and by an agony so awful, was the effect of a love that could only originate and dwell in the bosom of Jehovah. The God-man did not surround Himself with majesty, or array Himself in the splendours of heaven. He veiled His Deity, but allowed it to be felt in its characteristic beneficence.

And O what a labour He accomplished! He secured for us the best of boons — salvation. He has delivered us from the worst of evils, and brought us into the possession of supreme and eternal good. No other gift would have sufficed, and He died to procure it. 'He loved us, and gave himself for us.' The whole enterprise was one of love to us. And surely if we apprehend its source and nature aright, and are by faith participators in its blessings, then, as we cherish its memories, and revel in its hopes, we must 'love Him, because He first loved us.' Gratitude will surely warm into love at the view of eternal blessing. If we feel what we were, and what He, at such expense, has made us, we will love

Him. Is there any enthusiasm in loving one so worthy of our affection? Has not our love to Jesus the mightiest of arguments to rest upon, and the noblest of reasons to 'render' for itself—what He is in Himself, and what He has done for us. Such love, resting upon the purest conviction, is totally different from that aesthetic rapture which the devotee may feel as he gazes upon a picture of the Virgin's Son, to which genius has given either a countenance of celestial grandeur and beauty, or one expressive of the deepest anguish and sorrow. The artist's work only excites the imagination, and ministers but to the taste, and its impressions, either of awe or delight, are traceable to the common associations and instinctive sensibilities of our nature, not to the attachments of a sanctified heart. The tear may start as one gazes on such a wondrous effort of the pencil as the 'Man of Sorrows wearing the crown of thorns,' and the spirit may thrill under the subduing music of the chaunt, 'Now there stood by the cross his mother;' and yet there may be absent all that reliance on the Saviour, and sincere appreciation of His claims, which lead men to love Him with soul and strength.

In a word, if you look to Him as your Instructor, He cannot but secure your attachment, and you will love Him for the truth He teaches, the amount of such truth He has taught, and the spirit in which He has communicated it. Can there be really any bosom so callous and insensate as not to be entranced with the vision of the bleeding Lamb? Nay, though

He has gone to the right hand of the Father, and is clothed in royal dignity, He is not merely to be revered — He is still to be loved. For He stands not in calm and stern majesty, so far from you and so far above you that you are chilled at the idea of His elevation and distance; but He is yet with you — identified with you, sympathising with you, keeping heaven for you, and preparing you for it. Can you then refuse to love Him? You have not, indeed, seen Him; you know not the colour of His complexion, the height of His stature, or the tones of His voice. But you need not such information — you have His portraiture drawn by an inspired pencil, and preserved in the gospels. It is a perfect likeness. And as you gaze upon it in its beauty and charms, and feel its inquiring eye to be upon you and to be following you, will you not look up to the living Jesus, and say in a burst of sincerity, 'Lord, thou knowest all things; thou knowest that I love thee!'

II. Let us now consider how Jesus is to be loved. If our creed be, there is none like Christ, then the language of our heart will be — None but Christ! Had He common claims, He might be worthy of common love. Had He any rival — were there any truth but His that could enlighten, or any blood but His that could sanctify, or any power but His that could vanquish sin and lift the sinner to glory, then affection toward Him might be either endangered or divided. But His claims are paramount, and therefore love to Him must not only be ardent, but supreme. It must correspond to His merits and character, rising to the occasion, and, like Aaron's rod, swallowing up every rival emotion.

Now, it is not of the absence of love in the church we complain so much as of its lukewarmness. It is feeble, cold, and lifeless—unworthy of Him who is the brightness of His Father's glory. That sentiment, so dull and intermittent, cannot be called love, which only warms towards Christ on the first day of the week, but falls into oblivion and slumber on the other six days. The plant could not maintain its life by the enjoyment of air, soil, and water once a-week, and the animal would drag out an enfeebled existence if it depended on a similar periodical nutrition. No; it is of the nature of love to give its object an immediate and permanent existence in the heart. It keeps it enshrined there. It gives it a continued presence. It so carries it about, and so delights in it, that it lives in the dream by night, and the reverie by day. It rises unawares to the lips, and 'out of the abundance of the heart, the mouth speaketh.' So that if Christ were loved, His image would ever dwell within us; and were He, as He ought to be, loved supremely, that image would gather in upon itself our deepest attachment, and exercise an undivided sway over thought, purpose, speech, and action. The ultimate object of every thought, the one centre of every emotion, and the distinct boundary of every enterprise would be Christ. There may be other emotions, but this will be the master-passion — ever watching itself, and trembling for itself with 'a godly jealousy.' There are many occasions on which this ardour may display itself, and there are many incentives to its increase. You live among men to whom the Saviour is as 'a root out of a dry ground,' having 'no form nor comeliness,' and no beauty why He should be desired. Will their callousness reduce the temperature of your love, or rather, will not the glow of your affection radiate into the chilliness around it, and light it up and warm it? While they are silent in His praise, will you too have 'a dumb devil;' or rather, will not your tongue be loosened, that you may openly and loudly glorify your Redeemer?

O for supremacy to this christian affection! How eagerly it ought to be coveted, and how earnestly it ought to be wrestled for. What a struggle should be made to 'see the King in his beauty,' and to be ravished with it. And then, if the heart were filled with this sanctified attachment, what competing emotion would find an entrance? We may be pardoned the truism if we add, that were we to love Him with every power, no faculty would be chained and paralysed by the world. Were we to love Him with every feeling, no emotion would be left to go out toward any unworthy rival. Were we to love Him at every moment, there would be no leisure for any ignoble and disgraceful desire. The supremacy of this love is the true safeguard against its being dissipated and frittered down. Let it roll through your bosom in genial current; and then, though the rock may impede it, its seeming stagnation will allow it only to gather its strength, when it shall overleap the obstacle, and in its impetuosity dash aside every barrier. 'He that loveth father or mother more than me, is not worthy of me; and he that loveth son or daughter more than me, is not worthy of me.' If such love prevailed — such love as Jesus is entitled to, and does possess among the glorified saints — what a scene not only of enjoyment but of hallowed activity the church of Christ should be: 'He that hath my commandments, and keepeth them, he it is that loveth me; and he that loveth me, shall be loved of my Father, and I will love him, and will manifest myself unto him.' Again, 'If a man love me, he will keep my words; and my Father will love him, and we will come unto him, and make our abode with him.'

> 'Do not I love Thee, O my Lord?
>   Behold my heart and see,
> And turn each cursed idol out
>   That dares to rival Thee.

> 'Thou know'st I love Thee, gracious Lord;
>   But O I long to soar
> Far from the sphere of mortal joys,
>   And learn to love Thee more.'

III. Let us now consider the sin and danger of not loving Christ. The duty being so imperative, its neglect is so much the more awful. And therefore a very solemn form of phraseology is employed — he shall be Anathema Maran-atha—accursed when our Lord cometh. There is sin of peculiar aggravation in not loving Christ.

1. It implies ignorance of his person, claims, and work. All who know Him cannot but love Him. Nay, the more they know Him, the more does their heart burn with this gracious and absorbing affection.

There may, indeed, be a distant recognition of Him as a historical personage without any attachment to Him. But the soul that so views Him is beyond the sphere of His enlivening influence. The rays of the Sun of Righteousness fall not with such obliquity as to warn a spirit in this low and shrouded position. Still, every one who knows, in his own experience, the glory and riches of Christ, and whose consciousness testifies that 'virtue' has come down from Him and healed his soul, is induced to love Him. He does not need to be argued into it. It is not under the pressure of logic that he is forced into it. It rises spontaneously within him, as the vital glow and accompaniment of his knowledge of Christ. To know Him is to love Him, for such knowledge and love co-exist by a secret and constitutional connexion, like the bloom and odour of the flower. Where, then, there is no love to Christ, there is no genuine knowledge of Him; and surely ignorance of Him must bring a merited anathema. For such ignorance is wholly inexcusable, with the Bible before it and the cross in its view. Not to love Him because the soul is so uninformed as not to know Him, is surely to pine away in self-gathered gloom — a gloom which, alas! is congenial with the darkness of that terrible region where morning never breaks.

2. Again, what unbelief is implied in a loveless heart. It is by faith in Him that salvation is enjoyed. Through this belief, and by the Spirit of God, the soul becomes one with Him. This precious and living unity manifests itself in love. Faith worketh by love.' To believe Him to be robed in loveliness of character, and distinguished above all for loveliness in action — to believe Him possessed of a love to you whose fervour shone brightest amidst the darkness of death—a love which still surrounds you with His favour, and lavishes upon you transcendent goodness; so to believe in Him must be to love Him. This love everywhere adorns 'the faith of God's elect,' and everywhere accompanies it, as verdure and freshness attend the course of a stream. But if absence of love imply absence of faith, what a curse must follow: 'He that believeth is saved, but he that believeth not is condemned already.' Severed from Christ, the soul is lost for ever. Like a lopt-off branch, it can have no circulation of life and sap from the root. If to be loveless is to be faithless, no wonder that the apostle solemnly predicts such an anathema as that of our text—Our Lord cometh. And the spirit devoid of love, because devoid of saving faith, is exiled to a world where it shall have faith, and where it must have faith—where faith, as an element of its punishment, shall possess it and fill it, and by no means leave it — not belief

that it may have deliverance, but belief that it might have had it, in the period of grace and privilege now past, and past for ever.

3. Besides, how unlike God is a soul that does not love Christ. Now, this unlikeness to God must be positive deformity and misery. Every unfallen creature bears the divine image as its highest style of beauty. That the Father loves the Son, the very terms of relationship do certainly imply. He has infinite complacency in Him: 'The Father loveth the Son, and giveth all things into his hands.' Nay, Jehovah exclaims, ' Behold my Servant whom I have chosen, mine elect in whom my soul delighteth.' As one so like Himself, the Father loves Him.* He, therefore, who does not love Christ, is as unlike God as he possibly can be. And, if, on a point so tender, he is so unlike God, will not God frown upon him and punish him? Can He have any emotion but that of resentment toward one who is not like-minded and like-hearted with Himself toward His Son? It is also doing Himself discredit, not to believe and feel what He has said concerning the Beloved. If there be such antipathy in a human soul, there needs no formal sentence of anathema to be pronounced upon it. There needs to be no inquisition, no summons, no trial, no reverberation of thunder from the throne. Let but the mind retain this special element of dissimilarity to God—let it persevere in this indifference to Jesus, and it of necessity gathers in upon itself the elements of

* See Discourse VI.

wretchedness, brings a withering gloom over all its susceptibilities of happiness, banishes all those emotions which elevate and dignify, is disappointed in the unworthy and unsatisfying objects of its attachment, loses the power of appreciating what is noble, or of being flushed and regaled by what is lovely; becomes, in short, shrivelled and dead, capable of no feeling but remorse, and of no excitement but that of despair. The anathema comes surely, and the loveless heart woes it and nurses it. It has vitiated all its spiritual tastes, and it punishes itself in its own depravity. It curses itself, and under the double woe it shall be, and must be, Anathema; our Lord cometh.

4. And the curse is sure, too, from the fact, that the soul which does not love the Lord Jesus Christ has no preparation for heaven. Heaven is a region where love to Jesus predominates — where it gladdens every bosom, and gives music to every anthem. The glorified saints are freed from all misconception and numbness, and they 'love out of a pure heart fervently.' The ashes have been removed, and the flame ascends with a steady brilliance. As they remember what they once were, so guilty and polluted, and by what a miracle of grace they have been recovered; as they think how Jesus assumed their nature, died for them, to secure that pardon in which they now rejoice, and pleaded for that perfection in which they now are clothed; and as they see Him arrayed in royal splendour, the object of vision and theme of song to enraptured myriads,

can they refrain from joining in the halleluiah? Their happy consciousness finds its appropriate utterance in these hymns — the spirit of which is love to the Redeemer — for such song is but the dialect of love. But the unloving mind is not allowed to join in these warblings, it could sing neither 'with the spirit nor with the understanding.' It has not caught the soul of the melody, for none but the new heart can sing the new song. It would find no inducement to gaze on Christ, and none to celebrate His majesty. Without love to Him, because unconscious of any salvation from Him, it would feel no reason to bless Him. These praises would ring in its ears as unmeaning and distasteful sounds — and it would remain silent, lonely, surprised, and sullen amid the hymning choirs. But, alas! there is no neutral world where it can subsist, and snatch the means of enjoyment; and the loveless spirit must therefore be doomed away to that bleak and cheerless prison, filled and torn with mutual hostilities—that hell of conflicting passions, where, amidst a thousand battling rancours, there reigns over all an intense antipathy to God and to His Son Jesus Christ.

5. And the curse is certain—OUR LORD COMETH. The church rejoices in that motto, but it is the terror of the wicked. The cloud that guided Israel consumed and terrified the amazed Egyptian. There may be no notice of this loveless state on earth, and the church may have no penalty for it. But 'the Lord comes,' and it cannot escape unpunished. As

under the third commandment, though profane swearing may meet neither mulct nor imprisonment, nor any form of civil repression, though man may be unable to try and punish it, yet 'the Lord will not hold him guiltless that taketh his name in vain.' The heart that loves not Christ, though it may pass unobserved in the world, and may even secrete itself in the church, is under an eye which never slumbers, and beneath a hand which never fails in its aim, or misses its stroke. Our Lord cometh.

And He comes for the very purpose of making inquisition—of ascertaining who have responded to His love, and confided in His atonement. Nor can He be deceived. No one can evade His glance, or pass undetected in the crowd. His eye, as it looks upon the mass, scans every individual composing it, and looks down into his heart. Nay, the heart without love will at once discover itself by its tremor. The presence of Jesus will throw it into such frenzy, as will at once signalise its doom. Nor can it escape. Subterfuge and evasion are alike impossible. 'Though they dig into hell, thence shall mine hand take them; though they climb up to heaven, thence will I bring them down; and though they hide themselves on the top of Carmel, I will search and take them out thence; and though they be hid from my sight in the bottom of the sea, thence will I command the serpent and he shall bite them.'

But not only does the awful formula certify the curse, it also embitters it—Our Lord cometh. O it is He whom men are bound to love as Saviour—

whose grace has captivated so many hearts — He whom the Father loves, and who is enthroned in the bosom of the unfallen and the redeemed creation—He who sought their affection and did everything to win it in His blood — it is He who pronounces the dread anathema. From other lips it would not be so awful; but surely such an anathema from the lips of Love must arm itself with a burning and unbearable terror. Such gleams of his inexpressible loveliness will fall upon the soul as He pronounces its fearful sentence—that it will bow in helpless agony to the justice of its doom, and will confess with a shriek of sudden horror at its obtuseness and insensibility, that not to love one so lovely deserves the full weight of the curse. THE LORD HAS COME.

May God, of his great mercy, deliver us all from so frightful a penalty! The Lord direct our hearts into the love of His Son, and so win us to this holy emotion, that we shall rejoice in His coming, and then this Maran-atha, which frightens others, shall be the pledge of our dearest hopes. Amen, and Amen.

LECTURE IX.

THE LOVE OF INVITATION AND REVIVAL.

AN EXPOSITION.

HOSEA xiv.

'O Israel, return unto the Lord thy God; for thou hast fallen by thine iniquity. Take with you words, and turn to the Lord; say unto him, Take away all iniquity, and receive us graciously; so will we render the calves of our lips. Asshur shall not save us: we will not ride upon horses; neither will we say any more to the work of our hands, Ye are our gods; for in thee the fatherless findeth mercy. I will heal their backsliding, I will love them freely; for mine anger is turned away from them. I will be as the dew unto Israel; he shall grow as the lily, and cast forth his roots as Lebanon. His branches shall spread, and his beauty shall be as the olive-tree, and his smell as Lebanon. They that dwell under his shadow shall return; they shall revive as the corn, and grow as the vine; the scent thereof shall be as the wine of Lebanon. Ephraim shall say, What have I to do any more with idols? I have heard him, and observed him; I am like a green fir-tree; from me is thy fruit found. Who is wise, and he shall understand these things? prudent, and he shall know them? for the ways of the Lord are right, and the just shall walk in them; but the transgressors shall fall therein.'

PART I.

THE INVITATION AND WELCOME.

ISRAEL or EPHRAIM, on behalf of which Hosea prophesied, was the national name of the ten tribes which revolted from the house of David on the accession of Rehoboam, and chose Jeroboam, the son of Nebat, to be their king. Afraid lest his subjects should be seduced from their new allegiance by frequent journeys to the capital in observance of the great festivals—'lest the heart of the people should turn again to its lord'—the crafty monarch set up two calves as objects of worship, 'made priests of the lowest of the people, which were not of the tribe of Levi,' and caricatured the sacred seasons of Jerusalem. To this source may be traced the rapid degeneracy of the people. The ties of law were relaxed, the claims of religion disregarded, and the express commands of Jehovah opposed and nullified by the idolatrous policy of him who has been branded with the indelible stigma of Jeroboam 'who did sin, and who made Israel to sin.' Peace and prosperity fled the land of revolt and schism— faction and conspiracy revelled in it—might and murder became the twin sentinels of the throne—a false religion begat ferocity and sensuality, and the frown of Heaven rested on the fated confederacy. Only one child of Jeroboam came to the grave, and he died in early youth—the rest were doomed to the dogs and birds. His successor, Nadab, was assassinated by Baasha, of the 'house of Issachar,' and Elah, the son of Baasha, fell by the hands of Zimri, who put to death all his 'kinsfolk and friends.' But the usurper was hated by the people, and after a brief reign of a few days, and to escape the vengeance of Omri, his rival, he 'burned the king's house over him with fire, and died.' Omri enjoyed no peaceful period, for half the people adhered to Tibni the son of Ginath; but having triumphed over his competitor, he 'did worse than all that were before him.' His son and successor, Ahab, outdid even his father in infamy, 'sold himself to work wickedness in the sight of the Lord,' and died, in his ignoble disguise, on the fatal field of Ramoth-gilead. The house of Ahab was extirpated by Jehu, who yet followed the nefarious policy of Jeroboam. Foreign nations at this time rose in opposition, and 'in those days the Lord began to cut Israel short.' Jehoahaz had a disgraceful reign; but Jehoash, his son, was more successful, and internal prosperity was restored for a short interval under the second Jeroboam. His son, Zachariah, was murdered by Shallum, and Shallum's usurpation of a month was ended in his blood. Menahem, his assassin, bribed the king of Assyria with the extorted wealth of the kingdom; and his son, Pekahiah, reigned but two years when he was killed by the conspirator, Pekah, who, in turn, died by the stroke of one who followed his own example — Hoshea son of Elah. He soon became the vassal, and ultimately the prisoner of Shalmaneser, by whom Israel was depopulated and laid waste. What a history of rapine, misery, and bloodshed — almost without a parallel among the nations!

It was in the reign of Jeroboam II., that Hosea exercised the prophetic function. He felt that the crisis was fast approaching. The seer already saw the terrible penalty — the cantons of his land ravaged, and its tribes murdered or enslaved. Already his prophetic ear caught the tramp of accoutred squadrons, and the piercing shriek of hopeless misery. No wonder that his soul is thrown into that turmoil of agony, which gives his oracles their abrupt and awful significance. There are few menaced judgments couched in so dreadful language as his, and few promised mercies offered in such subduing pathos. The tender and the terrible are shaded off into each other. The book begins with severe expostulations. The blood of Jezreel is to be avenged on the house of Jehu, and national calamities of no common bitterness are announced. But love intervenes, and blessings interrupt the progress of the curse, or become the happy sequel. The thunder cloud that lightened and muttered, is at length dissolved in a shower of sunny tears. The whole of this last chapter is a scene of love — love of invitation and consequent revival.

Verse 1. 'O Israel, return unto the Lord thy God.' The love which had borne so long with their provocations, bears with them still. It is unwilling to leave them; but takes a last, and yet a last and lingering look, ere they pass out of its view. It is so loath to say farewell, that it will yet argue and remonstrate, take them by the hand and look through their eyes into their hearts, ere it give them up as hopeless and irreclaimable. 'O Israel return.' Thou hast wandered far and long, spurned, in wanton pride, the voice that would have wooed thee, and the hand that would have led thee back, yet thou hast another offer — another still — but it may be a last. Forward, there is certain destruction if thou perseverest; the path is darker, downward — hellward: 'Thou hast fallen by thine iniquity.' Sin is both separation and declension — it carries the soul away from God, and the depth increases with the distance. But God stoops in love to the lowest aspect of it, and reaches in His mercy to the farthest point of it.

The whole design of the dispensation of grace is to invite sinners to return to God. This is its pressing offer, its central injunction. Were its doctrines and histories, its invitations and warnings combined, and were they required to utter in one short word their whole, their eternal import, that one word would be 'return.' Sinners are still invited to return — not to purify themselves that God may love them, or to present any merits that Christ may the more readily accept them. To seek and enjoy a Saviour, it is enough that they be sinners claiming the warrant of the divine promise. Man is not bidden rise to heaven, because with Him to hear is to will, and to will is to accomplish. For the offer of pardon pre-supposes guilt, and the promise of the Spirit implies inability. The poor and guilty wanderer is enjoined to come back — and the command contains the assurance that he will be welcomed.

He is asked to 'return' — the divine love is content with nothing less; and nothing less, and nothing else, will give him safety. There must not only be a cessation of the present journey, but a definite and conclusive retracement of the steps. What the prophet sighs for, and what His God so earnestly commands, is not the mere inactive terror of proceeding onwards when the fiery abyss stretches to the view, nor the attempt, while that terror lasts, to breathe a hasty vow or utter a disordered prayer. No; what the divine love insists on is a decided and complete retreat, such, as when the wanderer turns his back to the danger and his face toward God, with a radical change of thought, purpose, and pursuit; when, conscious of peril, and aware of only one Refuge, and that in God, he eagerly seeks Him with the whole heart. 'I will arise and go to my Father,' is his earnest and practical resolution.

And the injunction, moreover, is peremptory—an instant compliance is demanded, and an instant acceptance is pledged. The God of infinite love does not deliberate whether He will receive sinners or not. There is in Him nothing but goodwill toward men; and, in spite of all they have done, they will meet with no frown on His brow, with no taunt from His lips, if they will only return. Alas that men should trifle with the offers of reconciliation — that they should still persist in wandering, or 'halt between two opinions!' Even while the conviction is gathering upon them that return to God can alone make them happy, do they still preserve their distance from Him. A more convenient season is confidently expected, but it may never be enjoyed. There may be a sudden and swift departure. Let not youth claim a few more years of thoughtless gaiety—and then; let not mercantile pursuit ask a few more busy seasons and profitable sales — and then; let not science demand further leisure for its discoveries and its fame — and then it will pause, and give itself to God. Ah! hell is paved with good intentions. If man would but prosecute his immediate convictions, and at once act on them — if he would take the first step backward to God as soon as persuaded of its duty, he would keep himself from deep anxiety and peril. Did not the Psalmist say, 'I thought upon my ways, and turned my feet unto thy testimonies. I made haste and delayed not to keep thy commandments?' Our safety is in instant compliance, for the next step away from God may be over the precipice, followed by a plunge into the vortex, out of which there is no rescue.

But let no one say, how am I to return? The love that invites you has paved a path for you. You are not left to grope your way in uncertainty. It is indeed a dismal thing for a traveller to be overtaken with darkness. He casts about in eager anxiety, and knows not whither he is going in the painful obscurity. Occasionally he stumbles and falls, and, so far from making progress, he only treads round and round again the same melancholy circle. The storm begins to moan in the distant forest, and his blood curdles at the sudden roar and rustle of a beast of prey. The owl cleaves the air so close to his head, that the flap of its wing startles him. The

THE LOVE OF INVITATION. 207

surf of a hidden lake is heard beating upon its bank, and he trembles to take another step lest he fall into it. As he gazes on all sides a bright point suddenly looks up into his eye — it is the glare of a crouching tiger. But as he waits and quakes, the clouds begin to part above him, and a solitary star shines out. How his spirit rejoices as star after star comes into view, and the bright edge of the moon gradually shows itself out of the rack that has been drifted to the eastern horizon. Such has been man's spiritual history. Sin involved him in gloom, and the early promises at length twinkled on his path. The lunar effulgence of the Mosaic economy next broke feebly upon him; but it waned and faded as the Sun of Righteousness arose in his majesty. Now the way of return lies in day-light. The sinner is accepted of grace and for the merits of his Saviour: 'I am the way, the truth, and the life; no man cometh unto the Father but by me.'

It is surely needless to urge on sinners any preparatory exercises, ere they return to God. Jesus has removed every barrier in their path. They have but to return. It is vain for any one of them to say, I am not worthy, let me prepare, or give me a place for repentance, ere I draw nigh. Is not this the fallacy of attempting to cure, that you may safely send for the physician. Such a plausible reformation is a deceitful refuge, for it tempts its victim to stay in the outer court, and not to pass the vail and lie low in 'the holiest of all.' The injunction is, 'Believe in the Lord Jesus Christ,' and the promise is, 'thou shalt be saved;' and to enforce any other duty is just as foolish and preposterous as if Christ had commanded Lazarus to step forth from the tomb, ere himself had restored the principle of animation. What then should hinder thy return? Has not love removed every obstacle — assured thee of welcome — given its 'angels charge concerning thee' — sustained thee by its promises when thy soul was apt to faint because of the way — given thee 'the hidden manna'— opened for thee the 'strait gate,' and enabled thee to enter, and secured thee against the overflow of the waters when thou passest through them. Return, O return, then — 'The Spirit of the Bride says, Come.' Refuse not the love that invites thee, the Spirit that wrestles with thee, and the Leader who beckons thee onward to God and glory.

The invitation to Israel is, Return to the 'Lord thy God.' They were to forsake the Egyptian worship of the calves at Bethel and Dan, and resort to the adoration of the one living and true God. Jehovah was their God, and to Him in this character they were to return. And still the wanderer is asked back to his God — his God in covenant, his God in Christ. Jehovah in Himself is an appalling vision to the transgressor. The brightness of His glory dazzles and overpowers, and the guilty spirit trembles, shrinks away, and would hide itself. It feels that to approach would be death, and that to look is to court destruction. It flees from the intolerable vision. But to thee, O sinner, Jehovah assumes, in

THE LOVE OF INVITATION.

His earnestness, the aspect and character of 'thy God.' He robes Himself in love, and His royal seat is a throne of grace. As in the vision of Ezekiel, the glow of the sapphire is tempered by the green of the emerald. The wanderer is amazed at the softness of the voice which invites him. He beholds God loving him and sending His Son to die for him. He wonders at the fact, and seeing the majesty of God dissolving in a flood of tenderness for him, he is emboldened to approach, and as he breathes freely, he exclaims, 'My Lord, and my God.'

The prophet now enforces the injunction by the true and terrible rebuke, 'Thou hast fallen by thine iniquity.' Their experience echoed the appeal. As a portion of the Hebrew church, they had fallen. To them, along with the tribes from which they had separated, had been 'committed the oracles of God.' The law had been given from Sinai, they had been freed from captivity, and brought into the promised land of rest. The temple had been built, the hierarchy consecrated, and the altar smoked with the morning and evening sacrifice. But, alas! how soon 'the gold became dim, how soon the most fine gold was changed!' The ten tribes in particular sadly apostatised—'changed the truth of God into a lie,' and His glory into an 'image made like to four-footed beasts.' Baal also became the rival of Jehovah, and in the dark recesses of their groves were practised the impure and murderous rites of heathen divinities. As a State, too, they had fallen. They had in earlier times held a high rank among eastern kingdoms, and the victorious arms of David had reached 'from the sea to the river.' The land of milk and honey had been signalised by its tranquillity. The mountains brought peace, and the little hills by righteousness. 'One chased a thousand, and two put ten thousand to flight.' 'The barns were filled with plenty, and the presses burst with new wine.' The dew of Hermon fell in profusion, and the balm of Gilead ripened in luxuriance. Ammon and Moab bowed before them, Amalek and Philistia licked the dust. The skill of Tyre and the gold of Ophir built and adorned the sacred fane. Sheba and Seba presented gifts. But as if victory had always been awarded to their own prowess, as if civil prosperity had been the result of their diplomacy and economic skill, and as if their own bow and sword had gotten them the triumph, they forgot the Lord of Hosts, whose 'right hand' and 'holy arm' had achieved their successes. Proud, luxurious, and discontented, they became a prey to invasion and internal commotion, and were threatened with famine and pestilence. The divine complaint is, 'For she did not know that I gave her corn, and wine, and oil, and multiplied her silver and gold, which they prepared for Baal. Therefore will I return, and take away my corn in the time thereof, and my wine in the season thereof, and will recover my wool and my flax given to cover her nakedness.' So it was that nature was summoned to vengeance. The flock was cut off from the fold, and there was no herd in the stall. Lebanon poured down the ferocious inhabitants of its dens. Jordan withheld the wonted fertility of its stream. The heaven hung forth its drapery of woe, and the earth drooped beneath the ominous canopy. What grace more needed than penitence, for—

> ' Our woes
> Are like the moon reversed — the broad, bright disc
> Turned heavenwards, the dark side toward us ;
> Till God, in His great mercy, turn them round,
> And roll them, with a wise and gentle hand,
> Into the dim horizon of the past,
> To bless us with their smile of tearful lustre.'

And Israel was but in spirit a symbol of humanity. Truly man has fallen. And who shall gauge the depth of his descent, or compute the leagues of his moral distance from God? Measured in its effects, it exceeds comprehension. It had already changed angels into devils, and prepared for them a prison-house. It has subjected man, and the creation around him, to groaning and travail, doomed the former to death, and the latter to final conflagration. It has made a wreck of humanity, and filled it with the elements of damage and disorder. There is no perception and appreciation of spiritual truth, no confidence in God, and no preparation for futurity. We do not libel humanity — we say not that it does not possess and exemplify many virtues. There are many instances of integrity, kindness, heroism, and philanthropy — warm domestic ties and filial affections — sympathy with affliction, and liberality in relieving it. Nor are all equally sinful; there are fairer ruins in the universal fall. But even where these virtues exist apart from the indirect influence of Christianity, and where they are not the mere promptings of animal instinct, still their existence is no proof against the assertion that man has fallen. That fall consists not in severing man from his fellows, but in severing man from God. The virtues of one rebel towards his brethren in crime are no compensation for the want of fealty to their common Sovereign.

And our present is not our original state; it is the loss of primeval purity and communion. Mysterious hints are given us of the agency of superior beings in producing that spiritual revolt which did so debase our race, that while the first man was a rebel, the second man was a murderer. But we know not how these beings lost their purity, how they arrived at the knowledge of this new-peopled orb and discovered its locality, how long time intervened between their own lapse and their entrance into Eden, how they were employed in the interval, or why they were permitted to ply our first parents with their wiles. The mode of the fall is wrapt in mystery, but the fact of it is matter of sad and daily experience. Therefore the gospel comes to us as a system of remedy and restoration, professing to bring us back to the favour and image of God. It edges its offer with the appeal, 'Thou hast fallen.'

And its return is a spiritual ascent. For if man will listen to divine love, and lay hold of the remedy, not only will he be forgiven, but he will be elevated to a higher than his first position.

It would have been a work of great mercy to have brought us back to our first condition, to have given us the image, and introduced us to the abode of the first Adam. We bear 'the image of the earthy' in his second and fallen condition, and it would have been a restoration of unspeakable magnitude to have re-stamped us with his image in its first and perfect form. To have given us such a soul as Adam's when it loved and served its Master amid the bowers of Paradise; to have spread the bounties of Eden over the world, eradicated all traces of the curse, cleared the sky, calmed the waves, refurnished the globe, and made it all like the garden of the Lord — this would have been a restorative enterprise which God alone could execute, and must have called forth a song of happy and unending harmony. But the ideal of God and His plan is higher. The love that has opened up the path of return, and that repeats this invitation, has provided a most glorious destiny. Not only shall the returned penitent be as high as he was, but he shall be indescribably higher. Man was, at his best, but a fallible creature; now he is confirmed in holiness, and beyond the possibility of apostasy. The serpent found his way into the garden, but he shrinks from intruding into glory. Eden was on earth, our inheritance is in the skies. It had one river parting into four streams, but the river of life has ever a current of undiminished volume. Then man was expelled lest he should eat of the tree of life, but now he shall have free access to it, and to the shedding of its monthly fruits. It is not the image of the first Adam, but that of the second, to which the redeemed sinner is to be conformed. Is not this higher enjoyment than we lost, nobler honour than we forfeited? That love which restores the fallen is not stinted in its blessings, for it lifts earth to heaven. What eye that pictures out such a vision will ever withdraw its grateful gaze; what ear that listens to such an invitation will not vibrate with its melody! Is there a heart that will not respond in the words of the prophet, 'Behold we come unto thee, for thou art the Lord our God?'

Verse 2. 'Take with you words, and turn to the Lord: say unto him, Take away all iniquity, and receive us graciously: so will we render the calves of our lips.' As the returning penitent no sooner feels his guilt and danger than he craves the divine assistance, and as his lips, unaccustomed to prayer, might stammer in his first petition, the divine love condescends to teach him, and not only to furnish him with ideas, but to put words into his mouth. There is no excuse—the form of supplication is provided. And the prayer He teaches us, is surely one which He will readily answer. He knows what is best for you, and He tells you to ask it, and how to ask it, in order that He may honour Himself in conferring it.

THE LOVE OF INVITATION.

'Take with you words, and turn to the Lord.' Words—mere words are wingless, and will never rise to heaven and enter into the ear of God. But these 'words' are symbols of thought; and the fervid thought suddenly and instinctively throws itself off in earnest words. 'Take with you words, and turn to the Lord.' To pray and not to turn is hollow impiety; and to attempt to turn without prayer is gross presumption. He who feels his danger shrieks for help; so that the accents of prayer are the first symptoms of spiritual life—the first sounds that fall from the lips of him who is born again. To quench all doubts in the mind of Ananias of the reality of Saul's conversion, it was said, as an argument not to be resisted, 'Behold he prayeth.'

'Say unto him.' Yes, speak to Him in open-faced confidence. What a privilege! 'Say unto him.' Fill His ear and touch His heart with human language. The 'words' of faith are never rejected. The power of prayer lies not in fluent expression or rich language—in chaste tones or graceful demeanour; these are not the odours 'in the golden vial full of prayers of all saints.' 'As a man thinketh in his heart, so is he;' so that these words to be spoken are the expression of emotions already felt. Insincerity damages many a prayer—words from the lips are not words from the heart. The heart must be in an agony of earnestness, lifting an eager and outstretched hand to receive the blessing and to grasp it as it descends. Surely it is a grievous mockery to approach the divine throne and repeat the form of prayer from mere mechanical habit; to utter admiration of the divine character we have never experienced; to present confessions which we have never felt; to ask pardon for sins we have no desire to abandon; and to offer petitions for mercy while we are wilfully braving His wrath and scorning His indignation. Is not such profanity enough to provoke Jehovah to pour down His vengeance in fiery ruin on our heads, and mingle our blood with our sacrifice?

The prayer here taught us has four parts—the PETITION, the THANKSGIVING, the DISCLAIMER, and the ARGUMENT.

And the petition, 'Take away all iniquity,' proves itself to be divine in its origin. Brief and simple though it be, it manifests its source — that it 'also cometh forth from the Lord of Hosts.' Left to themselves, the returning suppliants might have presented a very different supplication. Would they not at once have prayed for the removal of judgment, and the revival of prosperity — that God of His great mercy would arrest impending calamity, divert the march of the invader, inspirit their troops in the day of battle, clothe their pastures with flocks, and cover their valleys with corn? But in the wise benignity of Him who dictates the prayer, they are directed to the cause of disaster, and to pray for its removal. 'Take away all iniquity;' for iniquity is the origin of all suffering. Too often do sinners, when overtaken by a pricked conscience, a shattered constitution, public odium or detection, or swift and sudden penalty—too often do they then pray God, in the bitterness of their spirit, to save them from ruin, and restore them to health, comfort, and safety. But it is the punishment they hate, and not the sin which leads to it. The murderer dreams of the gibbet, the halter, the executioner, and the gaping multitude, and wakes in a sweat of agony; but he does not lift his heart's desire from violence and blood. What transgressor is there who does not abjure the chains and darkness of hell, and would not shudder as he gazed upon that lake, each wave of which breaks upon a living shore? Let it be iniquity itself which you seek to remove; for, it being taken out of the way, all saving results will follow. The divine love, which has taught you this cry, has made ample provision for listening to it, and granting your request, for 'in Him we have redemption through his blood, the forgiveness of sins, according to the riches of his grace.'

Besides, the prayer, in another of its features, shows that it is not the spontaneous production of fallen humanity. Their own desires, if indeed they had referred to the removal of iniquity at all, would have pointed to sins which they might easily abandon, or those which certainly involved them in open and alarming ruin. But He who knew their frame instructs them to pray for the removal, not of this or that, but of 'all iniquity;' not of such sins as brand us in the world, or eject us from the church which fashion condemns or interest forbids; but of all sins — those, too, which no eye can detect, and no human statute can reach, which lurk in the recesses of the heart, and are gratified in secret security. Nay, secret sins are specially included — those which we are so apt to indulge — which grow with our growth, and strengthen with our strength — form temptations out of every occurrence, and gather hardihood from every indulgence. For if any sin claim and wield the mastery, if we pray for the removal of all but it, ay, and loathe and abandon all but it, still our relation of enmity to God remains unchanged. 'He that offendeth in one point is guilty of all,' inasmuch as the spirit of insubordination reigns within him, and needs but opportunity for committing grosser outrage. The man possessed by one foul spirit was as really the slave of Satan as he who named and numbered a legion. The pardon of Christ respects every transgression, and the operation of His Spirit extends to all impurity. O pray then, we entreat you, pray to God for the removal of all iniquity, without exception, and without reservation, for all is hateful to God, and equally hurtful to yourselves.

And Jehovah directs them to look to Himself, and ask Him to 'take away all iniquity.' He alone can do it, and He is willing to do it. He invites the desire, and He will fulfil it. In His love He tells you where to apply, and in what words to make the application. Will not you, so equipped by Himself, look up to Him with confidence and say unto Him, 'Take away all iniquity?' Do not try it yourselves, the attempt will only convince you of your folly and add to your agony. But, sensible that you cannot cleanse yourselves, that you have no sacrifice to present, and that no punishment which you can suffer will be an equivalent satisfaction, look up to God and cry to Him for help, and He will hear the request which His own Spirit has prompted, when presented in the language which His own love has furnished. Man must be led to renounce all self-reliance, either to obey the law he has violated, or merit the salvation he is in quest of, to avert the wrath he has incurred, or elevate himself to that dignity and felicity which he covets as the end and glory of his existence.

The second part of the prayer is, 'Receive us graciously;' or as in the margin, 'give good.' The order of the petitions is to be adverted to. Sin is pardoned, ere any spiritual good can be enjoyed. The 'good' prayed for as the result of the removal of iniquity is incalculable—the indwelling of God's Spirit, peace of soul, adoption into His family, assimilation to His image, and assurance of His love. But the sinner's relation to God must be changed ere his nature be renovated, and pardon and purification are inseparably connected. This good is highest good—spiritual in its essence, and permanent in its results, fitting in to our moral nature, creating present satisfaction and the hope of ampler possession. 'The Lord shall give that which is good.' Knowing what is good for us, He gives it as it seemeth good to Him; at His own time, which is the best time; and in His own way, which is the best way. The heart is ever to be aspiring to it, ever asking it and asking more of it, till, grace upon grace being lavished upon it, it reaches perfection. What was the 'chief good,' was a vexed question in the ancient schools of philosophy. Some placed it in one thing, and some in another; some in pleasure, and some in progress; some in contemplative leisure, and others in intellectual superiority. It was only one phase of good which they saw when they caught a momentary and sudden glimpse of it. They knew not the appetences of their own spiritual nature, nor could they rise to the height of their destiny. They neither understood nor relished this purest good—which is at once the beautiful and the true. As then we merit so much evil, and are so devoid of good; nay, as so much evil lodges in us, presses so heavily upon us, and reigns so malignantly around us, ought it not to be our eager and incessant cry, 'Give good.'

Nor must it be thought that this 'good' is given always in a form to be at once enjoyed. What is good for a saint God will send, but 'God is judge.' What the saint reckons good for himself may be ultimately destructive of his comfort. What is good for him may be affliction, and it is 'not joyous but grievous.' Or it may be a battle, and he does not relish it; a time of trial, and he does not like it. Yet he has really gotten what was good for him. Or he may ask a deeper penitence, but because he might be 'swallowed up of over much sorrow,' God may vouchsafe him a gracious sense of His presence. He may long and pray for a fuller assurance, but lest he should be betrayed into high-mindedness, he is thrown back into the billows, and must anew maintain the conflict. He may earnestly long for this good, and he may wonder why the gift is deferred. But 'the times and the seasons' are God's prerogative. And this postponement makes him pant more earnestly after the gift, and value it more highly when it does descend upon him.

After prayer comes praise — 'So will we render the calves of our lips;' or, as the apostle quotes, 'the fruit of our lips, giving thanks unto his name.' Is there any wonder? 'So will we render.' So; that is, our prayer being granted. And well might they. If they did not offer praise, they did not merit the blessings which they asked. The Divine Love shows them how God is pleased with praise, how welcome to Him is a grateful heart. It was a merited rebuke of our Lord in the case of the healed lepers, 'Were there not ten cleansed? but where are the nine? There are not found that returned to give glory to God, save this stranger.' And if this prayer, brief but comprehensive, has been heard — if its blessings, so rich and varied, have been conferred — if sin has been pardoned, and its power laid low — if good, in all its germs, has been given — if such a change has taken place as frees from condemnation, brings into acceptance, creates a glowing holiness, and guarantees final perfection — then indeed the spirit so richly laden cannot but express its gratitude, and give relief to its sensations in song. If it has been forgiven much, it will love much, and bless much. For praise as naturally follows the pardon of sin as prayer does the conviction of guilt. The soul melts with the thought of its deliverance, and naturally bursts into praise, and often into melody. Its very passion seems to mould its words into harmony, and lend a music to its song. 'Praise ye the Lord: for it is good to sing praises unto our God; for it is pleasant; and praise is comely.' None can so praise but those who have prayed. The empty heart can have no cause. ' So — we will render the calves of our lips.'

But the lips can produce no melody, if the heart does not beat in unison. It is neither the beauty, nor the rapidity, nor the grace, nor the solemnity of execution that gives praise its acceptance with God. Let there be a spirit of genuine humility and dependence, with a true knowledge of self and its relation to the God against whom it has sinned so grievously, and by whose love it has been saved so graciously; let there be a true recognition of its utter helplessness, and of the magnitude of its spiritual gifts — God the one giver, and His fervid and spontaneous love the one source — and it cannot but pour itself out in loud and joyous minstrelsy: lamenting, all the while, that its emotions are so languid, its words so dull, and its strains so tame and unproportioned to the mighty theme. 'Praise ye the Lord. Praise the Lord, O my soul. While I live will I praise the Lord; I will sing praises unto my God while I have any being.' Nay, in the midst of so much to humble us, there is sometimes a plaintive melody and the tune is set to a minor key. But how frequently the note changes from that of sorrow to gladness, as in the experience of the sweet singer of Israel, who seems often lifted out of the depth of his moanings, and carried on seraph's wings to the midst of the choirs before the throne. O why should not praise be on every lip which might have borne upon it the howl of despair?—why should not an anthem be on every tongue that might, but for the intervention of Divine love, have been craving a drop of water from a finger's tip to fall upon it? If we call our walls 'salvation,' we must name our gates 'praise.' 'Rejoice in the Lord, O ye righteous; for praise is comely for the upright. Praise the Lord with harp; sing unto him with the psaltery and an instrument of ten strings. Sing unto him a new song, play skilfully with a loud noise; for the word of the Lord is right; and all his works are done in truth.' And when all ill shall have been surmounted, and the bliss of final purity shall have been enjoyed—when good commensurate with our desires shall have been conferred, and iniquity shall be a theme of memory, and the chief mention of it in songs of deliverance from it—then, indeed, shall the family of the redeemed soar into its noblest raptures, and raise its psalm of victory—

> 'Louder than the thunder's roar,
> Or the fulness of the sea,
> When it breaks upon the shore.'

Verse 3. 'Asshur shall not save us; we will not ride upon horses; neither will we say any more to the work of our hands, Ye are our gods: for in thee the fatherless findeth mercy.' In turning the penitent sinner to itself, the Divine Love is anxious to show the grounds of contrition, and to teach what ought to be forsaken when God is prayed to. Conduct must be in unison with profession. And the disclaimer is in these words: 'Asshur shall not save us; we will not ride upon horses; neither will we say any more to the work of our hands, Ye are our gods.'

'Asshur shall not save us.' Alliance with Assyria is a vain thing: any attempt to bribe off its hostility but postpones for a brief season the period of national overthrow. 'We will not ride upon horses;' — we will not use cavalry as a means of national defence. The allusion is to Egypt, famous for its war-steeds. The king of the Hebrews was not to multiply cavalry, lest he should be obliged to go down to Egypt for horses. The prophet Isaiah says, in his sternest mood, 'Woe to them that go down to Egypt for help, and stay on horses, and trust in chariots, because they are many; and in horsemen, because they are very strong: but they look not unto the Holy One of Israel, neither seek the Lord.' And they might be the more inclined to go down to Egypt, as Jeroboam the first had found an asylum there, and brought back the worship of its 'foddered gods.' In times of panic, they promise no longer to resort to an arm of flesh. Their king, in a civil sense, was God, for their government was a Theocracy. So long as they were true to his charter, He would be true to His promise, and defend them. 'The shields of the earth belong unto God,' and no weapon formed against them should have prospered. Every confederacy would have been broken. But the heraldry of heaven was such that their dull eye could not detect it; their sovereign dwelt not in visible pomp, and they longed to have a human king to emulate the neighbouring nations. They abandoned confidence in Jehovah—the Lord of hosts, whose 'stars in their courses' had fought against Sisera. And still nations are apt to trust in fleets, and armies, and mighty alliances, and to forget 'the Lord strong and mighty, the Lord mighty in battle.' Such expectations are often dashed—for they look not to the Eternal Thunderer, who 'brake the arrows of the bow, the shield, and the sword and the battle; at whose rebuke the chariots and horses are cast into a deep sleep.' It is remarkable that those two nations, here cast off as allies, have a special and blessed prophecy attached to them by a contemporary prophet: 'In that day shall there be a highway out of Egypt to Assyria, and the Assyrian shall come into Egypt, and the Egyptian into Assyria; and the Egyptians shall serve with the Assyrians. In that day shall Israel be the third with Egypt and with Assyria, even a blessing in the midst of the land: whom the Lord of hosts shall bless, saying, Blessed be Egypt my people, and Assyria the work of my hands, and Israel mine inheritance.'

And they are also taught to forswear idolatry — 'Neither will we say any more to the work of our hands, Ye are our gods.' A strange and humiliating confession indeed! The enlightened mind can scarce believe that any rational being should call that a god which his own fingers have formed. How vile and blinded does a man appear when before God he pledges himself to renounce idolatry. To see a creature in such an attitude, and with such a resolution on his tongue, what a startling proof of the degradation of our race! And yet what so common as polytheism — myriads have fallen under the unhappy delusion. 'Gods many and lords many' have been all but universally adored — some in the likeness of humanity, and others in the guise of quadrupeds and reptiles. The gods which the tribes had worshipped were calves, imitated from the base and bestial superstitions of Egypt, the love of which had never wholly left them, and to these tendencies Jeroboam had wickedly pandered as a matter of statecraft. We cannot comprehend how man can descend so far, and so miserably besot himself. How terribly the Hebrew prophets satirise idolaters, and how justly. Their finest idols want the ordinary attributes of humanity. The eye is there, but still and dark; the ear is there, but no sound enters it. The lips are sealed and mute.

The deifying process is ignoble. The god was once a stick, but compasses and planes are applied to it, and after being blocked out with an axe, and plated and nailed together by a 'cunning workman,' it needs to be 'borne upon the shoulder,' 'set in his place,' and there he stands; 'from his place he cannot move,' unless, perchance, he tumble from his niche, like Dagon at the presence of the ark. When such a deity changes his scene, 'Bel boweth and Nebo stoopeth,' 'the carriages are heavy laden,' and the divinities are 'a burden to the weary beast.' The one end of the tree burns to cook provisions, and the other end of the same tree has incense burned before it. There could not be a sin of more heinous aggravation for Israel than to break the first commandment of the decalogue, to call the calf a god, to bow the knee before the cloven hoof, and to ascribe power and prerogative to the golden brute, that could not, like its living type, brush a fly from its mane, or toss its horn in defiance, or bellow over its grass. Alas for humanity! These returning penitents are to renounce this worship; and no love but God's, deep and tender, could ever welcome them, after such sin and profanity, and teach them to make this confession and disclaimer.

And so it is that man must still be divested of all self-dependence as a necessary step to his spiritual acceptance and restoration. The church cannot save him, nor can the water of baptism secure his salvation. Existence in a Christian land, or descent from pious parents, is not identical with the second birth. The Lord's Supper is not to every one the bread of life. A place in the roll of ecclesiastical membership is no infallible proof of inscription on the pages of the book of life. Protestantism is no pledge of deliverance from the universal apostasy. God's grace alone, Christ's work alone, and the Spirit's influence alone, are the one basis of hope, and the one means of deliverance. Nor are we wholly free from idolatry. You may not worship an uncouth fetish—a stock or staff; but how many bow to those absorbing passions which rule the world as a divinity — the birth which ennobles, the talent which elevates, the accomplishments which adorn, the treasure which enriches, ay, and the pleasures which debase and brutify. Who is there that consecrates his whole mind and heart to the God who has given to the one all its powers, and to the other all its susceptibilities, and who therefore has an indefeasible claim for undivided and hearty service? Who has not some idol in the hidden chambers of imagery within, to which matins and vespers are regularly chaunted? O to be able to acknowledge God alone, not in theory, but in practical reality, to 'cast the idols to the moles and to the bats,' and so to level the mountains and fill up the valleys, that Jehovah alone may be exalted! Thou art the one Benefactor, to Thee may we ever turn; the one Preserver, in Thee may we ever trust. Who is a God like unto Thee? Be this our conviction and this the rule of our faith and worship. Let us encircle the one throne, and prostrate ourselves before its one loving and majestic Occupant. Thou art God alone, and beside Thee there is none else.

Feeling how far they had wandered away, and how deeply they had provoked Him; how they had wantonly broken the covenant, and in insane superstition had offered sacrifice to the calves, they needed some mighty inducement to go back, and they encourage themselves as they return by the blessed reflection, 'In thee the fatherless findeth mercy.' The pathos of the argument is equal to its logic. The poor orphan has a ready paternity and refuge in God. The bereaved child that strays in poverty and filth, in ignorance and wretchedness, turns him to a lordly portal, but he meets with a curt and surly refusal. He looks with wistful gaze to a passer by, but his appearance creates disgust, and he is spurned away as a loathsome thing. Children of his own age stand aloof from him, and the dogs instinctively snarl at him. And yet he may be sinned against, the victim of mystery, the waif of a dark and disastrous providence. But in the crisis of his fate some good Samaritan may discover him, and see God's image through incrusted filth, and may tend him, wash him, feed him, clothe him, educate and provide for him; develope his spiritual nature, and open up for him a path of usefulness and honour. It may be so — it has often been so — but there are many melancholy exceptions.

Yet though such compassion is not found universally among men, it never fails in God. It is ever true of Him, 'In thee the fatherless findeth mercy.'

Whoever, prompted by the declaration, seeks to Him will find the statement verified. No one who has in this spirit claimed fatherhood in God was ever dismissed, no orphan who comes because of his faith in this report, was ever repulsed. And he is not put off with some civil but useless inquiries, nor served with a few cheap counsels, nor cheated out of his expectations with a miserable verbal condolence. The fatherless finds what he most wants, he finds 'mercy' in God, and that mercy secures to him every needed blessing. Bread is given him, his water is sure. The filthy garment is taken from him, and he is dressed with a change of raiment. His flesh comes to him as the flesh of a little child. He had long fed upon ashes, but he has now the chief place at the feast—his Father's bosom. His heritage was want and the prospect of it, now he is an heir of God and a joint heir with Christ. The storm had often beaten on his brow, but a 'fair mitre' is set upon it; the feet had often been bruised and bleeding, but shoes are now put upon them. Yes; 'In thee the fatherless findeth mercy'—at once and without hesitation, always and without change. It is prompt and overflowing. It is mercy leading to acceptance, mercy that knows what to give, and how and when to bestow it. For the crowning mercy is that the fatherless finds a father, ay, his own father, finds the love of the paternal heart unchanged, and is welcomed across the threshold with outstretched arms. That Father will not scorn the wanderer, or taunt him with his folly. He will not chide him and say, you have now come back because you could find no better place; but He says, though you have found no better place, but a worse, yet you are welcome home. Repose again on the bosom of mercy, let the paternal arm again encircle you and wander no more.

It is, therefore, a truth which forms the argument — a truth that has its birth in the unquenchable ardour of the Divine Love. It has been verified again and again, and it will remain a truth for the solace of the fatherless in all succeeding ages. Could we but fix this conviction in your minds, that you are by your apostasy fatherless wanderers — no parent to protect you, no domicile to receive you, and no social board to welcome you; then would it not follow, that you should earnestly desire restoration? Knowing that God has successfully solved his self-proposed problem, 'How shall I put thee among the children;' rejoicing that He has said to the outcast 'ye shall be my sons and daughters;' looking up to Him and repeating the argument, 'in thee the fatherless findeth mercy,' and we shall find it too, — will you not return to the Lord your God? O will not the whole company of the ransomed encourage one another as they go back, and 'fill their mouth' with the cheering inducement? When man had sinned at first, and was expelled from Paradise, the cherubim and fiery sword prevented his return, lest he should eat of the tree of life; but a 'new and living' path has been opened up, and the angels are the servants and guardians of such as walk upon the high-way paved for the redeemed.

O, then, let me ask you to take but the first step back, and your feeble endeavour will be blessed. They who have returned, bid you follow. The Father, whose tenderness has been so often tested and never found wanting; the Son who shed His blood to open up the pathway by which the orphan might find his home; and the Spirit who shows the apostate how dreary he is, till he wonder at himself, and long to go back,—the Triune Jehovah has His heart set on your return. 'Turn, turn ye; why will ye die.' 'Let the wicked forsake his way, and the unrighteous man his thoughts, and let him return to the Lord, and he will have mercy upon him, and to our God, for he will abundantly pardon.'

PART II.

REVIVAL.

And now, it is supposed that the wanderers, so kindly and earnestly spoken to, have listened to and been won by the Divine Love; that they have turned, taken with them 'words' and offered this brief and cordial prayer; that they have been welcomed and accepted, and that the first notes of the song of praise are now springing out of their incipient bliss. Then bursts forth the glorious promise of revival, which is 'like ointment poured forth,' and the remainder of the chapter is filled with the odour. 'He joys over them with singing;' and the song of Divine Love thus begins:—'I will heal their backsliding, I will love them freely: for mine anger is turned away from him.'

'I will heal their backsliding.' Their alienation was not only offensive to God, but also hurtful to themselves. It had brought spiritual malady upon them: 'The whole head was sick, and the whole heart was faint.' They had strayed into a climate where the dew never fell, and the sun never shone through its damp and sickly vapours. 'Woe is me,' might each of them have said, 'my leanness, my leanness!' Health had left them, and what had the semblance of it was a hectic deception. Nor did the region into which they had wandered supply any antidote—what seemed to be so, only yielded a momentary relief followed by a deeper depression. But Jehovah assumes the function of healer, and He effects what He promises. There is a balm in Gilead which never fails, and a physician there who was never baffled, who never tries an experiment—never seeks counsel with any co-ordinate wisdom, and always effects a permanent cure — redeeming our 'life from destruction.' The God whom they had offended does not suffer them to perish, nor spurn them away as loathsome; but He revives and quickens them. The gangrene disappears, and they return to soundness and health, with the assured prospect of coming at length to 'the fulness of the stature of perfect men.'

'I will love them freely.' For their wandering deserved punishment, but it is remitted. Continuance in sin, especially when provision is made for deliverance from it, justly deserves the anger of God. Still to wander, when He wooes you back; still to be ignorant, when a Bible has been inspired; still to be in poverty, when the fulness of His wealth is offered; still to be under the curse, when means of reconciliation have been secured; still to be unaccepted, when 'words' have been found for you, and a throne of grace has been erected for you; still to be an orphan, exposed and destitute, when a father's heart yearns over you, and a home is 'swept and garnished' to receive you; O such infatuation is no ordinary sin, and must bring upon itself no ordinary penalty! But when you comply, and come back, His anger turns away: 'Who is a God like unto thee, that pardoneth iniquity, and passeth by the transgression of the remnant of his heritage; he retaineth not his anger for ever, because he delighteth in mercy. He will turn again, he will have compassion upon us; he will subdue our iniquities: and thou wilt cast all their sins into the depths of the sea.' And O remember what is implied in His free love; what stores of spiritual blessings, and what generosity to confer them. How He will lavish His riches upon you 'exceeding abundantly above all you can ask or think.'

> 'Human loves soon part,
> Like broken clouds, or like the stream
> That, smiling, left the mountain brow,
>   As though its waters ne'er could sever,
> Yet, ere it reach the plains below,
>   Breaks into floods that part for ever.'

But the Divine love endures like His own being! Nothing can tear us from it. What a gush of emotion rushes upon the apostle's mind as this high thought passes through it: 'I am persuaded, that neither death, nor life, nor angels, nor principalities, nor powers, nor things present, nor things to come, nor height, nor depth, nor any other creature, shall be able to separate us from the love of God, which is in Christ Jesus our Lord.'

The divine beneficence is next portrayed — rich, varied, and satisfying in its nature: 'I will be as the dew unto Israel: he shall grow as the lily, and cast forth his roots as Lebanon. His branches shall spread, and his beauty shall be as the olive-tree, and his smell as Lebanon. They that dwell under his shadow shall return; they shall revive as the corn, and grow as the vine: the scent thereof shall be as the wine of Lebanon.'

'I will be as the dew unto Israel.' Blessing is promised, and its glorious results are portrayed. The dew was a favourite symbol of divine influence with the Hebrew bards. It fell in copious drops after the hot day had passed. Every blade of grass, and every leaf, bore a refreshing globule, which threw out its prismatic sparkle as the next sun rose upon it. The dew comes not like the hurricane with a sweep and a howl, nor does it beat lustily upon the earth like a tropical shower. Calmly and insensibly it steals downward to its destiny, beyond human recognition or control, 'waiting not for man, nor tarrying for the sons of men.' 'Hath the rain a father? or who hath begotten the drops of dew?'

The mode in which divine influence operates is usually beyond human analysis and detection. It comes when many perceive it not — it comes when many expect it not. It comes to its own appointed place, and to none other, as when the fleece of Gideon was wet, and all was dry beyond it. We are not to seek to solve the mystery, but our special desire should be to feel the blessing. How divine influence descends is not for us the question; but the question is, how shall we enjoy it? We may not know how its impulses harmonise with the functions of reason; but we know that reason is not compelled while it cheerfully yields. What forms of access the Divine Spirit may have to my spirit, to move it and guide it, is a species of 'knowledge too high for me.' Yet I may rest contented that He has modes of entrance, not the less numerous and not the less real, though I cannot trace them. I may not feel the falling of the dew, but I see the wetted ground. Let us not therefore perplex our minds as to how God may perform this promise, but let us rest assured that He in His love will be true to it.

What fulness and richness of blessing in such a promise! The dew moistens all about it with its copious influence. His reviving blessing will not be stinted in its nature. The divine love will not be niggardly in its gifts. It gives like itself, and the church will be filled 'with all spiritual blessings.' Such powerful impulses, such healthful impressions, such a tone of deep self-consecration, such an amount of spiritual mindedness — these are the blessings of revival. And when they are found everywhere, and everywhere in fulness, then may we say that the promise is realised.

And the dew descends silently, and in the calm of the evening. It comes not from the thundercloud. The church should prepare itself for the fulfilment of the promise, and banish everything which would repel the Spirit. All earthiness of temper and fierceness of passion — all disunion and schism — all indulgence in sins of which anger, scorn, and sensual lusts are the representatives; these repress divine influence, and forbid its descent. Let the church hush every evil burst by the strains of her hallowed minstrelsy, and calm her bosom in holy expectancy of the promised gift. And it will come, and what a glorious epoch will the coming of it be! A second Pentecost. In order to secure such a large blessing, the best way is to improve what you have got. Such is the method of His love. Praise for past favours is the best prayer for future gifts.

The imagery employed by the prophet to portray the results of this reviving influence is of exceeding beauty. And there is no wonder. The rich and tranquil landscape is only a faint type of spiritual revival and abundance. 'He shall grow as the lily, and cast forth his roots like Lebanon. His branches shall spread, and his beauty shall be as the olive-tree, and his smell as Lebanon. They that dwell under his shadow shall return; they shall revive as the corn, and grow as the vine: the scent thereof shall be as the wine of Lebanon.'

The imagery is tenderly grouped. The lily sends up from the green bosom of the plain its tall and graceful stalk, surmounted with its brilliant cup. The cedars of Lebanon strike their roots deep into the earth, and shake their boughs in luxuriant wantonness. The brow of Hermon is crowned with their glory, and the storm that rocks them only so loosens the soil that their fibres creep outward and downward with rapidity and firmness. The olive rejoices in its fatness and fragrance, for its foliage never fails, and it still shows its silvery hue as it is ruffled by the breeze. The scent of Lebanon, borne upon the winds, is refreshing with its coolness and odours. Under the shadow of that mighty range, the fields and orchards are protected from the northern blast. The crops shoot up in healthful verdure. The soft tendrils of the vine burst and blossom on the slopes, and its laden boughs droop at length with the swelling cluster. The landscape is perfect, and as the eye gazes around it, it sees at one sweep hill and orchard, vineyard and field, each enriched with its appropriate blessing, and all rejoicing in the beneficence of God.

It is a picture of the church enjoying a revival. What will not the blessing of heaven effect? Had no dew fallen, bare cliffs and drooping cedars might have met the eye — the lily pale and withered, the fields parched and sickly, and the vine shorn of its pregnant loveliness. Were no divine influence to descend upon us, what spiritual sterility should characterise us! If the heaven be iron, the earth will be brass. But if the Spirit be poured out from on high, 'the wilderness will be counted for a fruitful field.' If, then, you see a Christian society growing in grace and abounding in love, its consecration to its divine Lord becoming fuller and more tender, striving with one heart for mutual edification, continuing 'steadfast in the apostles' doctrine and fellowship,' exhibiting a constant vigilance, self-denial, and energy that others may be brought in and blessed, are you not induced, on beholding such a delightful spectacle, thus to salute it — 'Hail, highly-favoured of the Lord, blessed art thou' among churches! Such a community, whatever its numbers or wealth, is enjoying a revival — has experience of the divine love. Which was the more blessed — the crowd of Jews bowing their turbaned heads in the courts of the temple as the smoke of the sacrifice ascended, or the hundred and twenty met with one accord in the upper room? Which was the more blessed — the Romish hierarchy in its pomp and magnificence, its cathedrals and palaces, its princes in scarlet, and its secular dominions; or the poor Waldenses gathered in some lonely glen, or escaping to the mountains for their life, bleeding among the snows, and wrapt at length in nature's purest winding-sheet? Barnabas, when he saw the grace of God, was glad; let us share in his joy.

We have before us also a picture of healthfulness. The cedars might have been scant in foliage, the 'goodly fruit' of the olive might have been deficient, the corn in ear might scarcely have covered the clod, and the clusters of the vine might have been light and few. But all here wears an aspect of exceeding health and promise. There may be real religion, but it may be in a sickly state. It needs to be nursed. Faith may want vigour and compass — love may be cold and languid. 'The things that remain' may be 'ready to die.' There may be too great conformity to the world, too great formality in all religious service. The people may still come before God as His people, but too much from habit, and too little from eagerness to see His power and glory, as they have seen Him in the sanctuary. That predominant motive has lost its freshness and predominance—'we would see Jesus.' In prayer, while blessings are sought, it may be without due appreciation of them, or earnest faith in Him by whose blood they have been provided. The word of God may be still read, but the mind may have lost its early docility and its first felt need of divine enlightenment. The thoughts may wander when they ought to be concentrated, and the pulsations of life may be slow and feeble. Too much and too often is this the case; and the churches ought ever to be on their guard lest they fall into this 'lukewarm' state. But if this promise be fulfilled, if the dew descend in its divine copiousness, health returns, and the 'well watered' church revives. The young will be filled with ardour, and the old enriched with a happy experience. The men of secular activity, while they are 'diligent in business,' will be at the same time 'fervent in spirit.' Mothers will nurse their babes for Christ, and fathers train their children not only for worldly advancement, but especially 'in the nurture and admonition of the Lord.' Every house will be a Bethel, and every heart a sanctuary. The rich will be 'poor in spirit,' and the poor 'rich in faith.' The flush of a holy enthusiasm will be spread over all. Would to God that we witnessed such scenes, and that there were no rarity among us! Then the churches would be 'edified'—'walking in the fear of the Lord, and in the comfort of the Holy Ghost.'

The picture presented to us is, at the same time, one of beauty. The landscape smiles upon us in its variety and richness, and its 'scent is as the wine of Lebanon.' What object can be so attractive as revived religion—every grace in lively exercise,—Christ loved with ardour, and the Spirit's influence earnestly cherished—prayer arising as incense—praise felt to be 'comely,' and therefore habitual—every believer as happy as he is useful, reflecting the divine image, and breathing the atmosphere of heaven. Men may scoff at such a scene, and wonder, and, it may be, caricature it, calling it fanatical excitement; but the church luxuriates in it, and is filled with grateful amazement at the divine goodness. Nay, such a scene would soon tell on the world, and compel it to admiration. When it saw such purity and happiness, such elevation and dignity, such an assemblage of all the virtues which adorn humanity—piety combined with patriotism—devotion nourishing philanthropy—science, art, and business hallowed and ennobled by the spirit in which they are pursued—earth enjoyed while heaven is looked for—time improved while eternity is prepared for—would not the world be moved by the spectacle, and brought to confess that religion has a power and a glory which proclaim its superhuman birth? A revived church would certainly be a mighty and successful agent in the conversion of the nations. The world would not then ask in taunt, 'What do ye more than others,' or how are ye better than others? but it would see and acknowledge an arm divine.

Again, the scene is one of great fertility. There is not only fragrance of blossom, but also exuberance of fruit — the fields growing 'white unto harvest,' and the ruddy clusters foretelling an early and ample vintage. There is not merely the show of fruit, but the reality. Under the outpoured influence of the Spirit, there are seen the fruits of deep practical piety. There is not only enjoyment, but activity: fruitfulness 'in every good work,' as there is added 'to faith, virtue; and to virtue, knowledge; and to knowledge, temperance; and to temperance, patience; and to patience, godliness; and to godliness, brotherly-kindness; and to brotherly-kindness, charity.' Whatever good needs to be done, the earnest church does it. Whatever be the form of activity, physical or spiritual, it meets with a ready response. Neither wealth nor labour is grudged; neither patience nor travail is spared. Whatever interests humanity, interests the church; whatever gives man social elevation or civil freedom — whatever removes any disturbing element on his health or industry — whatever, in short, has a tendency to 'roll the stone from the well's mouth,' comes home to the bosom and sympathies of the church of Christ. He cleansed the leper, as well as proclaimed the kingdom — supplied wine to a feast, as well as preached the gospel—fed the multitudes, as well as expelled the demon. Especially will the spiritual interests of the world engage the efforts of the church. Revived piety is recruited strength for the task. The gospel is not merely enshrined in the heart, but borne upon the lips, carried in the hand, and commended by the life. Divine fruit!— and the end is 'glory to God in the highest.'

What an unbroken harmony pervades the prophetic landscape! There is no conflicting prominence in any part of the imagery. The cedar is not proudly overshadowing the lily—the olive is not struggling to dwarf the vine; and there is no thicket to choke the reviving corn. A spirit of unity reigns throughout. The church enjoying the divine blessing, is one—each part rejoicing in every other; for asperities are smothered, and past bitternesses are mellowed. The pre-eminent does not boast itself over the retiring—the wealth that gains itself a noble name, does not arrogate any superiority over the sympathy that washes a beggar's feet. Divested of prejudices, men 'see eye to eye,' and wonder why they came aforetime to so different conclusions. Controversy lays aside its mail, and difference of position does not create sectarian rivalry. The believer, whoever he be, is hailed as a brother; for your arm may embrace him whom Christ's arm has encircled and blessed. The 'one mind' receives the one truth; the 'one heart' is filled with the one love; and there is the 'one mouth' to glorify God. So near Christ, all the members of His church are near one another. The realisation of their union to Christ, leads them to feel their brotherhood in Him. The whole church will breathe that 'charity which is the bond of perfectness,' loving and loved, by an indissoluble tie. When shall such love be exhibited in this distracted world, and amidst its feuds and factions? What prayer for the Spirit must precede it — prayer that He may reign until the 'one Lord' is confessed, and the 'one baptism' has been enjoyed. The foul flap of the raven's wing has too often darkened the scene. O for the brooding of the gentle dove! Nations covet the eagle of quick eye, strong pinion, and bloody talon as their humble symbol; but the church has for her's the dove — the Spirit that alighted on her Master, and 'abode upon Him.'

There is also, and in fine, the prospect of increase. It is no evanescent scene. 'He shall cast forth his roots as Lebanon.' What is now seen is only as the first-fruits of a richer verdure and plenty. And to the enjoyment of this spiritual plenty, the prayers and energies of the church be directed. Amidst all exercises and functions, this one end should ever be in view. When an emigrant goes to a new country, he may engage in many kinds of rural labour; but his heart is borne up by the prospect of a crop. Whether he fells timber and clears the soil, or drains it or ploughs it — the one motive is to see his fields laden with promise. Now, to enjoy such spiritual plenty, from the descent of the promised dew, should animate the church to exertion and prayer. O did we feel our need of the Spirit, with our own insignificance and feebleness — did we feel how dry and parched is the land where there is no water, then should we eagerly long for and pray for the fulfilment of the promise. And in answer to such prayer, the atmosphere, surcharged with blessing, will moisten the earth, and the 'fruits of righteousness' will gladden the heart of the Divine Husbandman; — the gleanings of Abiezer shall be better than the vintage of Ephraim,' and the handful of corn on the top of the mountains shall shake with fruit like Lebanon. It will come. God speed the time! O that it would come, and that soon — be this our fervent and repeated prayer. Till then, we believe, and wait, and hope.

Verse 8. 'Ephraim shall say, What have I to do any more with idols? I have heard him, and observed him: I am like a green fir-tree: from me is thy fruit found.'

And what is the immediate effect of such blessings on his people? 'Ephraim shall say, What have I to do any more with idols?'

> 'Gods they had tried of every shape and size
> That godsmiths could produce, or priests devise.'

But now Ephraim wonders why he ever should have had to do with them, and he is heartily ashamed of them. None of them could do for him what God has done; none of the 'vanities of the Gentiles' could either promise or send the dew. So thoroughly convinced is he now of God's unity and supremacy, that he is effectually cured of all propensity to idolatry. There is no word so ominous to him as idol — no practice so revolting as that of idolatry. That sin now stands out to him as 'exceeding sinful.' His penitence is sincere, and it is accepted. When Ephraim says, in this contrite spirit, 'What have I to do any more with idols?' Jehovah responds, 'I have heard him and observed him.' His actions declare his intentions to be honest — his practice justifies his declared resolution. God had observed him. The eye of heaven was upon him, but it had not detected any lurking inclination to bow in secret, or to make any compromise with the calves. His confession and vow are therefore accepted and registered.

The humbled Ephraim hears the glorious promise; but as he gazes on the imagery taken from hill, field, and orchard, he feels as if none of it was realised in him. 'I am,' he sobs, 'like a green fir-tree.' That tree is fruitless, only a piece of timber. Ephraim, in his humility, can see in himself neither the vine, nor the olive, nor the field of cereal crop. He feels as if reviving influence was only partially enjoyed by him as yet; for he is but 'a green *fir-tree.*' But Jehovah responds at once to his moaning, and says, 'From Me is thy fruit found.' Ephraim shall have fruit, and it will be from God. Let not despair seize thee: the power to bear fruit is fast descending upon thee, and it comes from Me. If men complain of spiritual sterility, and if their complaint be genuine, the Hearer of Prayer will not disregard it, but will graciously impart His fructifying influences; so that 'they shall bring forth fruit in old age, they shall be fat and flourishing.' Such is the last and blessed tenderness of the Divine love.

And now this change or revival is so peculiar as not to be understood by ordinary intellect. Verse 9, 'Who is wise, and he shall understand these things? prudent, and he shall know them? for the ways of the Lord are right, and the just shall walk in them: but the transgressors shall fall therein.'

'Who is wise, and he shall understand these things? prudent, and he shall know them?' It needs wisdom and prudence not our own to learn the blessedness and reality of a revival. The sphere of spiritual influence is beyond the cognizance of our senses. While many scoff and toss their heads in credulity, let us experience it — then shall we really know it. Let us not be content with admiring it; let us seek, aye seek above all things, to share in it. 'For the ways of the Lord are right, and the just shall walk in them.' God's procedure is always just, and His people at all times acknowledge its equity: 'But the transgressors shall fall therein;' they cannot comprehend it. It offends them by its seeming mystery and inequality, and they stumble and fall — declaring it to be a hard and uneven path, and exclaiming in bitterness that 'the ways of the Lord are not equal.'

But surely you will rejoice in the magnificent manifestation of Divine Love which this chapter has brought before us. What can be more refreshing? — its language is so full of pathos; its imagery reposes in tranquil brightness; and its spirit is that of deepest solicitation and most gorgeous promise. O that the period were come, and that all our churches felt it! Never let us regard it as a romantic impossibility. It has been partially witnessed, and it will be more fully experienced. Christ's church has not been forgotten by Him. No: as his bride sighs for Him, will He not respond? And as He advances, will not she recognise Him in the distance, and joyfully exclaim, 'The voice of my Beloved: behold He cometh leaping upon the mountains, skipping upon the hills!' Let the spirit of prayerful and confident anticipation 'prepare the way of the Lord.' And Thou, whose Name is Love, do Thou grant 'times of refreshing.' Send forth Thy pioneers to prepare the church for this overshadowing power of the Highest. Revive by Thy gracious influences Thy withered and mourning possession. Let Thy dews come thick, heavy, and prolonged, as 'floods upon the dry ground.' O give sap and verdure to Thy 'trees of righteousness,' Thine own planting, that Thou mayest be glorified. Let not Lebanon be ashamed, nor Sharon be as a wilderness; let not Bashan languish, nor the top of Carmel wither. Fulfil Thine old promise —'I will hear the heaven, and the heaven shall hear the earth, and the earth shall hear the corn, and the wine, and the oil.' And then Thy revived and satisfied church shall respond to this love, and cry in her eagerness, 'Awake, O north wind, and come thou south, blow upon my garden, that the spices thereof may flow out. Let my beloved come into his garden, and eat his pleasant fruits.'

LECTURE X.

THE DIVINE LOVE IN ITS REFLEX POWER AND MANIFESTATIONS.

DETACHED ANNOTATIONS.

1. THE MOMENTOUS QUESTION.

'So when they had dined, Jesus saith to Simon Peter, Simon, son of Jonas, lovest thou me more than these? He saith unto him, Yea, Lord; thou knowest that I love thee. He saith unto him, Feed my Lambs. He saith to him again the second time, Simon, son of Jonas, lovest thou me? He saith unto him, Yea, Lord; thou knowest that I love thee. He saith unto him, Feed my sheep. He saith unto him the third time, Simon, Son of Jonas, lovest thou me? Peter was grieved because he said unto him the third time, Lovest thou me? And he said unto him, Lord, thou knowest all things; thou knowest that I love thee. Jesus saith unto him, Feed my sheep.'—JOHN xxii. 15—17.

PETER had denied his Lord. The heart of the bold man had failed; and in fright at the gossip of a waiting maiden, he who had drawn a sword in presence of the Roman soldiers, told a deliberate falsehood—once and again, and the third time confirmed his denial with an oath. 'I know not the man,' he solemnly avowed — that man with whom but a few hours before he had pledged himself to die — that man who, as the words of repudiation reached His ear, turned such a look of pity upon the recreant apostle, that he went out and wept bitterly.' Precious tears of thine, Peter, for they relieved the oppression of thy sorrow, and were the signs of thy genuine contrition. Judas had none to shed, and he 'went and hanged himself.' But Jesus still loved Peter, and the message about His own resurrection ran thus; 'Go and tell his disciples, and Peter.' O what kindness to the penitent!—and he needed it. Nay, early on the very day He rose, the Lord appeared to Simon. And now, when the Master met him, He saw his returning love; for as soon as he knew that it was the Lord, he tightened his robe, flung himself into the cold sea, and, bravely buffetting the waves, swam to the shore — more than a hundred yards. The whole company then got the invitation from the mysterious purveyor, 'Come and dine.'* And they dined, and the meal being ended, Peter was accosted with the startling question, 'Lovest thou me? His smitten heart at once replied, 'Yea, Lord, thou knowest that I love thee.' Again was the question put, and again was the same answer given. A third time did the Lord make the unvarying interrogation, and a third time, Peter answered with a broader assurance, 'Lord, thou knowest all things; thou knowest that I love thee.' Three times had he denied his Master, and three times was he questioned

---

* Dinner is here simply the forenoon, in contrast with supper, or the afternoon meal.

as to his love. But his mind was now chastened—there was no bold asseveration—no pledge of going to death — no boast of superior attachment. The humble appeal was at length to Christ's own omniscience and His knowledge of the speaker's heart.

Now, does not the same authority put the same question to us? Has not He the right to put it? Dare we demur to answer it? Can we challenge the Saviour's claim to our love? If He has loved us, and died for us—given us such a pledge of His love as cannot be rivalled; and if He is bestowing upon us the fruits of that love in forms of blessing which He only could think of and confer—beyond all question we are summoned to love Him. Surely as He points to Calvary in the past, and to the Heaven prepared by Him and held by Him for the future, He has the unchallengeable claim of asking, 'Lovest thou me?' And is it not to bestir us to self-examination that He so shapes the question? He is anxious that we love Him. And the formal question is meant to put us on our guard. He questions you, to prompt you to question yourselves. Let us look in and examine. Is love to Christ there at all; or, is it so overlaid that we cannot detect it? Is it there in power as it ought to be; or, is it, as in a coffin, feeble and useless? Is it the ruling passion, or but an incidental guest? Does it constrain you to self-consecration; or rather, do you repress and stifle it? You have certainly done many things unworthy of that love, and probably some things in defiance of it; there is, therefore, just cause that you subject yourselves to a searching scrutiny. Of the woman welcomed by the Lord, he said, 'she loved much.' O that He could bear such a testimony of us!

May not Jesus be suspecting you, when He puts the testing question? Has He not just grounds? Peter had thrice denied Him; and have you never acted in a similar spirit? You may not, in so many words, have disclaimed all knowledge of Him; but, alas, how often have you acted as if He did not exist! as if there were no Christ, or you had no faith in Him, and no love to Him — as if you had renounced all His claims upon you. You do not say so — you would shrink from saying it; but you have acted as if it were so. Ah yes; when that pursuit so engrossed you that you could think of nothing else but it, according to your own confession; when that object you set your heart upon was the thought of the day and the dream of the night; when that child became so much of an idol, or that fame so much of a passion; when that affliction suddenly struck you, and in your first paroxysm you did not think at once of telling Jesus; when that temptation overcame you, and you forgot Him in its early blandishments; when that company treated His name lightly, and you interposed not to rebuke or argue; or when that enterprise of Christian beneficence was set on foot, and you allowed it to go on without one word of approbation, one prayer for its success, or one mite for its support. May not Christ suspect you, to induce you to suspect yourselves, and have you not just grounds of suspicion? Be jealous over yourselves 'with a godly jealousy,' and slacken not your efforts, and abate not your scrutiny, till you can appeal to His omniscience, and say, 'Lord, thou knowest that I love thee.' See that you do this as honestly as Peter. O to be warranted to do so, with yet higher assurance!

The grand proof of Peter's love was to be seen in his obedience to the command, 'Feed my lambs: feed my sheep.' This 'shepherding' of the flock was to be his special care; and nobly he discharged its duties, till at length he sealed his testimony with his blood. And still the cause of Christ represents Himself, and it is neither an unworthy nor an uncommissioned representative. He that loves Him, will love it. Where there is love to Him, there must be love to it.

> 'Hast Thou a lamb in all Thy flock
> I would disdain to feed?
> Hast Thou a foe before whose face
> I fear Thy cause to plead?'

For whatever reminds, and is so moulded and placed as to remind one of the absent object of love, creates attachment to itself. The cause of Christ so stands to us; and if we love Christ, we cannot but love it. It is His: His heart is set upon it, it bears upon it His image, and He has left it in charge to His people. The furtherance of that cause can rightly proceed only from love to Him in it. If we are indifferent to it—if we care not about the purity, the union, and the extension of the church — if we pray not, labour not, and give not for it — if we prefer not Jerusalem to our chiefest joy, how can any one of us dare to say to the risen Redeemer, 'Lord, thou knowest all things : thou knowest that I love thee?' Would not His immediate, if not indignant answer be, 'If ye love me, keep my commandments;' and in My absence, cherish My cause —the cause I bled for, and then committed to you— the cause involving My glory and My full reward?

And that cause of His is no abstract or impersonal thing. His people are identified with it — they are its embodiment. They bear His likeness, and each one that loves Him, will also love His image. And therefore He who challenges our love has, in order to warn and direct us, left behind Him —

II. THE NEW COMMANDMENT.

'A new commandment I give unto you, That ye love one another; as I have loved you, that ye also love one another. By this shall all men know that ye are my disciples, if ye have love one to another.' — JOHN xiii. 34, 35.

THE DIVINE LOVE produces in the believer's heart the reflection of itself. Not only does it incite him to love the Lord Jesus Christ, but to love all who bear Christ's image. Love to the brethren is only another form of loving Christ, for it is loving Christ in them. The Redeemer is absent Himself, but He has left behind Him visible representatives; and they are, for His sake, to share in our affection. Of Him it is said, 'Whom, having not seen, ye love;' but of them it is true, that because we see them, therefore do we love them. To His disciples at the Paschal board, and over the symbols of His holy suffering humanity, our Lord said, 'Whither I go, ye cannot come.' I am about to leave you, and ye cannot in the meantime follow Me. It is on your errand I am going, and ye must remain behind to do My work. So long as He was with them, He was the bond of union among them: loving Him, they loved one another in Him. But He was soon to be withdrawn from them, and therefore it was needful to lay upon them the injunction still to love one another. In their new circumstances, there was need of the new commandment. The family had the more need to cling closely together after the Elder Brother had left them. While they followed Him, if two of them happened to disagree, a word from Him removed the misunderstanding, and a look from Him brought reconciliation and harmony. But now, if offences should come, and He be away, it was only in the spirit of mutual attachment that peace and concord could be preserved among them.

Such a command as that of brother-love* was not

---

* We render the term usually translated 'brotherly-kindness,' by the more correct equivalent, 'brother-love.' Such is the literal meaning of the Greek compound. Brotherly-love is love which in its nature is brotherly, but brother-love is such love as every brother is entitled to demand and receive. In calling it brotherly-love, one might suppose that it signified such love as wholly new in its spirit. Even under the sternness of the Old Testament, men were summoned to love their neighbour as themselves. But this love was somewhat different from brotherly-kindness. The one is the love of man as man, the other is the love of man as a fellow-believer. Love to the human family is not identical with love to the household of faith. The law had also already taught some points of this duty. Thus the Mosaic statute said, 'Thou shalt not suffer sin upon thy brother,'—a mode of brother-love which, though negative in its form, was genuine in its spirit. But in its expressness and comprehensiveness this command was new. It was now given in direct phraseology, and it developed the one principle to which all preceding enactments were to be traced. Incidental injunctions had contained some one or other of the features of this brother-love; but all such commands were absorbed in this novel and engrossing declaration, 'Love one another.' Various practical elements

---

should be cherished toward us; whereas, by calling it brother-love, the true meaning is brought out — such love as every one sustaining the relation of a brother has the right to expect. In short, the affection is not brotherly-love named subjectively from him who cherishes it; but brother-love named objectively from him who is the authorised object of it. So in other Greek terms similarly constructed — *philosophia* is not wise love, but love of wisdom; *philanthropia* is not manly love, but love of man; *philarguria* is not monied love, but love of money; *philotimia* is not honourable love, but love of honour; and *philoponia* is not laborious love, but love of labour, etc.

had been previously delineated; but now, and for the first time, the theory was enforced.

The commandment was new also in its origin and place. It had come, in some of its dictates, from the lips of prophets; but now it was enjoined by the incarnation of love. As received of old, it was found in the vicinity of other statutes, which cast a shadow over it, for they spoke of the sword, of the stern execution of law, and of some nations doomed to extinction, and of others which could never be naturalised in the Hebrew commonwealth. But now the command is freed from all such neighbourhood, from all that might modify its power, or impede its results. For the church is not confined to one nation, but receives its members out of every tribe; and her brotherhood is not broken by difference of rank or colour, of language or social position.

Need we add that it is new in the example by which it is enforced — 'as I have loved you.' Such a model almost deters us from attempting to comply. Can we come up to Christ's practice? Can that heart of ours, in which love is an implanted and not an original affection, ever resemble that heart where love had ever dwelt?

'As I have loved you.' As if He had said, recall your past intercourse with Me, and summon up to your memory the numerous proofs of My attachment to you. When I first called you, how I bore with your reluctance, and yet loved you. When you interposed so ignorantly and cruelly between

Me and the little children, between Me and the Syrophenician women, I did not disband you. When some of you tried to expel the demon and failed, I did not throw you from Me as disgracing your functions, and for ever disqualified from exercising them. When Peter's forwardness and his rash sayings provoked Me, and the ambition of the sons of Zebedee chagrined Me; when the moodiness of Thomas grieved Me, and the treachery of Judas was apparent to Me, I did not exclude them from the list of apostles. When all of you misunderstood My parables, as your subsequent questions so often indicated; when you saw not the purpose of My miracles, and failed in your conceptions of the end of My mission, I did not depose you, and summon others to succeed you. When there arose the strife among you which should be the greatest, that recent outburst of selfish ambition has not quenched My love for you, or prompted Me to blast all your anticipations. Bear with one another, as I have borne with you. Let your love to one another be as Mine to you — too ardent to be cooled, too tenacious to be severed; like Mine, let it be unaltered amidst changes, unshaken by disappointments, and unextinguished by the occasional coldness it may meet, and even by the hostility which its ardour and honesty may happen to provoke.

'As I have loved you.' Such love as His was a novelty, and therefore the injunction that was at once prompted by it and illustrated in it was certainly 'a new commandment.' The essence of the

second table of the law was love; but that love was
inculcated in prohibitions of injury to our neighbour, and the code was published amidst 'blackness, and darkness, and tempest;' but now the
ruling motive of conduct has been placed in the
fulness of light. For as the Master said, 'I have
loved you,' there lay on the table before Him the
fragments of a feast designed to set out and commemorate a love the noblest and tenderest the world
had ever seen.

'As I have loved you:' and do you ask what is
meant, or what measure of love is requisite? Had
he not said but a few minutes ago, 'This is my body
broken for you?' and over that cup that so lately
passed round, did He not utter these awful words,
'This cup is the New Testament in my blood, shed
for remission of sins unto many.'

'As I have loved you'—is not this declaration
still set before us as our model? Such love, pure,
unselfish, and ready to deny itself—such love as
brought Him down, 'not to be ministered unto,
but to minister'—such love as prompted Him to
endure the cross, 'despising the shame'—such love
as still sustains His uplifted arm while He pleads—
the image of this love ought to characterise our love
to the brethren. But such love as His was 'a new
thing in the earth,' and therefore the commandment
based upon it and exemplified in it was 'a new commandment.'

Besides one of the ends our Lord had in view
was indeed till then unheard of: 'By this shall all

men know that ye are my disciples, if ye have love one to another.' Discipleship had been evinced in various shapes, and discovered by numerous tests. But no 'master' ever dreamed of imposing such an obligation, and creating by it such a characteristic. The scholars of the Academy, the Portico, or the Lyceum were at once known by their modes of reasoning, their attachment to distinctive theories, and their frequent appeals to Plato, Zeno, or Aristotle. The Jew was recognised by his dress and language, his reverence for Moses, his selection among meats and drinks, and his antipathy to all the races of the Uncircumcision. If you entered a company of Greeks, and found them theorising upon pleasure, its nature, enjoyment, and modes, you would at once pronounce them to be Epicureans; or if, mixing with another crowd, you were met with such sounds as fate, liberty, necessity, wisdom, and chief good, you would feel in a moment that you were among the Stoics. Did you, in any city of Judea, see a man clothed with a robe deeper than common, and adorned with a phylactery of unusual breadth —did you follow him, and hear him pray with a stentorian voice to attract all passers by, or see him give alms so ostentatiously as to draw upon him the public gaze and admiration, you would have no doubt that you beheld a Pharisee. And if, on the streets of Jerusalem, you met with one in whose dress the prominent portions of the national uniform were carefully pared down, who, as he passed with you near the temple, observed with a quiet sneer that the scent of the burning sacrifice tainted the air, or who, as he looked on the place of sepulchres, assumed a philosophic air and spoke of death as the debt of nature, as a hard and universal necessity; smiled at the idea of a spirit-land, and hinted that the prevailing belief on that point was not consonant to reason, or based on a rational interpretation of scripture — you would have no difficulty in detecting the speaker to be a Sadducee. But our Lord discards what is external; and His followers are to be known not by dress, language, or occupation, but by the mutual kindness which they cherished and exercised toward one another. They were to be known not by mind, but by heart — not by intellect, but by soul.

How, then, should such love prove and glorify their Christianity? In this way. Love had never so belonged to any system. There might have been selfish attachments, but there was no genuine affection. Christ, however, came into the world to teach and illustrate love. Love is the very genius of his system. All its doctrines lead to love as their centre, and all its duties depend upon it for their fulfilment. Love is the essence of all its promises, and the lustre of all its hopes. It teaches that love to Jesus should fill the heart, and that the entire life should be swayed and consecrated by its influence. In imitation of the God of Love, it inculcates love to every living thing, and a special attachment toward all that bear His likeness. He who loved us and gave Himself for us, is the model we are summoned to copy in all our words and deeds. Love of the purest, fullest, and most disinterested nature is enjoined upon His disciples, and is to be uniformly exemplified by them.

> 'He prayeth best who loveth best
> All things, both great and small;
> For the dear God who loveth us,
> He made and loveth all.'

Now, if men see such love, and observe its unselfish nature — if they witness its self-denial and nobleness, overleaping all conventionalities, and laying low every barrier which pride so often erects, and surviving also those shocks and trials which convert common affection into enmity or jealous rivalry, then they must feel that it is an uncommon and unearthly principle; and as it exists only among persons of a certain creed, they at once 'take knowledge of them that they have been with Jesus.' No other system breathed such a spirit. The Greek sneered at all the world beyond himself as barbarian, and the Jew scowled upon it as uncircumcised. In Rome the word denoting a stranger meant also an enemy; and the classic tongues have no term to signify those erections where the sick and aged are sheltered and healed. In the eye of law, the slave was a thing; but the gospel made him a brother, and more than a brother. Creed is not enough, for there may be a dead orthodoxy; but this warm love, an image of His own, is the test of discipleship. Alas that it should be so feebly manifested, and that we should so seldom make 'full proof' of our discipleship! The world may not be inclined to study books on the Evidences; it may not busy itself in analysing the reality of miracles, or proving the fulfilment of prophecy; but here is a proof which commands attention, while no profound scrutiny is needed to detect it, and no earnest logic to reach its resistless conclusion — 'hereby shall all men know that ye are my disciples, if ye have love one to another.'

But there is another reason why such brother-love should characterise us, and that is, the enmity of the world round about us. We are thus led to contemplate—

III. THE NECESSITY AND GROWTH OF LOVE IN THE MIDST OF PERSECUTION.

'This is my commandment, That ye love one another, as I have loved you. . . . These things I command you, that ye love one another. If the world hate you, ye know that it hated me before it hated you.'—JOHN xv. 12, 17, 18.

THE Lord here repeats His injunction. He had made them all His friends, and in being His friends they were to be mutual friends. The magnet that drew them to Himself, did, by the same process, attract them to one another. The nearer they came to Him, the nearer they came to one another. But they were left in a world of hostility—a world that loathed them, scorned them, and scrupled not to shed their blood. If such rancour reigned around them, there was surely all the more reason why among themselves they should 'walk in love.' A small army in an enemy's country clings tenaciously together. The little company exposed to persecution should comfort one another, and put on that 'love which is the bond of perfectness.' Love in the midst of themselves would be productive of peace and joy, would be a holy fire which the adverse winds could not extinguish, but only fan into a flame. Such love was to be as a family feeling, which becomes the stronger the more the family interests are threatened by external opposition. The world may bite and devour—there may be in it envying and strife, confusion and every evil work—it may be marked by its fierce competitions, springing from its motto that there is no friendship in trade; but surely in the church, the law of kindness should be devoutly and universally recognised—its members not only 'forbearing one another and forgiving one another' in love, but striving for one another's welfare, 'in honour preferring one another,' ready to lay down their lives for the brethren, as Christ laid down His for them, and exemplifying in their practice their belief in the statement, 'Now abideth faith, hope, love, these three; but the greatest of these is love.'

But brother-love is not only an evidence of discipleship to the world, it is also—

IV. THE CONSCIOUS TEST OF A SAVING CHANGE TO OURSELVES.

'We know that we have passed from death unto life, because we love the brethren: he that loveth not his brother abideth in death.'—1 JOHN iii. 14.

To pass from death to life—how momentous and necessary the change!—to pass from gloom and sorrow, insensibility and wrath, to light, health, activity, and blessedness. It is a change which divine power and love alone can effect. The ear of death wakes up to no voice but that of God. What joy to be warranted in saying, 'we live.' Now, the apostle proposes a test of the reality of this life. We know it, 'because we love the brethren.' This is no ambiguous declaration or criterion. And it is a sure one. These brethren bear the image of Christ; and only in so far as they bear that image, can we recognise them as brethren. Our love to them is but another form of love to Christ; and there can be no love to Christ where His salvation is not enjoyed. Faith is the means of life, and love exists as the result of saving faith. There can be no capability of love without the quickening power of such faith. For the human heart has by nature no attachment to the beauty of holiness. It finds no attraction in it. It does not appreciate spirituality of character. Therefore, not until it feel the influence of Divine Love upon itself, can it be drawn toward the results of that love in others. But it will be so drawn, as soon as it is conscious of 'the love of God shed abroad' within it. If, then, it pass out of a state of enmity or indifference into that of love, it knows that it has 'passed from death unto life.' So that if you do not love Christ's image in a brother, nor hail as a brother him in whose bosom that image is enshrined, you are yet in death, 'as Cain, who was of that wicked one.' 'He that loveth not his brother abideth in death.' Hatred is the nurse of murder, and 'no murderer hath eternal life abiding in him.' The loveless heart is at once a faithless and a lifeless heart.

And among the results of this brother-love there is one form which occupies a prominent place, and that is love to the poorer brethren, leading us to sympathise with them and to relieve them. So that this love is—

V. THE BASIS OF THE CHRISTIAN POOR LAW.

'But whoso hath this world's good, and seeth his brother have need, and shutteth up his bowels of compassion from him, how dwelleth the love of God in him?'—1 JOHN iii. 17.

THE gospel does not produce uniformity of social condition. 'The poor have ye always with you.' Some ride in chariots, and some are humble pedestrians. Some have abundance, others are denied it. Some have increasing stores, and others, with the utmost frugality, are still touching the verge of poverty and debt. But this inequality is the means, under God, of developing the choicest of the Christian virtues. Were all rich, there would be no room for Christian benevolence; were all happy and prosperous, there would be no space nor call for Christian sympathy. Were there no brethren in need, we should be denied the luxury of doing good. If there were no distress, 'pure religion and undefiled' would never be fully exhibited. Nor could we copy Christ's example in many of its noblest features, or drink into the spirit of His work, if the church did not present such opportunities. Therefore the fairest graces of the Holy Spirit, and the noblest and loveliest adornments of the Christian character, would never be seen, but for the inequalities and hardships of social life within the pale of the church. Homage to the absent Christ in His members would also be impossible, if there were no prison with its inmates, and no sick-bed with its sufferers. No wonder that love takes this form, and rejoices in it. In doing good to the needy, it imitates Him who came into the world to serve. It pictures Him girt with the towel, and in the act of stooping to the basin and washing the disciples' feet. It tastes the blessedness of giving. It does not deal in cheap commiseration: 'If a brother or sister be naked, and destitute of daily food, and one of you say unto them, Depart in peace, be ye warmed and filled; notwithstanding ye give them not those things which are needful to the body, what doth it profit?' The Christian heart will be thankful for the opportunity of imparting relief to a Christian brother, and proving itself a faithful steward: 'Is it not to deal thy bread to the hungry, and that thou bring the poor that are cast out to thy house? when thou seest the naked, that thou cover him; and that thou hide not thyself from thine own flesh?' In opening itself to distress, it feeds itself with sublime enjoyment: 'And if thou draw out thy soul to the hungry, and satisfy the afflicted soul; then shall thy light rise in obscurity, and thy darkness be as the noon-day: and the Lord shall guide thee continually, and satisfy thy soul in drought, and make fat thy bones: and thou shalt be like a watered garden, and like a spring of water, whose waters fail not.'

But, specially, it is glad in this accredited way to manifest its love to Christ; for He and His are identified. It is in this spirit that relief should be offered or beneficence conferred, so as to receive the commendation, 'Inasmuch as ye have done it unto one of the least of these my brethren, ye have done it unto me.' 'Me,' said He, 'ye have not always.' But He never wants representatives; and this love to Him through them, is so pleasing to Jesus, that on the day of judgment He shall openly refer to it, as if to vindicate His sentence of acceptance by it, or as if it were the highest proof of the power of faith, and of the reality of their salvation. 'Then shall the King say unto them on his right hand, Come, ye blessed of my Father, inherit the kingdom prepared for you from the foundation of the world: for I was an hungered, and ye gave me meat; I was thirsty, and ye gave me drink; I was a stranger, and ye took me in; naked, and ye clothed me; I was sick, and ye visited me; I was in prison, and ye came unto me. Then shall the righteous answer him, saying, Lord, when saw we thee an hungered, and fed thee? or thirsty, and gave thee drink? When saw we thee a stranger, and took thee in? or naked, and clothed thee? Or when saw we thee sick, or in prison, and came unto thee? And the King shall answer and say unto them, Verily I say unto you, Inasmuch as ye have done it unto one of the least of these my brethren, ye have done it unto me.' And thus we find the church in Antioch, when a famine had been predicted, resolving at once 'to send relief unto the brethren which dwelt in Judea.' 'Let us not love in word, neither in tongue, but in deed and in truth.' We do not further pursue these sentiments of the beloved disciple, who rejoiced to his dying day in exhorting the members of the church to love one another, and who was privileged especially to make the sublime announcement that 'God is Love.'

Again, all who love Christ will rejoice in holding fellowship with Him. Therefore it is that they have special attachment to the 'Law, the Prophets, and the Psalms,' which are so full of Him. So that love to Christ is indicated by —

VI. LOVE TO THE BIBLE.

'And they are they which testify of me.' — JOHN v. 29.

ALL who love another, and who love Christ, also 'His appearance and coming.' 'Amen. So come,' is the language of their hearts. On this account they cherish the book which contains the promise of his advent, and often have recourse to it as a communication from Himself. In and by the Bible they hold correspondence with Jesus. They meet Him in it—Him who is the great promise of the Old Testament, and the great fact of the New. There is indeed much about the book to interest them, but its Christ is the principal attraction. There they see Him in His love—there they hear His words, and behold His wondrous deeds. They can there bend over His cradle, and kneel by His cross—sail with Him on the lake, and journey with Him on His errands of mercy. The New Testament, therefore, has exercised a supremacy of love in the church. It consists of only two modes of composition—telling a story and writing a letter. But the book is immortal, for believers love it, and will not let it die. And they have felt its influence in a variety of forms.

For no volume ever commanded such a profusion of readers, or has been translated into so many languages. Such is the universality of its spirit, that no book loses less by translation—none has been so frequently copied in manuscript, and none so often printed. King and noble, peasant and pauper, are delighted students of its pages. Philosophers have humbly gleaned from it, and legislation has been thankfully indebted to it. Its stories charm the child, its hopes inspirit the aged, and its promises soothe the bed of death. The maiden is wedded under its sanction, and the grave is closed under its comforting assurances. Its lessons are the essence of religion, the seminal truths of theology, the first principles of morals, and the guiding axioms of political economy. Martyrs have often bled and been burnt for attachment to it. It is the theme of universal appeal. In the entire range of literature, no book is so frequently quoted or referred to. The majority of all the books ever published have been in connection with it. The Fathers commented upon it, and the subtle divines of the middle ages refined upon its doctrines. It sustained Origen's scholarship and Chrysostom's rhetoric. It whetted the penetration of Abelard, and exercised the keen ingenuity of Aquinas. It gave life to the revival of letters, and Dante and Petrarch revelled in its imagery. It augmented the erudition of Erasmus, and roused and blessed the intrepidity of Luther. Its temples are the finest specimens of architecture, and the brightest triumphs of music are associated with its poetry. The text of no ancient author has summoned into operation such an amount of labour and learning, and it has furnished occasion for the most masterly examples of criticism and comment, grammatical investigation, and logical analysis. It has also inspired the English muse with her loftiest strains. Its beams gladdened Milton in his darkness, and cheered the song of Cowper in his sadness. It was the star which guided Columbus to the discovery of the new world. It furnished the panoply of that Puritan valour which shivered tyranny in days gone by. It is the magna charta of the world's regeneration and liberties. The records of false religion, from the Koran to the

Book of Mormon, have owned its superiority, and surreptitiously purloined its jewels. Among the Christian classics it loaded the treasures of Owen, charged the fulness of Hooker, barbed the point of Baxter, gave colours to the palette and sweep to the pencil of Bunyan, enriched the fragrant fancy of Taylor, sustained the loftiness of Howe, and strung the plummet of Edwards. In short, this collection of artless lives and letters has changed the face of the world, and ennobled myriads of its population.

May we not, then, sum up these various precepts, and say with the apostle —

VII. 'WALK IN LOVE?'
EPH. V. 2.

YES, 'Walk in love.' Not simply, pray in love, or 'keep the feast' in love; not simply, hold the doctrine of the communion of the saints in love, or give relief to the poorer brethren in love; but 'Walk in love.' Every step is to be one of love. The whole tenor and course of life are to be characterised by love—not only on the Sabbath, but on every day; not only in the sanctuary, but in the house, the workshop, the counting-room, and the exchange. Love is to reign, not only in the language of congratulation, but also in that of reproof; and to hold its sway, not merely when Christians meet in the oratory, but when they offer one another civilities on the streets. Nor is it suddenly to forsake them when they are making a bargain, and each is looking for his own profit by the transaction. Are you injured? Love forbids you to retaliate. You might perhaps derive from some business considerable advantage, and yet keep within the limits of commercial usage, though you certainly would go beyond the bounds of Christian equity, — then love interdicts you. It may be that one who has done you some harm has come into your power, and you could easily and safely let him feel your memory of his past offence: love 'worketh no ill to his neighbour,' but bids you 'heap coals of fire upon his head.' Is there any one whom you could oblige and benefit without being under any formal or legal obligation to do so? Love requires you to 'do good,' as you have opportunity. Perhaps there is another in whom you do not feel a very great interest, but in some moment when you might be of service to him, and direct him to some useful opening in life, love will keep your tongue from justifying your indifference, and saying, 'Am I my brother's keeper.'

'Walk in love.' Were this walk of love to be always trodden, how very soon would ecclesiastical and civil discords cease. Were nations to observe this precept, there would speedily come to an end all forms of selfish monopoly and tariff; all attempts to convert might into right, and to enforce an ambitious and grasping policy by the cannon and the sword. Love would far outweigh diplomacy. Were churches to remember this injunction, alienation because of differences in ritual and government would disappear, truth would be spoken in love, the jagon of sectarianism would never be heard, and catholicity and conscientiousness would not only co-exist, but coalesce. And if individuals were to keep the Christian statute in their hearts, no little animosity and misunderstanding would be avoided. But how often has the 'dead fly' fallen into the apothecary's ointment. One drop of the 'gall of bitterness' has an infinitesimal power of self-diffusion; for they who taste it, and they who behold the result, are alike under temptation to forget themselves. It is a strange thing that any rational mind should be guilty of this 'little folly,' which in so many forms frets itself and embroils others — either haunted by the suspicion that it is slighted or overlooked, and for ever guarding itself against the baseless fancy by hard and rash accusations of others, or set on edge by the slightest occurrence, and ingeniously construing accident into design — claiming independence of speech, yet hurt and ruffled into surly displeasure should others speak and act under the very same plea — utterly regardless of the annoyance it causes to others, or the obstacles it raises to Christian fellowship — loving, above all things, to utter a truth which may be distasteful to others, and yet annoyed beyond measure when any truth is spoken distasteful to itself — stiff and unyielding, not in defence of principle, but only in obedience to its own inherent and unreasonable obstinacy — mistaking narrow-mindedness for fidelity, and baptizing its censorious surmises by the sacred title of conscientiousness or rectitude. Such infirmities of temper are all of them deviations from this path of love. No apology can vindicate them either in church or market. It is a shame for any disciple of the religion of love either, on the one hand, to be thrown off his balance by a fit of indignation, or, on the other hand, to cherish a grudge, and to feed it against any one who may have given him offence. The prayer of Robert Hall in a moment of provocation was a very fitting one: 'Lamb of God; Lamb of God, calm my perturbed spirit.' 'Slow to speak, slow to wrath,' is a maxim of prudence and inspiration. The Master, 'when he was reviled, reviled not again; when suffering, he threatened not.' There is nothing so remote from Christ's example as a hard and uncharitable disposition.

'Walk in love.' There are no thorns in the path, but all deviations from it lead into thickets of distress, and the transgressor lacerates his own feet with briars and thistles. He grieves others, and, in proportion to the tenderness of his conscience, he is a plague and sorrow to himself. 'Walk in love,' and you induce others to tread in your steps. But all such loveless and repulsive features of character do not and cannot commend the gospel around you.

'Walk in love.' It is 'the more excellent way,' for it leads to perfection. Were the path fully recognised and entered on by professing Christians, and were those around them again to be urged to exclaim, 'See these Christians how they love one another,' we might safely hail such a period as the dawn of the world's jubilee. Let us, therefore, commend the grace of Christian love. 'The fruit of the Spirit is love.' Ought not Himself to be loved, as He is 'altogether lovely?' and should not His hold a place in our heart of hearts? O if we or our churches were to meet 'with one accord,' as on the morning of Pentecost, and present our united supplications for reviving influence, its effusion would develop our mutual affinities, and bring us into sympathetic contact and final unity. Men have struggled for the faith—let them now contend for love. With a pure theology, let us have a warm and outflowing religion. Loving Him who begat, let us love 'him that is begotten.' 'Above all things,' says an apostle, 'have fervent charity among yourselves.' Let prejudice be charmed away by calm and dignified appeal. Let there be a constant desire to accommodate. 'See that ye fall not out by the way,' is an admonition as appropriate in our days as in those of Joseph. Let the spirit of mutual condescension pervade our every arrangement. No one is to deem his opinion infallible, or his character in all respects invulnerable. Again, Jesus is our model. At the last supper, he was among his disciples 'as one that serveth;' and he taught them the nature and spirit of that service of love which they ought ever to render to one another: 'So, after he had washed their feet, and had taken his garments, and was set down again, he said unto them, Know ye what I have done to you? Ye call me Master and Lord: and ye say well; for so I am.

If I then, your Lord and Master, have washed your feet, ye also ought to wash one another's feet. For I have given you an example, that ye should do as I have done to you. Verily, verily I say unto you, The servant is not greater than his lord; neither he that is sent greater than he that sent him. If ye know these things, happy are ye if ye do them.'

And now, perhaps, we are able to understand the apostle's statement when he says, 'The greatest of these is charity.' Let us, then, in conclusion, try and enter into the spirit of—

VIII. THE APOSTLE'S ADJUDICATION AMONG THE GRACES.

'And now abideth faith, hope, charity, these three; but the greatest of these is charity.'—1 COR. xiii. 13.

THE apostle in this chapter proves the superiority of love by two comparisons. He compares it first with the miraculous endowments of the primitive age, and his conclusion is, that they shall disappear, but love shall survive, and always keep its place in the church. The gifts of the early church were of a bright and dazzling order — prophecy, tongues, and knowledge. They have passsd away with the age that needed them. But 'love never faileth.' It can never be superseded. The church, bereft of the extraordinary, has still the ordinary graces of the Spirit: for the apostle, in his second comparison, says, 'And now abideth faith, hope, love — these three.' We dare not disparage faith, for according to our faith so is it unto us; and we cannot look lightly on hope, 'for we are saved by hope.' 'But the greatest of these is love.' It leavens all other graces with its spirit. 'Love is the fulfilling of the law.' 'Owe no man anything, but to love one another; for he that loveth another hath fulfilled the law.' 'Thou shalt love the Lord thy God. . . Thou shalt love thy neighbour as thyself. On these two commandments hang all the law and the prophets.' Every precept of the Decalogue is thus resolved into love, which is thereby enthroned on an eminence to which faith and hope cannot be elevated.

Farther, eloquence such as would befit an angel's lips is, without it, only 'as sounding brass or a tinkling cymbal.' Profound insight into the depths of faith, and supernatural ability to disclose its mysteries, are 'nothing,' if love be absent. The labours and sacrifices of professed philanthropy, if not prompted and sustained by it, 'profit nothing. Such love is not soon exhausted, is filled with unwearying sympathy, never grudges what another enjoys, never boasts of its efforts, is purely disinterested in all its labours, never rashly withdraws its kindness, imputes no sinister motives, longs to advance God's glory and man's good, is patient under provocation, indulges in no suspicions, forms no censorious judgments, perseveres though it be thwarted, never dreams of rendering evil for evil, and still holds on its course amidst malignity and insult. This noblest of the graces has faith and hope as its supporters, and it therefore rises as far above them, as the end surpasses the means. And when faith and hope shall have ceased to exist in their present forms and aspects, it shall survive unchanged but in intensity. Nay, more, it gives its happy possessor the closest approach to Him who is Love, for faith and hope cannot properly be ascribed to God, but 'God is love,' and 'he that dwelleth in love, dwelleth in God,' and shall dwell with Him for ever. We are, therefore, brought to the irresistible conclusion that 'The greatest of these is love,' excelling them all on earth and absorbing them all into itself in heaven; for

'Love is heaven, and heaven is love.'

LECTURE XI.

THE FRIENDSHIP AND SYMPATHY OF JESUS.

JOHN xi. 5, 35.

'Now Jesus loved Martha, and her sister, and Lazarus. . . . Jesus wept.'

IT is difficult to realise the fact of our Lord's true humanity. It fades away from our view in the splendour of His Divinity, so close was the union of man with God. But it was nevertheless a distinct manhood, as perfect in itself as that worn by any of our race. The entire record of Christ's life proves the assertion. He was born as the children are born — a partaker of their 'flesh and blood;' and He was nursed as the children are nursed — growing 'in wisdom and stature.' He was hungry, and He ate; He was thirsty, and He drank; He was weary, and He lay down; He was fatigued, and He slept; He was smitten, and He died. Still it is no easy task to picture out to ourselves the merely human sensations and tendencies which characterised the man Jesus. We believe that His human nature, sin excepted, was as ours; but it is scarcely possible for us to feel it and imagine it, from the overshadowing glory of His higher essence. In consequence of this failure, we are apt to miss no little instruction and comfort as we read the incidents and travel over the scenes of His life. We invest the man with attributes belonging to the God, and unconsciously deify His humanity. Let us, therefore, humbly endeavour to form a just conception of one element of His veritable humanity — his friendship and sympathy. Both are purely human emotions, and both existed unmistakeably in Christ. The Divine Love showed itself in these earthly forms. We are not to throw a veil over them, and regard them as shapes of saving grace; but we are to look upon them as essentially the same with such virtues and affections in ourselves. As a man, our Lord had His own attachments and predilections, distinct altogether from His love as a God, and His compassion as a Saviour. There was among His apostles one singled out as 'the disciple whom Jesus loved; and among his acquaintances and entertainers in general society there was one circle specially endeared to Him. The sacred record states that 'Jesus loved Martha, and her sister, and Lazarus.' Let us approach with reverence, and contemplate with amazement—

I. THE REALITY OF CHRIST'S FRIENDSHIP. That Jesus should have passed His life in solitude was impossible; nor could it be that His spirit, wrapped up within itself, should be alien to all human impulses. He did not move through society in cold isolation, or teach and act as one whose soul dwelt in a sphere of its own, far apart and high. Nay more, as He mingled among men and women, He must have met certain forms of character which had special attractions for Him. He was moved to friendship by what He liked, as really as to sympathy by the suffering which He saw. What disposes our hearts to friendship, must have operated on His spirit with a similar result. So it was; and how it was will be seen in the following paragraphs.

In that village which lies at the base of the eastern slope of the Mount of Olives, there lived a family noted for their harmony and piety. It consisted of a brother and two sisters. The neighbours noted the earnest welcome which they uniformly gave to an occasional visitor, who was also invited sometimes to partake of the hospitality of Simon the leper. This visitor was of serene and august appearance, and it was soon noised abroad that He who so came and went was Jesus of Nazareth, whose appearance had created such sensation in various parts of the country. He who had 'not where to lay His head,' found a home under the roof of Martha, who 'received Him into her house.' After the work of the day was over, and the crowds had dispersed, He felt special relief in this domestic retirement. It must have been a happy circle which assembled around that hearth — bosom opening to bosom without reserve, thought eliciting thought in free and happy conversation. Jesus Himself was at ease, unbending from all His public cares, conscious of being out of the reach of spies and slanderers, reposing in confidence on the love of His hostess, quietly telling what was in His heart, and partaking cheerfully of the fare set before Him; while Lazarus enjoyed His precious company, drinking wisdom from His lips, and Mary sat at His feet, listening devoutly to His lessons, and looking up into His face with awe and wonder. This hallowed intercourse was continued for some time, till it ripened into earnest and steady friendship. The family grew into Christ's affection, and His heart intertwined itself with theirs. At length they regarded Him as one of themselves, and He responded to their congenial attachment. He was the friend of the family of Bethany, joyed with them when they joyed, and we know that He wept with them when they wept. Had any one of the sisters been wedded, His presence at the nuptial feast would have been as heartily coveted as it was at the sickness, death, and funeral of the brother. In all that concerned them, He sympathised, and He made no secret of His interest in them, but spoke to His disciples of 'our friend Lazarus.'

This friendship grew as do other human friendships. How and when He and they met we know not. There may have been some air of restraint at their first interview. When Martha invited Him, she might wonder whether He would accept her offer; and she and the family might not well know how to treat Him the first night He feasted and slept under their roof. Their demeanour would be that of reverent attention. But frequency of interview soon produced a respectful familiarity, and as there followed a perfect understanding and appreciation of one another, the forms of courtesy soon became the easy and living tokens of reciprocal union. Heart was knit to heart in amity, and Jesus was no longer as a guest, but as an inmate.

The Saviour condescended to accept of various entertainments. He sat a guest at many a table, and must have always endeared Himself to those about Him by His amiability and wisdom. The love of His bosom must have shown itself in the commonest acts of convivial intercourse, and in the interchange of the ordinary civilities of social life. But it did not always mature into friendship. To love another as a sinner, and labour for his salvation; to love him as a Jew, and have a special anxiety for a countryman's spiritual welfare; to love him as a townsman with whom he had once held juvenile communion, and, urged by such a reminiscence, to seek his benefit in his riper years; to love him as a relative, and to feel his kinship in blood to be a very tender motive for blessing him; — all these forms of love must have been often felt by Jesus, and as often exemplified by Him. But none of them are identical with that affection which He cherished towards Lazarus and his sisters. They were *his friends* — He loved them as one loves the confidants of his soul. He loved humanity, indeed, and came down to die for it; but general philanthropy did not absorb his special likings. He preached with power, and crowds listened to His addresses; but He 'did not commit himself' to them. He pitied and healed the sick and maimed — received their professions of gratitude, and then dismissed them. Amidst multitudes of disciples in whom He rejoiced, there was yet an inner circle, of which alone he said, 'ye are my friends.' In other words, apart from His high and generous sympathies as Redeemer, and His pure and fervent patriotism as the Jewish Messiah, and different still from His mediatorial grace as the God-man, the Lord had perfectly human attachments. Human, we call them, as they sprang from those instinctive sensibilities which everywhere characterise our nature.

We may not be able to tell all the reasons of Christ's friendship. But we doubt not that it was based on mutual esteem and like-mindedness, on certain elements of character which the four possessed in common, and which were so blended and harmonised as not to be easily detected or specified. There must have been in the family of Bethany a vital piety lying deep in an ardent nature, feelings of rare delicacy, and quick susceptibility; integrity crowned with generosity, innate sympathy with the good and noble: the open mind and the gentle heart — all yearning to meet with their own likeness, and rejoicing to find it so fully in Him, whom they first 'took in' as a stranger, then entertained as a guest, and finally cherished as a friend. Jesus and they were instinctively drawn to each other: 'Jesus loved Martha, and her sister, and Lazarus.' It was not divine grace, nor redeeming kindness, nor relational union, nor neighbourly good-will, nor a vague liking, nor official attachment; but it was the affectionate fondness of a man — the love of a friend.

Let it not be objected that among its inculcation of virtues, the gospel forgets friendship, when its Author sets so true an example of it. Let it not be objected that friendship is swallowed up in general good-will to the race, or special attachment to the church. We are summoned to love one another; but within the sphere of this love there may be closer circles of Christian friends, formed on kindred tastes and mutual intimacy. There are various fields of Christian labour, and associates in it are ever ready to embrace each other in a dearer fellowship, if they are 'true yoke-fellows.' There are also assemblages and consultations for more special objects, and they who there speak 'often one to another' usually pass into the bonds of companionship. They whose natures are cast in the same mould, or who have been educated by the same experience — whose mental constitution is not dissimilar, or whose history has been chequered by the same vicissitudes, are prepared to become each to each 'a friend that sticketh closer than a brother.' And if there be in this procedure no exclusive partiality or selfish predilection, it is a friendship formed on the model of Jesus and the household of Bethany. Still piety must lay the foundation. It alone can secure lasting confidence and cement friendship on earth by the thought, that though it be interrupted for an interval it shall be renewed in glory. It divests such alliances of all selfishness, refines them from earthly grossness, and preserves them unbroken by human frailty. Heathen sages have expatiated on the pleasures of friendship; but have not Christians better reason? Theirs is a closer fellowship; for it is that of spirit as well as of mind — linked together not only by the sameness of creed, but by oneness of destiny. It is a fellowship exercised in tastes not merely refined, but sanctified; and in pleasures not only dignified, but divine; while it is associated with hopes that are not bounded by the grave, and with enjoyments that rise from the imperfection of earth into the tranquil rapture of heaven. Ours is an immortal friendship; for it rests on an imperishable basis. It is not union so long as we travel together, but union, too, in our everlasting rest.

> 'A few short years of evil past,
> We reach the happy shore,
> Where death-divided friends at last
> Shall meet, to part no more.'

II. We remark, that the FRIENDSHIP OF JESUS IS NOT AFFECTED BY VARIETIES OF INDIVIDUAL TEMPERAMENT. This family was one in spirit; but there was diversity in the midst of unity. The one living faith dwelt in their hearts and filled them; but each heart had its special and distinctive peculiarities.

We do not know much of Lazarus. It is plain, however, that his character endeared him to Jesus. The appeal of his sisters for him was, 'Lord, behold, he whom thou lovest is sick.' When Jesus stood by the grave of him whom He had called 'friend,' and as the tears rolled down his cheeks, the spectators truly said, 'Behold how he loved him.' He had 'sat at meat' with Jesus, and enjoyed a close and tender intimacy with Him.

The character of Martha is marked by broad and distinctive lines. In some sense, the mansion at Bethany was hers—she 'received him,' the evangelist tells us, 'into her house.' The management of the family was also devolved upon her. Her sphere was activity, and she honoured Jesus in specially ministering to His physical comforts. When she was 'cumbered about much serving,' she requested Jesus to urge her sister to assist her. Not that she was unwilling to prolong her service, or grudged that her sister was disengaged; but her desire was to abridge the labour, by dividing it, that she too might listen to the Divine Instructor. Nor is she to be wholly blamed. Such duties as belonged to her must be attended to in their place; and had not Martha been working, Mary could not have been sitting at the feet of Jesus. Were there no Marthas, there could be no Marys. But probably Martha attached too much importance to her housekeeping, and erred in showing, so much in this way, her kindness to the Master. She laboured to set forth a feast worthy of the occasion, and Jesus hinted to her that honour meant for Him might assume another form. 'One thing is needful,' and to it everything else should yield. He required but little serving, and much serving only troubled the mistress of the mansion.

The mind of Martha was robust. Under the sad bereavement that fell upon her, she did not lose self-possession. When she heard that Jesus was coming to visit her, she went and met Him; 'but Mary sat still in the house.' At once did she accost Him with the declaration, 'Lord, if thou hadst been here, my brother had not died.' The statement has the semblance of a complaint, that Jesus might have hastened His steps on receiving the news of the illness of Lazarus. But she indulged in no paroxysm of sorrow — being able to add a declaration, of the full meaning and force of which she was not aware, 'I know, that even now, whatsoever thou wilt ask of God, God will give it thee.' The Saviour assured her of her brother's resurrection, and she replied at once, 'I know that he shall rise again in the resurrection at the last day.' This article of her creed gave her solace in the hour of sorrow. The Saviour spoke yet again to her of His own function as the resurrection and the life, and she avowed her belief in His Messiahship. The mind that could thus express its hopes and give its reasons, was a mind whose natural strength had been augmented by a healthy and vigorous faith.

On the other hand, Mary was calm and pensive. She had chosen the 'good part,' and it formed the theme of continuous meditation. What was fixed and intelligent belief in her sister, was in her deep and tender sentiment. The conversation of Jesus had a special charm for her, and her favourite posture was at His feet. He was to her the incarnation of wisdom and love. She might admire the busy hands and nimble feet of Martha, but she would not stir to assist her, lest she should lose one of the pearls that dropped from the Loved One's lips. Under the shock of bereavement her sensitive spirit was sorely crushed. She sat and mourned, brooded over her loss, and felt it the more keenly, as she had so twined herself round her brother's heart. Her's was one of those delicate natures that feel their need of some one to lean on, as the soft tendril that clings instinctively to the oak for support. When the visit of Christ was announced, her sister rose up to meet Him, 'but Mary sat still in the house.' The thought of seeing her brother's friend, brought so vividly their past intercourse to remembrance, that her heart bled afresh. When at length Martha roused her by the secret intelligence, 'the Master is come and calleth for thee,' 'she rose up quickly,' and yet when she met Him she could not speak like her sister; but 'she fell at his feet.' Those happy evenings when her brother sat with Him and she listened had come to an end, and Lazarus was now in his tomb. The shadow of death that had fallen upon her dwelling, had also descended upon her heart. The friends who had come to offer their condolence intimated their perfect knowledge of her character, when they conjectured, as they saw her so hastily leave the house, that she had gone to the grave 'to weep there.'

The character of the two sisters is thus quite distinct. Both were pious — both believed in Christ. Both were warmly attached to Him, and in their kindness to strangers, had entertained a higher than angels. Both delighted to honour the Messiah. But Martha showed it more as a hostess, Mary more as a disciple; Martha spared no pains on her feast, and Mary none in her efforts to hear and learn. Activity for Him characterised the one, submission to Him filled the other. That the distinguished stranger should be entertained as He ought to be was Martha's motive — that His visit should be spiritually blessed to herself was Mary's ruling passion. Martha's was an active, energetic nature; Mary's a more passive and confiding temperament. When 'they made him a supper,' Martha was happy in serving; but during the feast, Mary, with true womanly devotion, slipped behind the couch on which He reclined, knelt and anointed his feet with a very costly perfume, 'and wiped them with her hair.' When Jesus went to the grave of Lazarus and said, 'Take away the stone,' Martha at once interposed, but Mary offered no resistance. Martha imagined that Jesus wished to obtain the natural gratification of looking on His deceased friend's face; but believing that the process of decomposition was far advanced, she shrunk from the prospect of looking again on her brother's ghastly remains, and would have arrested the process of opening the sepulchre; but Mary, in the courage of her unresisting weakness, could have endured the sight; at least she made no objection to the Lord's proposal.

Now, such varieties of temperament have existed in all ages. Mental characteristics are not obliterated by conversion. Divine grace does not produce uniformity in human nature. It left in their own prominence, the valour of David, the genius of Isaiah, the pathos of Jeremiah, the fervour of John, and the reasoning powers of Paul. The innate elements of the mind and character stamp an individualising distinction on us. No two individuals have precisely the same features, nor have they the same intellectual conformation. Partakers of the 'common salvation,' their Christianity is tinged by their personal peculiarities. Nay, it is also affected by difference in race and blood, as may be seen in the ancient and modern churches of Europe, and in missionary stations over the world. Simplicity, docility, and a confidence that does not seek to analyse its warrant, and explain all its grounds, are found in one region; while another is distinguished by a marvellous subtlety of intellect, and a love of argument, which are not uniformly promotive of faith or love. Thus, while the lakes are filled with water — each of them has its own shape and dimensions — its own species of herbage and shrubbery upon its banks. There may be sameness in confidence and hope, in devotion and service, but there will be minor differences of aspect and manifestation.

For religion, though it sanctify mental power in

the children of God, does not give it an equal strength in all of them; and while it elevates and purifies the heart, it does not produce a uniform evenness of ardour and love. There are some believers in whom intellect predominates, and the 'full assurance of understanding' is their goal; others in whom emotion has a constitutional empire, and who find a more natural delight in devout meditation than in profound reflection. Some have an instinctive tendency to ruminate on the past, and on what He has done for their soul; others are led forward to sanguine expectation, and find their paradise in the 'full assurance of hope.' One class tends to look more to Christ without them in His atonement; and another class inclines to look more to Christ within them by His Spirit. There are those of a darker hue, who prefer to walk in the valley, humming psalms of penitence; and there are those of a bright nature, who love to traverse the mountains, chaunting hymns of triumph. Babes are found by the side of perfect men. Activity has its sphere contiguous to that of quiet contemplation. This one is forward to tell his experience, and that one shrinks from laying bare his bosom. One member of the church gives largely and cheerfully; another is concussed into liberality by the repeated protestations of his conscience. On the one hand, you meet with one who carries his religious spirit into his business, firmly and without ostentation; and, on the other hand, you meet with another, who is afraid to mingle with the world, and who leaves its bustle, that in his retirement he may walk with God. I feed on doctrine, says one; I live in practice, responds another. The world is dangerous — beware of it, is the motto of this party. The world is sinful — but try and better it, is the maxim of another party. The nature of one excites him to battle as a missionary; and the nature of another fits him to endure as a martyr. To this one, earth appears as a scene of duty, on which to 'fight the good fight;' and, to that one, as a field of trial — a valley of Baca, where the pilgrims weep as they go. And lastly, some expire in calmness, and others die in triumph.

Now all such complexional varieties of piety are the result, not of education or training, but of original temperament. Men are born so; and these inborn peculiarities, though they may be greatly modified, are never erased. They resemble the features of the face, the larger lines of which, amidst many changes, remain unaltered; and they serve, like them, to produce recognition. Besides, every gift is useful in its place; no talent is superfluous — all being consecrated to the glory of God. The prayer for revival is as needful as the effort for extension. Adherence to principle is useful, if it rise not to intolerance; but so is catholicity of spirit, if it sink not into latitudinarianism. The prayer of Moses on the hill sustained the courage of Joshua in the vale. The tongue that pleads for 'liberal things,' and the enterprise that acts upon them, are as important as the 'liberal soul' which 'deviseth' them. 'The Lord hath need' of every variety of gift and grace in His church. When, therefore, faith dwells in the heart, and the Divine Spirit occupies it, amidst all the diversities created by Him who gave us existence, the friendship of Christ may be enjoyed. Various as were the mental habits and spiritual tendencies of the members of the family of Bethany, it is nevertheless a blessed fact, that 'Jesus loved Martha, and her sister, and Lazarus.'

III. We remark, that the FRIENDSHIP OF JESUS DOES NOT EXEMPT ITS POSSESSORS FROM AFFLICTION. He put forth no miraculous power to prevent Lazarus from falling into sickness. The good man was seized with some overpowering malady, and gradually sunk beneath it and died. Jesus might easily have ordered it otherwise, for the effect of a miracle did not depend upon his personal presence at the scene of operation. Nor was it in ignorance of his suffering that Jesus allowed him to descend into the grave, for He was well aware of the instant of his death, and intimated it, in His own form, to His disciples. Nay more, on being informed of his illness, not only did He not haste to his relief, but actually, on receipt of the intelligence, He 'abode two days still in the same place where he was.' Even the appeal to His friendship did not move Him; for the message was couched in these terms of simple pathos, 'Lord, behold he whom thou lovest is sick.' Severe agony and death were thus permitted to Lazarus; and a heavy trial of bereavement were allowed to fall on the family whom Jesus loved.

The religion of Christ does not free us from suffering. It often leads to it. Not only are we liable to the ills which press upon humanity, but special chastenings are set apart for us. Believers have sufferings in common with others; but they have also trials adapted particularly to themselves. The object of Christianity is to train the mind; and it takes advantage of suffering to aid it in the process of tuition. It works in the sphere of experience. It does not simply set lessons before us, but it produces changes within us. It does not do with us, as the sculptor with the block of marble, when he gives it only the external form, aspect, and drapery of humanity; but it descends into the recesses of our nature, and there operates so mightily that, under its guidance, the sharp edge of affliction traces out the living image of God.

Experience is the offspring of religion. We should never know thoroughly the character of God, unless we felt our need of His grace. We read of His 'tender mercies;' but their tenderness is never really understood save by the sufferer who feels it. Who but she who has been made a widow, can truly fathom the depth of grace in the statement, that He is 'the husband of the widow?' The orphan, solitary and unbefriended, has the only clue to the whole meaning of the promise, 'Leave thy fatherless children: I will preserve them alive.' The bright stars appear as the gloom falls upon the earth; so

promises assume a new lustre and power to the
spirit lying under the shadow of suffering. They
only know what God is, who have experience of
what He has done to themselves. They may
imagine that they knew such things before, for their
creed was pure and full, and they might be able to
expatiate on the perfection and loveliness of the
Divine character; but now, since they have been in
trouble, they have received a deeper insight, for
themselves are a living lesson and argument of
God's goodness and pity. I may rejoice in the attachment of my friend, though I have never put it
to a severe trial; but if I am suddenly brought to
ruin, and he as promptly rescues me, even at great
sacrifice to himself, I may safely say that I never
knew the profoundness and value of his friendship.
It is therefore in the period of suffering and bereavement that the soul is brought into nearer contact
with God, and knows Him, not from what it believes, but from what it enjoys — not from what it
has been taught, but from what it has experienced.
We are all aware that our Lord is named the 'Man
of sorrows,' and we are taught that He is 'touched
with the feeling of our infirmities;' but we do not
adequately comprehend the truth, till, under the
pressure of infirmity, we enjoy His sympathy; and
then we can say, Now we know it, for we have felt
it. There is truly a sublime meaning in the words
which He spoke to Martha, 'I am the Resurrection
and the Life;' but only those circumstanced as she
was — the grave having closed over her brother —

can really enter into their nobility and triumph. He who has never felt the pang or desolation of bereavement — whose heart has never been pierced by the barbed and mortal shaft — who has never gazed on the corpse of parent, brother, or child, and seen it closed up from view — who has never made one of the group of weeping mourners that stand, in inexpressible solemnity, by the grave, and feel a sad sinking of heart as they leave behind them, in dust and darkness, that form which they shall not see again till Christ descend and the trumpet sound — such a scathless and untried believer cannot, though he would, unfold to himself the sweetness and comfort of the saying, 'I am the Resurrection and the Life.' There is no Christian heart that does not hold by the pledge, 'My grace is sufficient for thee;' but it is only when 'weakness' overpowers it, that it can really find that His 'strength is made perfect.' Without affliction, the purest and closest knowledge of God could never be acquired; a vail would still seem to lie upon Him. The glory that surrounds Him might dazzle us; but we should still be comparative strangers to the tenderness and love of His heart. Still at a distance from Him, we would indeed trust Him; but when He lays His hand upon us and brings us nearer Him, then do we acquaint ourselves with His loving-kindness, no longer by report, but by tasting it. You may have seen the solar beam thrown back in yellow splendour from the crystal rocks, as they glistened with gold; but now you have found and gathered the precious ore. It is one thing to admire the beauty of His pavilion, and another thing to be in it; one thing to know Him from what He has said, and another to know Him in what He has done. Surely experimental intimacy far excels theoretic information; but it is gained only in the school of affliction.

Did, therefore, the friendship of Christ secure us against suffering, it would shade from our view these prime and happy lessons. But Christ is anxious that we learn them, and therefore, though He loves us, He permits us to suffer, that we may yearn for a fuller sense of His presence, and, penetrating into His heart, know, because we feel, the love and power of our Beloved and Friend.

There was some lesson which the family of Bethany needed to learn. Perhaps they indulged the thought that Christ's friendship might ward off all affliction from them. They might fondly dream, that as He ministered such help to others in healing their diseases, He would guard them from the very approach of sickness. It would, they might reason, be as loving a token of His regard to prevent affliction altogether, as to remove it after it had been sent. And thus they gradually presumed upon His friendship as a safeguard, for each of the sisters by herself, in this spirit, thus accosted Him, 'Lord, if thou hadst been here, my brother had not died.' A similar impression rested on the minds of such as knew the Saviour's previous intimacy with the family. 'And some of them said, Could not this man, which opened the eyes of the blind, have caused that even this man should not have died?'

Now, such a notion, however naturally formed, was based on an erroneous estimate of His character and relationship. It was lifting their own wisdom to a level with His; it was deciding by themselves what was best for them; it was, in short, prescribing a channel for Christ's affection. Therefore Lazarus sickened when Christ was away, and the kindest of friends did on purpose prolong His absence. An earnest message came, but He obeyed it not. The sisters were then effectually taught that they were not to interfere with Christ's modes of operation, and that they enjoyed no undue favouritism from their intercourse with Him. How anxiously they must have looked, hour after hour, for His approach! How brightly they would picture out their brother's immediate restoration to health from His presence and touch! How their souls would sink in gloom when Lazarus became worse and worse, and his pale and collapsed countenance betokened the near and sure approach of the last enemy! With what 'searchings of heart' they would try and frame reasons for Christ's seeming indifference to them in the period of trial and sorrow! And at length when they had closed their brother's eyes, and swathed him in the dress of the tomb, how they would still ponder over the reasons of Christ's inexplicable conduct towards them. It was on the fourth day that their Friend came to them—not as they had anticipated, to heal the sick, but to condole over the dead, and mingle His tears with those of the bereaved household. But now, in Christ's studied refusal to their touching solicitation, and in the subsequent resurrection of their brother, they learned that God's ways are higher than man's ways, and are therefore not to be judged of in human weakness — that it is dangerous to pass an opinion upon any divine process till we have seen the result—that affliction is one of God's most effective methods of tuition, and that the endurance of it is no proof of any failure in Christ's friendship, for His love assumed a new tenderness and a more glorious form of manifestation in the day of their visitation and anguish.

They might have questioned His friendship during the lapse of those four mysterious days, but now they saw, as they could not have seen it otherwise, how He loved them. He did not begin to comfort them with the usual appliances — did not bid them adore the awfulness of the dispensation, and pray for grace to improve it—did not point them forward to a happy re-union—did not say that their loss was gain to Lazarus, and that they were not to sorrow 'even as others which have no hope'—but He went to the tomb and there He wept, commanded the stone to be rolled aside, summoned the sleeper back to life, and gave him to the embrace of his sisters. But for the sickness, death, and funeral of Lazarus, and Christ's absence in the interval, this miracle, set in such love, would not have greeted them. As they returned, in company with their brother, from the tomb, and saw him again in his own raiment, in health and happiness, did they wonder now why his sickness was permitted, and why Jesus was absent? The greater evil fell upon them that the greater good might be possessed. The joy of the rebound was in proportion to the depth of the previous descent. Their gladness in his resurrection derived its glow and fervour from the agony of the preceding death and bereavement. The triumph of love was mightier by far at the sepulchre than it could have been at the sick-bed. They had learned the lesson which they needed, their faith was confirmed in Jesus as Messiah, and their hope rested on Him as 'the Resurrection and the Life.'

Wonder not, then, Christian, thou that lovest Jesus and feelest, too, that Jesus loves thee, why thou art afflicted or why thou art bereaved. Never suppose for a moment that Christ has forgotten thee, or that His friendship toward thee has cooled. But seek in very earnest to feel the benefit of the discipline, and in its issue thou shalt behold new and multiplied tokens of His love. True, He has power to guard thee from suffering, but He loves thee better, and He consults thy interests more wisely than to give thee total exemption. Is not this His own language: 'For a small moment have I forsaken thee; but with great mercies will I gather thee. In a little wrath I hid my face from thee for a moment; but with everlasting kindness will I have mercy on thee, saith the Lord, thy Redeemer.' Do not perplex thy mind with insoluble questions, but listen again: 'Beloved, think it not strange concerning the fiery trial which is to try you, as though some strange thing happened unto you; but rejoice, inasmuch as ye are partakers of Christ's sufferings; that, when his glory shall be revealed, ye may be glad also with exceeding joy.' Do not, in fine, compare thy case with that of others, and gather in upon thee dark and shadowy conclusions. O rather lay hold on the apostle's assertion, and find unfailing comfort in it: 'There hath no temptation taken you but such as is common to man; but God is faithful, who will not suffer you to be tempted above that ye are able; but will with the temptation also make a way to escape, that ye may be able to bear it.' But we remark—

IV. While the friendship of Jesus does not exempt from affliction, IT DEEPENS INTO SYMPATHY WITH THOSE WHO ENDURE IT. Even during His absence, the soul of Jesus was in Bethany. Once and again, as if the matter was dwelling upon His mind, did He refer to it in speaking with the disciples. At first he told them generally, 'this sickness is not unto death.' Then He proposed to go back to Judea; and next He said, 'Our friend Lazarus sleepeth; but I go that I may awake him out of sleep.' The disciples thought that their Master spoke of a natural sleep — the common index that the crisis is past; and they answered, 'Lord, if he sleep he shall do well.'* At last Jesus told them

---

* The Scottish mode of expressing the same idea would be, 'He has got the turn.'

plainly, 'Lazarus is dead.' His mind was thus brooding over the scene, and the sympathy of His heart was all the while extended to the bereaved and sorrowing sisters. Though His enemies had threatened to stone Him in Judea, He had now no hesitation in returning to the province on this errand of love. He felt that He was immortal till His work was done; and therefore he set out for Bethany. By the time He arrived, Lazarus had been four days dead, and Himself had not been more than a day's journey distant. The family He had loved were in deep distress, and 'many of the Jews came to comfort Martha and Mary concerning their brother.' Both sisters had deeply loved him, and both must have felt forlorn and desolate. It may be that each sister would not have felt the loss of the other so keenly as both felt the loss of Lazarus — the representative to them of a deceased father, and a head and protector to the household. Many things he could do for them or with them, which, according to the usage of their country, and the barriers thrown around their sex, they were not permitted to do for themselves. So that to them he was clothed with a parent's authority, tempered with the equality of a brother's affection. The Saviour, as He met Martha, could speak in a firm tone of assurance to her; but when He saw Mary lying at His feet, weeping in the bitterness of her soul, and the mourners and relatives weeping in company with her, He was deeply moved — 'He groaned in the spirit, and was troubled.' Under the pressure of deep emotion, He could only command Himself so far as briefly to ask, 'Where have ye laid him?' The reply was, 'Come and see.' And as He took the first step to the tomb of His friend, His emotion could no longer be restrained; His bosom heaved, and His eye filled: 'Jesus wept.'

Marvellous spectacle! Jesus wept, as the mourners about Him wept! The sight of such sorrow overpowered Him, and He could not refrain. That was a true manhood, which felt this touch of nature, and burst into tears. There was no Stoicism in His constitution. There was no attempt to train down His sympathies, and educate Himself to a hard and inhuman indifference. Neither was He ashamed of His possession of our ordinary sensibilities. He felt it no weakness to weep in public with them that wept. So sinful did sin appear in its penalty of death—so saddening was the desolation which death had brought into that happy home—so humbling was the picture of Lazarus, alive and active but a few days before, but now laid in the narrow vault, and carefully concealed from view, that the Saviour bowed to the stroke, and in the impulse of genuine sympathy, 'Jesus wept.' Perhaps the prospect of His own death and entombment rose up suddenly before Him — the thought that He should soon be as Lazarus now was, a cold and inanimate corpse, with weeping mourners making a similar procession to His tomb. And though He had but to take a few steps more, and the greatest of His miracles should be achieved, and he that was dead should be raised — so powerful and tender were His mingled sensations, that 'Jesus wept.'

Shall we use the common term, and say that He was, 'unmanned?' No. Such an epithet originates in a grievous misinterpretation of our nature. Is man to be denied the relief of tears, and woman only to be so privileged? Is it beneath his masculine robustness to show a moistened eye? Is he to be a traitor to deepest and purest emotion, and to attempt to cauterise the fountain of tears? No. Christ, the model of manhood, the mirror of all that was noble and dignified, did not deny Himself the relief; and shall men be looked upon as effeminate, as falling from the dignity of their sex, if, with emotions like Christ, they shed tears like Him? No. Perish that dignity which would aspire to a transcendental apathy that man was not made for, and which Jesus despised. The tear is as genuine as the smile. He who would do such violence to his nature, insults his Creator, and would foolishly set himself above the example of his Redeemer. Instead of raising himself above humanity, he sinks beneath its level. The brow that never wore a smile, is not more unnatural than the eye that never glistened with a tear.

Therefore do we vindicate for the afflicted mourner the privilege of tears. You are not giving way to sin, when you are giving way to tears. Man is not disgracing his manhood, nor woman showing herself to be but a woman, when they weep under bereavement. Try not to be above the Saviour. It is not sin to mourn, but the sin is to murmur — to fall into querulous repining, as if God had wronged you, and it needed an effort on your part to forgive Him. We are sure that Jesus harboured no grudge of this nature against His Father in Heaven; and yet He wept. To forbid tears is to impose a cruel penance — is to deny a luxury to the mourner in which his Lord indulged. O thou of the bruised. heart, when thou goest to the sepulchre where the beloved dust is garnered, weep, but not in dejection — weep, but repine not; disturb not the unbidden tear, as thou art in the place of burials. The dust thou sorrowest over cannot indeed respond; but the time is coming when thy tears shall be wiped away by the very hand that inflicted the stroke.

Did Jesus ever smile? The question is superfluous. His brow had not always a cloud upon it. He was no anchorite; He came 'eating and drinking,' and He wrought his first miracle at a marriage feast. But there is no record that He did smile, and there needed none. But He wept, and we are told of it; for it might be surmised that One so pure might be above the reach of all infirmity—that One who healed disease might be untouched by the aspect of it; and that He who had shown His power over death, might be disturbed by no human emotions in view of the tomb. But lest we should associate such callousness with perfection, and reckon His elevation of character a proof that He could not stoop to be touched by the sorrows of a sinful world, the shortest verse of scripture tells us that 'Jesus wept.'

These tears are proof of His genuine humanity, that He was moved as we are moved to weep. Had that humanity been of a higher order than ours, or been a mere phantom in the guise of man, such as that which an angel might take upon him, the spectacle of the weeping Saviour would never have given assurance of His sympathy to the world. Let not the spectators of His life imagine that He cannot be 'touched with the feeling of their infirmities.' As they hear Him speak in those tones of sublimity, and rebuke in those accents of sternness, they may say of Him, 'not a man, but more than a man.' As they see Him still the winds and walk upon the waves, hush the demoniac and feed the crowds, their inward thought may again be, 'not a man, but more than a man.' Or again, when they behold Him seeming to disown all relationship of blood with His mother, His brothers, and His sisters, and affirming that a true disciple was to Him as 'brother, sister, and mother,' the conclusion would only be strengthened, 'not a man, but either different from humanity, or far above it.' But did they follow Him on this journey to Bethany, and watch Him as He spoke arguments of consolation to Martha, and breathed His words of sympathy into the ear of Mary; and did they accompany Him to the tomb of Lazarus, and mark that as His bosom heaved, His countenance quivered, and His eyes at length overflowed, would they not retract their previous inference, and cry, 'Yes, more than a man it may be, but beyond all doubt a man still—the wearer of a real humanity?' And therefore the mourners may reckon on His sympathy. These tears were shed not for Himself, but for the sorrows of others.

Many have wept for themselves, and some with selfish intensity. As she cast her son under a shrub to die, Hagar wept for her loss. When Esau found that he had been forestalled in his father's blessing, the chivalrous hunter wept under his disappointment. The wife of Samson employed her tears as her best weapon of victory over her weak-minded spouse. Hannah wept under the taunts and provocation of her domestic rival. The king and his people wept as they were forced into exile by the unnatural rebellion of Absalom. Often, too, have tears been shed under a sense of pain and bereavement. 'Abraham came to mourn for Sarah, and to weep for her.' The face of Job was 'foul with weeping.' Rachel is depicted as 'weeping for her children, and refusing to be comforted.' David wept over his dying child; and Hezekiah, as he felt himself under sentence of death, 'turned his face to the wall, and wept sore.' But tears have also sprung from other than selfish sources. Joseph wept once and again as he beheld his brethren, and a flood of early and tender recollections rushed upon him. Job says of himself, 'Did I not weep for him that was in trouble?' and his own friends, when they came to comfort him, and could scarcely recognise him, 'lifted up their voice and wept.' In the bonds of a pure and steady friendship, Jonathan and David 'wept with one another, until David exceeded;' and after he ascended the throne, he was moved to tears at the grave of Abner, and with him 'all the people wept.' Under the reproof of the angel, the camp of Israel wept so violently that the place was called Bochim, or the scene of weepers. Elisha wept as his mind's eye took in the future atrocities of Hazael. The captives mingled their tears with the streams of Babel. As Jeremiah thought of the desolation of his country, he wished that his head were 'waters' and his eyes 'a fountain of tears.' The priests who had seen the first temple, wept at the inauguration of the second and humbler edifice. Peter wept as the look of Christ entered his soul, and the Ephesian elders taking farewell of the apostle at Miletus, 'fell upon his neck, and wept.'

But the tears of Jesus were those of purest sympathy, and He was moved to them by the tears of others. May not those who weep be assured that their tears will still command His fellow-feeling— that He will 'hear the voice of their weeping?'

For what a variety of suffering our Lord passed through!—such experience being the basis of His sympathy. For sympathy is not innate goodness, it is *acquired* from suffering. It belongs not to the Father, but it has opened a place for itself in the bosom of the Son—'In that He Himself hath suffered, being tried, and He is able to succour them that are tried.' Are any of you in poverty? He had not where to lay His head; His cradle belonged to the beasts, and His corpse lay in a borrowed grave. Is any one frowned upon by the world? 'He was despised and rejected of men.' Do you complain of Satan's malignant assaults? Ah, He knew the hour and felt the 'power of darkness.' Does there seem to be an eclipse on your Father's face? O listen to that awful wail, 'My God, my God, why hast thou forsaken me?' Or is it that suffering lies heavily upon you, and your fevered lips are parched, and long to be moistened? He felt the same sensation, and cried, 'I thirst.' Or must it be that when you come to die there will be a new and terrible bitterness in death, in that you leave behind you those so near and so dear to you wholly unprovided for? Did not He suffer a similar pang, sharper than any of the nails that pierced Him? and from His cross He commended His aged and widowed mother to the care of the beloved disciple. Or perhaps bereavement has been producing desolation of soul. Is it a father who has laid in the grave his child of winning looks, and in the first bloom of existence? Or has death snatched from thee a youth as he was ripening into a manhood so like thine own, or a daughter, the lovely memorial of a mother under whose premature decease thou hast bowed and wept? Or is it a mother grieving over the babe, that still clung to her bosom as its fountain of life; or over the boy, whose rosy lips were learning to lisp out her name, and prattle in the witchery of broken language on her knee; or over that little girl, whose ways and works have reminded her so often of her own maiden years? Or it may be that death has severed that union which is significantly called 'one flesh,' and the husband sees his other self laid low in the dust. Or, alas! it is the widow, in lonely sorrow, bereaved indeed — deprived, in one hour, of partner and friend, shield and provider — an empty hearth and an unfurnished table — a dark present and a darker future. Or is it the child that has followed a parent's remains to the dark and narrow house — those of a father who had watched its budding years, and trained it with affectionate success — or those of a mother, of all names the holiest and tenderest, whose every look beamed with love, and whose smile will remain for ever engraven on the memory? Whichever of these forms of bereavement oppresses you, O be comforted by the thought that 'Jesus wept'—that He who so wept is still unchanged in nature—that the heart which was so troubled is as susceptible now as then, and will beat in unison and sympathy with you under such trials and sorrows. What a comforter is the Elder Brother! who knows what it is to be bereaved, and will, out of such experience, soothe and solace His people. Nay more, for eighteen hundred years the man Jesus has been employed in binding up the bleeding in heart, and healing all their wounds. Every variety of grief He has dealt with, and with every element and form of it He is perfectly familiar.

THE DIVINE LOVE.

If there be power in human sympathy to lighten the load of woe, O how much more in the sympathy of Him who 'bore our griefs and carried our sorrows' — whose words of comfort reach the heart — who gives Himself to be loved in room of the object taken away—and gathers the departed into a blessed company before the throne, with the prospect of a happy and unclouded reunion! Let the mourner never forget the image of the weeping Saviour. O how it will reassure him, and fill him with unspeakable consolation! Thou weepest — but 'JESUS WEPT!'

V. But we remark in the last place, that the FRIENDSHIP OF JESUS IS NOT INTERRUPTED BY DEATH. What breaks up all other ties has no such effect upon it. It survives that shock, which, from its awful power, men have named dissolution, as it unbinds every connection and relationship. Even that union founded in Eden, and chosen from its closeness to symbolise the oneness of Christ with His church, is, according to the apostle, so completely sundered by death, that, the husband being dead, the wife is 'loosed from the law of her husband,' and free to be 'married to another man.' Friends walk arm-in-arm, till they come to the tomb, and then one of them resumes his solitary path. The family presents a happy and a numerous circle; but years roll on, and death comes in and thins it, till at length but one is left, the sole survivor of his father's house. All societies experience the same constant changes, and ever and anon some one stands out in the isolation of a hoary age, the last representative of a bygone generation. Who has not felt link after link giving way round about him; and when he thinks of his friends, how many of them are now in eternity! That companion of youth, that friend of riper years, that colleague in office, that partner in business, that neighbour or fellow-traveller — ah, how soon you miss them! — death has intervened, and all connection is severed. They are associated in the memory of the past: but the hearty embrace is to be felt no more — no more the voice of wisdom will be heard, or the courtesies of social life exchanged. Each one feels, 'I shall go to him, but he shall not return to me.' How often in general conversation does the expression turn up, ' our late friend,'—a confession that such friendship in its earthly form is for ever at an end.

> 'My thoughts are with the dead, with them
>   I live in long past years,
> Their virtues love, their faults condemn,
>   Partake their hopes and fears.
>
> 'My hopes are with the dead — anon
>   My place with them shall be:
> And I with them shall travel on
>   Through all futurity.'

But the friendship of Christ brooks not any interruption. Our Lord said of him who had died, ' Our friend Lazareth sleepeth.' He recognised the friendship as still existing. Lazarus was yet His friend, after he had expired — His friend after he had been entombed. And He proved the reality of that enduring friendship. In spite of the enmity existing against Him 'in Jewry,' He went to Bethany, spoke with both his sisters, and proceeded to the tomb. Then He wept with the mourners, whose sorrow had again broken out at the place where, but a few days before, they had laid the dead in the dust. In profound and mysterious agitation, Jesus approached the sepulchral cave, commanded the stone to be rolled away, and, as tears almost choked His utterance, He offered up a brief prayer to His Father. Then rolled from His lips those brief words of power, LAZARUS COME FORTH, and Lazarus obeying came forth arrayed as he had been buried. What a thrill, approaching to alarm, must have shot through the spectators as they beheld the apparition of the moving grave-clothes. With what curiosity they must have gazed upon that face when the napkin was removed; and with what strange sensations they who perhaps had wrapped him in his winding sheet helped now to unroll it, and saw again the free action of hand and limb! We cannot, though we would, conjecture the conflicting emotions of Lazarus as he awoke at the voice of friendship. His last agony as he died, the couch at Bethany, and his weeping sisters, would be associated in his memory with the feeling of unaccountable relief as he rose. And then on his sudden restoration to consciousness to find himself in the garb of a corpse, lying in the family tomb, the vaults of parents and relations round about him, and making what effort he could, tightly swathed as he was, to come out to the light of day. Nor could he perhaps fully comprehend the scene as he saw Martha and Mary, the mourners, Jesus, and His disciples, in groups round about himself — an object as much of wonder as affection. How the leal heart of Mary would turn from her brother to Christ, and feel Him to be in truth a friend! When the command to loose him was given, Martha's busy hands would soon assist in performing the task; but the deep feeling of Mary's heart would hold her in motionless rapture and gratitude. Truly Christ proved Himself 'a friend that sticketh closer than a brother,' or even a sister. The sisters had laid Lazarus in his grave, and left him there; they could stick no longer to him, save in spirit and memory: but Christ's friendship was not to be barred out by the sepulchre, and He brought His dead friend back to fellowship and life. They had spent some evenings without their brother; but Christ would spend none in Bethany without him, and so He filled the vacant seat with its former occupant, ere He entered their house. The circle was not complete without Lazarus; Jesus would have him by His side, and therefore He raised him.

Will it be doubted that Christ's friendship dictated the miracle? The entire record seems to prove that this mightiest of His works sprang from His attachment and sympathy. His friendship descended to the grave, and brought up again its object. Nor is it otherwise now: Jesus is unchanged.

The objects of Christ's affection, when taken out of the world, are brought into closer union with Himself. We feel that death puts an end to our friendships; but Christ's friendship only moves a step closer when mortality intervenes. It is not for a moment suspended. The spirit rises to Himself, to the enjoyment of His presence, and to forms of intercourse and endearment which cannot now be imagined. So it was in the history of Enoch: to-day he 'walked with God' on earth—to-morrow he walked with Him in heaven. So far then from severing Christ and His friends, death only destroys the distance existing between them, and brings them face to face. Nor is the body forgotten or dismissed from His regards. It is His, and He claims it, though it be in the tomb. What He did for Lazarus, He will do for it; ay, and more. He will call it forth from its concealment. His power will not fail to achieve its resurrection, though it have lain centuries in the tomb, and have long faded away into dust. And it will be raised a glorious structure — flexile, ethereal, spiritual, and immortal — fitted for the pure soul which shall again inhabit it, and capable of enjoying Christ's friendship without fatigue and without end. It is said of Lazarus after he had been raised, that on one occasion he 'sat at meat' with Jesus; but the glorified saints shall have an endless feast with Him in His banqueting chamber, and His banner over them shall be love. Tradition reports of Lazarus, that after this solemn crisis in his life, he was never seen again to smile; the occupant of the tomb could never throw off the shadow of death. But His friends are for ever to be happy with Him — no vestige of their previous mortality clings to them, for they have shaken themselves so completely from the dust — and they live and love 'with songs and everlasting joy upon their heads.' Did not Lazarus descend again to the tomb at his appointed time? Those, however, raised by His love at the last day, are for ever beyond the attack of disease, and above the stroke of death. And thus they are with Him — ever with Him — in His presence, and under His smile.

And now, how shall we compute the value of Christ's friendship, and by what means shall we acquire an interest in it? The unbelieving heart can have no share in it: he who will not have Christ as Saviour, cannot enjoy Him as friend. Come to Him, then, in His official character, and you will soon possess His personal regard. Despair of yourselves, and trust in Him, and He will admit you to His confidence. The path to His bosom is by His cross. Strive, too, to be like Him in everything; and if you two are so agreed, you will walk together in undivided fellowship. How terrible it must be to have Christ for a foe! The Lamb of God is also the Lion of the tribe of Judah. The soul which is unlike Him, must be exiled from His presence. It shall blast itself, and the whole universe shall unite in condemning it.

Ye friends of Jesus, stand not aloof, but surround Him in closer circle. Is there not a true interchange of thought and sentiment between you and Him? Prove the reality of your friendship by doing whatsoever He has commanded you. Avow it and glory in it, and long for a fuller enjoyment of it. Have ye not tasted and seen that it is good, and that no earthly tie can be compared with it? What solace it has given you in times of distress and bereavement! You may have had trials, but you had His welcome presence.

> 'Hast thou lost a friend or brother?
> Seen a father's parting breath?
> Or gazed upon a lifeless mother
> Till she seemed to start from death?'—

Then thou knowest how thy Friend did visit thee, weep with thee, and cheer thee; and as thou rememberest what He said and what He did, thou wilt also indulge the hope that the missing one has gone to His embrace, and that the grave, now filled and closed up, will give back its tenant on the morning of the resurrection. Indulge no bitter regrets —use not the cold and unmeaning language of the world—give way to no frantic sorrow. Let those around thee see that the Comforter has spoken with thee. And in that better world friendship will never be broken in upon. Immortality is stamped upon it. The great and good of former ages—Abel and Noah, Abraham and Moses, David and Isaiah — prophets and apostles, saints and martyrs, shall all rejoice in undying union and intercourse with one another and with Christ. O to be found at length in that happy company, and the praise shall be Thine, Thou Friend of Friends. To Thee, with the Father and the Holy Spirit, be all glory, for ever and ever. Amen.

LECTURE XII.

THE LOVE OF CHRIST, THE SUSTAINING MOTIVE IN THE MISSIONARY ENTERPRISE.

AN APPEAL.

'*And he said unto them, Go ye into all the world, and preach the Gospel to every creature.*'—Mark xvi. 15.

'*He that hath my commandments, and keepeth them, he it is that loveth me.*'—John xiv. 21.

'*For the love of Christ constraineth us.*'—2 Cor. v. 14.

'THE love of Christ,' in the last clause quoted, is Christ's love to us, and it 'constraineth us' to earnest self-consecration. His love proved its fervour in His death — that death brings life to us — and a life so originated is to be devoted 'not to ourselves, but to him who died for us, and who rose again.' Such a result springs from our deliberate decision— 'we thus judge;' for it is but a reasonable thing that they who live by Christ should live to Him. The cross unites them to Him who bled upon it for them, and creates that love which is the passion of the sanctified heart, and comprises in it the sum of Christian ethics.

> ' Talk they of morals, O Thou bleeding Lamb —
> The grand morality is love of Thee !'

It is so in all duty, as the one grand motive is love; we engage in it, for 'the love of Christ constraineth us.' It is especially so in that sphere of duty which we propose to illustrate and enforce.

The motive which ought to guide you and prompt you in the prosecution of the missionary enterprise, you will find in the love of Christ. Motive is moving power, and in proportion to its strength and purity will be the amount of result, or the extent of success. If it be feeble — if it be only a quiet inducement, it will scarcely arouse the spirit to labour; and if it be not the offspring of intelligence and faith, then it is only a mere excitement, which shall live out its brief and fitful fever, and soon die of collapse. Motives of such a nature have had their day and their influence. At the commencement of modern missions there was novelty. All hearts were stirred, and the charm of romance was thrown around the work. It seemed to be the beginning of a new era — the dawning of the promised jubilee. But this epoch of admiration has passed away, and must be succeeded by the epoch of labour. At first, too, men formed sanguine anticipations, thought of rapid and extensive conquests, dreamed of a sure and speedy millennium, and saw in fancy idols burnt, temples ruined, altars overturned, paganism subverted, Judaism restored, and the reign of Christianity universally established. But these immediate results have not followed in all their fulness, and, therefore, the era of unwarranted expectation must be followed by an era of positive and persevering industry and toil. What we want now is a moving power which shall not soon or easily expend its energies; which shall not faint in the midst of difficulties, but shall ever be fanned into mightier strength by the blasts of opposition. What we want is a motive which combines perseverance with enthusiasm, which grows bolder in the midst of discouragement, and which persists, and still persists, with all the ardour and freshness of a first love, till the end be achieved. It is such a motive in living force and duration, as ruled the spirit of Columbus, when he turned the prow of his barque to the west, and held on cheerily and steadily in the same direction, and fainted not amidst growing murmurs and dissatisfaction, but still steered toward the setting sun under strange skies and amidst unexplored waters, till drift and sea-weed told him that he was nearing land; and then, as his vessel grazed the beach, the mariner leapt out in the fulness of his joy, and took possession of a new world. Thus, let the church, under the firm persuasion that she is doing the will of God, engage in this glorious work; let her gather faith from promise and prophecy; let her, like her own illustrious Head, 'not faint nor be discouraged' till she have set judgment in the earth; let her not be intimidated by obstacles, nor dismayed either by scanty success, the fickleness of heathen converts, the death of missionaries, or the languor and avarice of so many of her own adherents at home; let the one motive fill her, and then, by God's blessing, and in

God's good time, she shall achieve the conquest of the globe.

And whence shall this motive be brought but from the cross? There is only one source, and that is love to Christ. It is when 'the love of Christ constraineth us,' and we 'thus judge' ourselves to be under solemn obligation to live to Him, that we are furnished with power sufficient to labour without weariness, and with the prospect of success. This is a power which should be in every heart, in all its impetuous majesty. For were it there, then it would induce us to contemplate the spiritual wants of the world in the spirit of Christ. If we loved Him, we should love whatever He loves; and be disposed to form the same views of man and of the world as He does. He loved the world, and died for its salvation; shall not we, who love Him, love the same world, and commiserate its want of a salvation provided in the Saviour's blood? What we now complain of is, that men so often survey the world in all its aspects but that of spiritual want. The world is often under the eye of science, but how seldom under that of compassionate Christianity! We hear much of its population and their manners, of its soils and their capabilities, of its various climates and their peculiarities, its rivers and their navigation, its kingdoms and their policy; yet how seldom does the common traveller, the physical geographer, or the statist dwell upon the evils produced by the want of the gospel! You are told of the brawny Indian of North America — his noble form and warlike mien, his stoical endurance of suffering, and his hope of a future spirit-land. There is pictured to you the Mahomedan, his fierce hatred of idolatry, his oriental origin, and his fierce conquests, which resemble the dreams of romance in their rapidity and extent. And you are reminded of the Jew, of his cringing temper and love of money, of the cruelties he has undergone, and of the slavery to which, in spite of his gold, he has been subjected. And yet there are too often kept back from your view the wretchedness, cruelty, and degradation of the godless pagan — the licentiousness and fanaticism of the Moslem — and the promises made to the 'children of the covenant,' when God shall bring in His ancient people with the fulness of the gentile nations. Let us therefore view the world as the Christ we love views it — guilty, helpless, and miserable; but with a salvation provided for it and adapted to it — a salvation secured at the most awful expense, and waiting the period of its presentation to all tribes and tongues. Let the churches feel what the world is in want of; and feel it under the conviction that Christianity alone can meet its necessities. For commerce and civilization are inadequate; they cannot educate man's spiritual nature. You may send through the world the produce of the looms of Glasgow and Manchester, and of the forges of Sheffield and Birmingham, to refine and civilize its myriads; but yet if this iron and cloth be all your boon, you leave them still in their godless and hopeless state. Such an extension of temporal blessings may bind the demon, but it cannot expel him. To every one, therefore, who surveys the spiritual condition of the globe, and feels what its wants are, and how alone they can be met and gratified, there will appear, as to Paul, not one but many imploring him, 'Come over and help us.'

And what help shall you carry to them? Shall you teach them to name and number the stars, and say nothing of the heaven that stretches above and beyond them? Shall you show them how to change a hut into a house, without leading them to the knowledge and hope of the 'building of God,' the mansion of eternal bliss? No. Science without religion is an eyeless giant, and without its impulse art might show its genius and power in erecting and adorning temples for false divinities. 'Ye that make mention of the Lord keep not silence, and give him no rest, till he establish and till he make Jerusalem a praise in the earth.' Let the point of this prayer impress you: JERUSALEM, not Athens, the scene of intellectual splendour, nor Rome, the type of martial greatness, nor London, the mart of a world's merchandise; but Jerusalem, the ancient city of God — 'till he make Jerusalem a praise in the earth.' So long as there is a child without its school, or a man without his Bible, or a village without its pulpit; so long shall this prayer be presented by all who love the Lord Jesus — who see the world as He sees it, and love His salvation as He loves it.

Nor can you fail to look at the means to be employed. This instrumentality is of Christ's appointment — the result of His wisdom and love; and it is given in charge to you. Thus regarding it, your hearts must also be set upon it, to work it for its great design. Already have we alluded to it, as 'the glorious gospel,' that meets every want of humanity, and is fitted and offered to men of every colour and clime. It carries with it the choicest blessings. It brings pardon and peace. It quiets the conscience, and begets the hope of glory. It makes man what he should be in temper and action. It clothes present obligation in the most impressive form, for it places all duty in the light of eternity. It satisfies our cravings, and gives the soul its only portion. It is God's voice as it speaks, and God's arm as it guards us. In it, heaven stoops to earth, to raise up earth to itself. Nor is it cramped with any national peculiarities. What fits it for one man, fits it for every man; what adapts it to Britain, adapts it to Madagascar. The old economy was organised but for one people, and resembled its own Jordan, which, after traversing its narrow territory, lost itself in a sullen lake. But Christianity is the river of water of life, flowing onward with undiminished current; no barrier can withstand its expansive energy, no time nor numbers exhaust its pure and copious streams.

Now, the motive to employ this instrumentality is also supplied. It is not set before you that you may admire it, and simply handle it in curiosity;

but you cannot look upon it without being impelled at once to put it to its use, for you look at it as Christ does, and you love it from its connection with Him. O then, by the value of an immortal soul, greater by far than that of the physical universe — by the love you bear to Him who loved you and gave Himself for you—by the tears and prayers and agony which secured that salvation yourselves enjoy, we implore you to send the gospel to a perishing world. O seek not to creep up to heaven in selfish solitude; take others with you. Think with what you have been entrusted. So far as means go, the conversion of the world is in your power—within your reach. Not that any power on earth can convert a soul, or that the ordinances of the church can by themselves change and purify the heart. This has, indeed, been too common an error. It is in fact the very essence of Popery. Join yourself to the church, and the junction will unite you to the Saviour, is the motto of Rome; but the spirit of the Bible is, Christ first, the church next. For union to Christ is essentially union with His church: 'first to the Lord,' and afterward 'unto us by the will of God.' Every one in Christ is a member of His church; but every member of the church is alas not necessarily in Christ. But while these things are so, it is nevertheless true that means are to be put forth; and he who withholds the means does all in his power to frustrate the result. 'For whosoever shall call on the name of the Lord shall be saved. How then shall they call on him in whom they have not believed? and how shall they believe in him of whom they have not heard? and how shall they hear without a preacher? And how shall they preach except they be sent? as it is written, How beautiful are the feet of them that preach the gospel of peace, and bring glad tidings of good things!' The concatenation of means is plain. If there be no mission, there is no preaching; if there is no preaching, then there is no hearing; if no hearing, then no faith; if no faith, then no prayer; and if no prayer, then no salvation. If you refuse the first, you annihilate all that follows. Mere mission does not save, and mere preaching does not save; but saving faith and prayer depend upon mission and preaching. You cannot command faith—the Spirit of God alone can create it; but you can organise the ordinary means which the Spirit does employ for its origination. So that if you employ not the means which are in your power, you negative the end which is not in your power. How, then, will you justify yourselves in withholding the means at the starting point? But you cannot withhold this instrumentality, if you breathe His Spirit—the Sent of God; if you look upon a human soul, and see it made in God's image, and feel its immeasurable value, in the ransom-price of Calvary; if you remember the change which has passed over yourselves — from gloom to light, from misery to peace, from death to life; and reflect that such a change is needed by the heathen as much as by you, that the means of its production are at your disposal, and that you are solemnly commanded by Him you love to labour, and pray, and give, that the Bible may be circulated, the church extended, and the Redeemer Himself rewarded and glorified.

In fact, the saved are appointed to make conquests for their Saviour. And they respond to the commission, because they love the Master and love the work. They long to see His glory advanced, and they rejoice to clasp in brotherhood the partakers of the 'common salvation.' They know that there is no blessing for a man like salvation; and that though he has all, yet if he is without it he is poor indeed. And therefore you preach Christ to him. The preaching may not be from your own lips, or from your own example, but it may be from the lips of another sustained by your liberality and prayers. Your connection with this duty cannot be sundered. You may not go in person to the heathen, but you can speak to the irreligious nearer you. You may not cross the seas, but you have a personal interest in the missionary adventurer. For you he leaves home and kindred, and it is only in strict justice that you support him. Do not, therefore, call by the name of benevolence what is a work of purest equity,—that he who labours for you be compensated by you.

So that giving is a Christian obligation. Not only ought you to support those who labour for you, but you acknowledge Christ's claim in all you are, in all you have. He is the giver, and demands a proportion of the silver and gold to Himself. To withhold it is sacrilege, and as of yore He still sits 'over against the treasury,' and estimates what is given, not by its actual bulk, but by its proportional value. Will you then be so selfish as to keep back what it is in your power to confer? Having drunk of the river of water of life yourselves, and yet standing on the margin of the sacred stream, let your voice reach to the farthest shores: 'Ho, every one that thirsteth, come ye to the waters, and he that hath no money: come ye, buy and eat; yea, come, buy wine and milk, without money and without price.'

Besides, as love to Jesus is the grand motive, think what satisfaction you bring to the Saviour Himself. No one has such an interest in that work as He. As each soul is converted, a thrill of exalted joy passes through His bosom, and to be instrumental in producing this — O, what an honour! You may not be able fully to realise it, but be it yours to share in it, so that through you He may 'see of the travail of His soul, and be satisfied.' When a sinner is converted and blessed for ever, gladness also fills the heart of angels. Heaven is moved to ecstasy with the tidings of the success of the missionary enterprise. The redeemed spirit, as it feels its obligations to Christ, will thus become steadfast and immovable in His work. It will identify itself with all His desires, and among them is paramount the conversion of the world. For this He reigns and pleads, for this He dispenses the gifts of His Spirit, for this He has planted His church and brought you by His grace within its pale. As then you set your heart on what He has set His heart, and pray for it, labour for it, and contribute for its advancement, be this your aspiration —

> 'Come then, and, added to Thy many crowns,
> Receive yet one, the crown of all the earth,
> Thou who alone art worthy. It was Thine
> By ancient covenant, ere nature's birth;
> And Thou hast made it Thine by purchase since,
> And overpaid its value with Thy blood.
> Thy saints proclaim Thee king; and in their heart
> Thy title is engraven with a pen
> Dipped in the fountain of eternal love.'

And if it be Christ's work, so loved by Him, and so loved by you because it is loved by Him, it must be successful. The assurance based on such a fact must sustain you in it. Shall I turn you to the remarkable prophecies of Scripture? Is not their language precise and full, the imagery bold and varied, and their spirit that of earnest penetration. The earliest promise contained the assurance of victory over the serpent. The covenant made with Abraham imbosomed a blessing to all nations of the earth. Dominion from sea to sea was predicted of the Son of David. The restoration of the Jews was to be to Him a 'light thing,' compared with the conversion of the Gentiles. The mountain of the Lord's house was to be elevated to a conspicuous eminence on the top of the hill, that it might be a sanctuary for the world. Heathen kings are to lay their crowns at the feet of Messiah, and mountains are to sink into plains before His victorious progress. Ambitious men, from Nimrod down to Bonaparte, have fought and toiled to found a universal monarchy, but they have signally failed. Yet He shall succeed, and the glorious cry shall be heard: 'The kingdoms of this world are become the kingdoms of our Lord and of his Christ.'

For your exalted Lord has all influences at His supreme and unchallenged disposal. Whatever happens forwards His cause. Discoveries in science, revolutions in kingdoms, wars and persecution, are made to contribute to His success. He sits king on the floods, alike in their stillness and in their raging. The one Head of the Church, and Head at the same time over all things to the church,—can He be turned from any purpose, or can He fail in any enterprise? Wiser than the wisest, stronger than the strongest, and better than the best; if He be for us who can be against us? Thus runs the declaration and the command based upon it: 'All power is given unto me in heaven and in earth, go ye, therefore, and teach all nations, baptizing them in the name of the Father, and of the Son, and of the Holy Ghost; and, lo, I am with you alway, even unto the end of the world.' The populace of the world has been debased by fables and impostures, but Jesus the prophet has given a complete revelation, before which the fabrics of delusion fall, their oracles are silenced, and the dark and mysterious rites of their temples are exposed and supplanted. Humanity, under the pressure of a guilty conscience, has often resorted to impure and cruel lacerations and sacrifices; but Jesus the Priest has offered up a perfect oblation — infinite in its merits — these merits freely dispensed, and their reception bringing peace and hope; so that on that atonement we safely rest all the hopes and hazards of an eternal futurity. And though error has obtained such a hold in the world, and grasps its wide empire with such tenacity, and will not let it go, Jesus the King possesses unlimited sway, and when He revives and unites His church, then, girding His sword upon His thigh, He will go forth conquering and to conquer.

Nor is this all theory. It has been often realised. Our present churches are themselves the fruit of missionary enterprise. It was but a small band that met in the upper room at Jerusalem; but they were filled with that holiest of heroism which is based on the love of Christ. Three thousand at Pentecost believed in Him, who a few weeks before had died a felon's death. The sword of persecution was unsheathed — they fled; but they 'went everywhere preaching the word.' Samaria was greeted with the glad tidings, and they flew through Galilee beyond the limits of the country. The wisdom of Athens bowed to them, and the corruption of Corinth could not resist them. At Antioch the disciples grew so rapidly as to receive a distinctive name from the Divine Teacher; and the iron valour of Rome was conquered by the invisible might of the crucified Nazarene. The temple of Diana was abandoned at Ephesus, and books of magic were burned. Macedonia, famed of old for its phalanx, yielded to the Victor. Christianity came, and saw, and conquered. It surmounted the Alps, and descended into Gaul; scaled the Pyrenees, and gathered converts in Spain; crossed the channel, and founded its churches in the British Isles.

Nor is it different in more modern times. The snowy regions of Greenland have been thawed. Among the dwellings of the South Seas a change has come over the population which was once as far beyond control as the surf that beats on their coral reefs. Breaches have been made in the great wall of China, and Brahma is retiring sullenly from the shores of the Ganges. The throne of Mahomet begins to shake; the crescent is waning, ere long to be eclipsed; and the lamps which have burned for ages in the shrine of Mecca, are glimmering with a feeble and dying lustre. In the islands of the West Indies many a sable countenance has been lighted up with joy, and emancipation from human bondage has been felt to be second to a happier and nobler freedom. Yea, among the children of Ham, steeped in superstition and barbarity, the beginning has been made — a prelude to the coming epoch when Ethiopia's outstretched hands shall be loaded with the blessings she so earnestly craves. May we not also perceive, that in popish countries there is a shaking among the dry bones; the terror that inspires and increases persecution being to us a token of partial and incipient successes. The Anglo-Saxon races in Canada, the States of America, the

Cape of Good Hope, New Zealand, and Australia; the English rule in India, and its settlement at Canton, have been planted in these various localities, in providence, not simply for purposes of commerce and colonization, but for a higher and ultimate design—that as centres of influence they may evangelise the globe. O for mightier prayer and redoubled energy, enlarged liberality and more hearty consecration, that the few labourers may be multiplied, that efforts made may be blessed, that the mites may become shekels, that the church may awake to its mission, and the world be speedily won over to Messiah, the Prince! The world shall be so won: 'I have sworn by myself, the word is gone out of my mouth in righteousness, and shall not return, That unto me every knee shall bow, every tongue shall swear.' 'O earth, earth, earth, hear the word of the Lord.'

> 'Arabia's desert ranger
>   To Him shall bow the knee;
> The Ethiopian stranger
>   His glory come to see:
> With off'rings of devotion,
>   Ships from the Isles shall meet,
> To pour the wealth of ocean
>   In tribute at His feet.
>
> 'Kings shall fall down before Him,
>   And gold and incense bring:
> All nations shall adore Him;
>   His praise all people sing:

> For He shall have dominion
> O'er river, sea, and shore,
> Far as the eagle's pinion
> Or dove's light wing can soar.'

In fine, when any command of Christ is obeyed from love to Him, such obedience brings its own reward. How nobly will missionary prayer, liberality, and effort bless yourselves. They will return sevenfold into your bosom. You will enjoy the gospel in proportion to your efforts to diffuse it. And you will also retain it among you. The early churches, so soon as they ceased to be missionary, died out. The candle was put under a bushel, and it soon expired; and then, as it was of no further use, the candlestick itself was removed out of his place. Thus perished the African church — the church of Tertullian, the prince of orators — of Augustine, the first of theologians—and of Cyprian, the meekest of martyrs. Your activity will give health to your piety, and keep it free from morbid casuistry and pernicious slumber. 'There is that scattereth and yet increaseth.' God is able to make all grace abound toward you. The ocean which, from its generous bosom, sends up the vapour which is condensed into rain, is not thereby diminished in volume; for it receives its waters back again; having lent them for a season to refresh and fertilise the earth.

Thus, wherever you look all is full of encouragement. The world is in immediate want, but provision has been made for it in a complete and gracious gospel, and a motive of sufficient power has also been furnished. There is room for work, and there is but brief time for you to engage in it. O, then, let the love of Christ constrain you to immediate action, and sustain you under it. The success that has been already reaped is surely an inducement to persevere. Let it not be said in despondency over any of you, 'ye did run well, who did hinder you?' 'Look to yourselves, that we lose not those things which we have wrought, but that we receive a full reward.' Be ever imploring the blessing of the Divine Spirit. Your labour is only as the building of the altar and the preparation of the victim; unless the fire from God descend and consume the offering, the enterprise cannot be crowned with success. In the Acts of the Apostles there is a uniform recognition of the divine hand. Homage is not done to the zeal of Paul or the eloquence of Barnabas, but always to the Spirit of God.

In one word, then, begin and carry on under the stimulus of this mighty motive. Clamour not for immediate results, but still persevere in duty. In spite of their unbelief and rejection of Him, it never repented Christ that He died for men, let it never repent you that you have sought above all things their conversion. Be 'always abounding' in this work. It is Christ's work, O let it be yours. Ever be drawing fresh encouragement from all that happens around you, and ever be 'looking unto Jesus.' While you work yourselves, enlist others.

Let the leaven of your zeal and energy leaven the whole lump. And when that result is reached, as it will be reached, the end is at hand. Then shall the intelligence of Europe be exalted and sanctified, and the spiritual fruits of Asia shall resemble its own tropical productions in profuseness and beauty, and the isles of the South Seas shall lift up the voice together and sing, and Africa shall be washed and made white in the blood of the Lamb, and the great American continent shall, through all its zones, glow under the free and equal radiance of the Sun of Righteousness, and the globe shall be vocal with one continuous melody to the God who made it, — to the Saviour who redeemed it. 'The whole earth shall be filled with His glory. Amen, and Amen.'

THE END.

Other John Eadie Titles

Solid Ground Christian Books is delighted to announce that we have been privileged to republish several volumes by John Eadie. In addition to the volume in your hand we have also brought the following back into print:

Commentary on the Greek Text of Paul's Letter to the Galatians
Part of the classic five-volume set that brought world-wide renown to this humble man, Eadie expounds this letter with passion and precision. In the words of Spurgeon, "This is a most careful attempt to ascertain the meaning of the Apostle by painstaking analysis of his words."

Commentary on the Greek Text of Paul's Letter to the Ephesians
Spurgeon said, "This book is one of prodigious learning and research. The author seems to have read all, in every language, that has been written on the Epistle. It is also a work of independent criticism, and casts much new light upon many passages."

Commentary on the Greek Text of Paul's Letter to the Philippians
Robert Paul Martin wrote, "Everything that John Eadie wrote is pure gold. He was simply the best exegete of his generation. His commentaries on Paul's epistles are valued highly by careful expositors. Solid Ground Christian Books has done a great service by bringing Eadie's works back into print."

Commentary on the Greek Text of Paul's Letter to the Colossians
According to the New Schaff-Herzog Encyclopedia of Religious Knowledge, "These commentaries of John Eadie are marked by candor and clearness as well as by an evangelical unction not common in works of the kind." Spurgeon said, "Very full and reliable. A work of utmost value."

Commentary on the Greek Text of Paul's Letters to the Thessalonians
Published posthumously, this volume completes the series that has been highly acclaimed for more than a century. Invaluable.

Paul the Preacher: A Popular and Practical Exposition of His Discourses and Speeches as Recorded in the Acts of the Apostles
Very rare volume intended for a more popular audience, this volume begins with Saul's conversion and ends with Paul preaching the Gospel of the Kingdom in Rome. It perfectly fills in the gaps in the commentaries. Outstanding work!

Lectures on the Bible to the Young for their Instruction and Excitement
Buried over a century, this rare volume reveals pastoral wisdom of Eadie as he seeks to warms the hearts while filling the minds of his young readers. Every pastor should read this book to learn how to communicate great truths in very simple ways. While written with children in mind, it is pure gold for all ages.

Other Solid Ground Titles

THE COMMUNICANT'S COMPANION by Matthew Henry
THE SECRET OF COMMUNION WITH GOD by Matthew Henry
THE CHILD AT HOME by John S.C. Abbott
THE LIFE OF JESUS CHRIST FOR THE YOUNG by Richard Newton
THE KING'S HIGHWAY: *10 Commandments for the Young* by Richard Newton
HEROES OF THE REFORMATION by Richard Newton
FEED MY LAMBS: *Lectures to Children on Vital Subjects* by John Todd
LET THE CANNON BLAZE AWAY by Joseph P. Thompson
THE STILL HOUR: *Communion with God in Prayer* by Austin Phelps
COLLECTED WORKS of James Henley Thornwell (4 vols.)
CALVINISM IN HISTORY *by Nathaniel S. McFetridge*
OPENING SCRIPTURE: *Hermeneutical Manual by Patrick Fairbairn*
THE ASSURANCE OF FAITH *by Louis Berkhof*
THE PASTOR IN THE SICK ROOM *by John D. Wells*
THE BUNYAN OF BROOKLYN: *Life & Sermons of I.S. Spencer*
THE NATIONAL PREACHER: Sermons from 2nd Great Awakening
FIRST THINGS: First Lessons God Taught Mankind *Gardiner Spring*
BIBLICAL & THEOLOGICAL STUDIES *by 1912 Faculty of Princeton*
THE POWER OF GOD UNTO SALVATION by B.B. Warfield
THE LORD OF GLORY *by B.B. Warfield*
A GENTLEMAN & A SCHOLAR: *Memoir of J.P. Boyce by J. Broadus*
SERMONS TO THE NATURAL MAN *by W.G.T. Shedd*
SERMONS TO THE SPIRITUAL MAN *by W.G.T. Shedd*
HOMILETICS AND PASTORAL THEOLOGY *by W.G.T. Shedd*
A PASTOR'S SKETCHES 1 & 2 *by Ichabod S. Spencer*
THE PREACHER AND HIS MODELS *by James Stalker*
IMAGO CHRISTI: *The Example of Jesus Christ by James Stalker*
LECTURES ON THE HISTORY OF PREACHING *by J. A. Broadus*
THE SHORTER CATECHISM ILLUSTRATED *by John Whitecross*
THE CHURCH MEMBER'S GUIDE *by John Angell James*
THE SUNDAY SCHOOL TEACHER'S GUIDE *by John A. James*
CHRIST IN SONG: *Hymns of Immanuel from All Ages by Philip Schaff*
DEVOTIONAL LIFE OF THE S.S. TEACHER *by J.R. Miller*

Call us Toll Free at 1-877-666-9469
Send us an e-mail at sgcb@charter.net
Visit us on line at solid-ground-books.com
Uncovering Buried Treasure to the Glory of God

www.ingramcontent.com/pod-product-compliance
Lightning Source LLC
Chambersburg PA
CBHW031308150426
43191CB00005B/123